FAERIE QUEENE

BOOK ONE: ST. GEORGE & THE DRAGON

EDMUND SPENSER

PARALLEL VERSE TO PROSE VERSION
BY SARAH KOUS

The Faerie Queene: Book One
St George and the Dragon
Edmund Spenser
Parallel Verse to Prose Version by Sarah Kous

Copyright © by Sarah Kous 2018
Cover Art © Lori Follett of WickedDesignStudio.com

TABLE OF CONTENTS

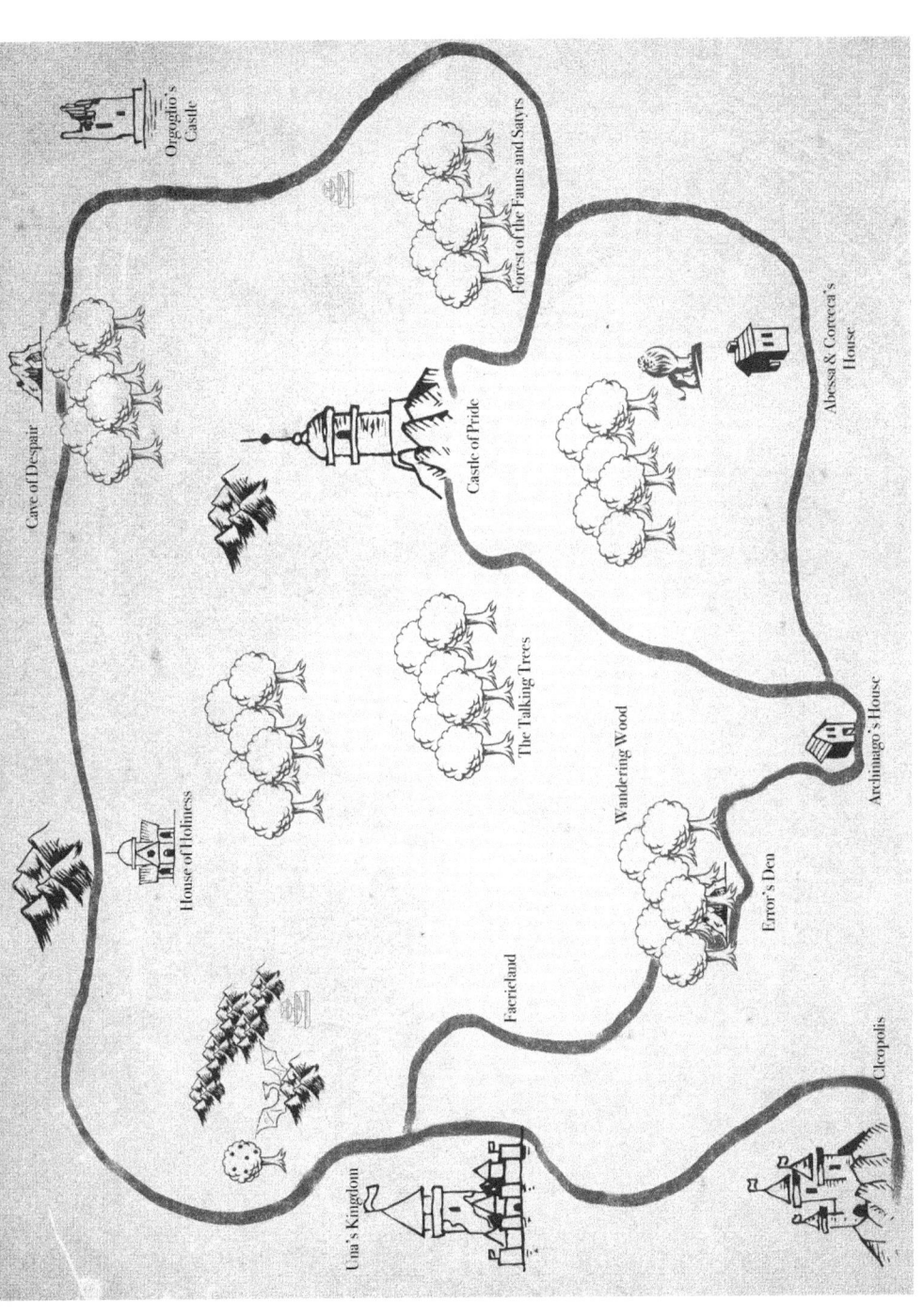

PREFACE TO THIS PARALLEL VERSE TO PROSE VERSION

Edmund Spenser's original verse version of *The Faerie Queene* can be challenging to read today because of the unfamiliar syntax, archaic words and multiple footnotes. This parallel version is designed to provide the reader with both the original verse on one side, and an accessible parallel prose version[1] which faithfully adheres to the story, rich language, tone and vigor, on the facing page.

Commentary, clarifications and footnotes from scholarly sources, such as AC Hamilton (2007)[2], Wauchope (1921)[3] and Spenser's letter to Sir Walter Raleigh, have been woven into the prose version where possible, or included in each Canto's notes, to enable a smoother reading experience.

I also received some assistance from leading Spenser scholar, Dr Richard Danson Brown (Open University), who generously helped with some of Spenser's more obscure lines and offered valuable feedback.

May this fresh translation of a magical epic inspire a new generation of readers and initiators of chivalrous deeds.

Sarah Kous
BA(Engl) *ECowan University*
Long Term Classical Home Educator

1 Prose Only Version: ISBN 0648164802

2 Hamilton, AC. *Spenser The Faerie Queene.* New York: Routledge, 2007. Print

3 The Project Gutenberg eBook, *Spenser's The Faerie Queene, Book I,* by Edmund Spenser, et al, Edited by George Armstrong Wauchope, 1921, http://www.gutenberg.org/files/15272/15272-h/15272-h.htm

"Since it is so likely that (children) will meet cruel enemies, let them at least have heard of brave knights and heroic courage."

— C.S. Lewis

LETTER TO SIR WALTER RALEIGH

The beginning therefore of my historie, if it were to be told by an Histo-riographer, should be the twelfth booke, which is the last; where I devise that the Faery Queene kept her annuall feast twelve daies; uppon which twelve severall dayes, the occasions of the twelve severall adventures hapned, which being undertaken by XII severall knights, are in these twelve books severally handled and discoursed.

The first was this. In the beginning of the feast, there presented him selfe a tall clownish younge man, who falling before the Queene of Faeries desired a boone (as the manner then was) which during that feast she might not refuse: which was that hee might have the atchieve-ment of any adventure, which during that feast should happen; that being granted, he rested him selfe on the floore, unfit through his rusticitie for a better place. Soone after entred a faire Ladie in mourning weedes, riding on a white Asse, with a dwarfe behind her leading a warlike steed, that bore the Armes of a knight, and his speare in the dwarfes hand. She falling before the Queene of Faeries, complayned that her father and mother, an ancient King and Queene, had bene by an huge dragon many yeers shut up in a brazen Castle, who thence suffered them not to issew: and therefore besought the Faery Queene to assigne her some one of her knights to take on him that exployt. Presently that clownish person upstarting, desired that adventure; whereat the Queene much wondering, and the Lady much gaine-saying, yet he earnestly importuned his desire. In the end the Lady told him, that unlesse that armour which she brought would serve him (that is, the armour of a Christian man specified by Saint Paul, V. Ephes.) that he could not succeed in that enterprise: which being forth with put upon him with due furnitures thereunto, he seemed the goodliest man in al that company, and was well liked of the Lady. And eftesoones taking on him knighthood, and mounting on that straunge Courser, he went forth with her on that adventure: where beginneth the first booke, viz.

Every year, the Faerie Queene held the feast of Twelve Days to celebrate the Twelve Virtues. It was the custom that, upon each of the twelve days, anyone in trouble could appear before the court and ask for a defender.

On the first day of the feast that year, a tall, clumsy, peasant boy presented himself, and bowing deeply before the Queene of Faeries, made a surprising request. He entreated that her majesty might not refuse him any quest presented during the feast that day, so that he might prove himself in trial and combat.

The Queene granted his request, and he seated himself upon the floor to wait, unfit through his rustic status for a better place.

Soon after, a fair lady entered, dressed in black mourning and riding on a white donkey. A dwarf followed, holding a lance, and leading a warlike horse that bore the arms of a knight. The lady fell before the queen, complaining that her father and mother, king and queen of an ancient kingdom, had been shut up in a brazen castle by a huge dragon, and were suffering greatly. Therefore, she begged the Faerie Queene to assign one of her famed knights to take on the monster.

Presently, the young peasant, rising to his feet and bowing deeply, declared that he desired that quest. While the queen much wondered, and the lady much contested, the youth earnestly persisted in being put to the test with the dragon.

Finally, the lady told him that, unless the armor that she brought would fit him, that is, the armor of a Christian man as specified by Saint Paul, he could not succeed in that enterprise.

Bowing again deeply, he accepted the lady's terms, and was led forward to be fitted out as a knight. Once clad, he resembled the bravest knight in all that company, and was well liked by that lady. Then, after taking the pledge of knighthood, and being given the name Redcross, he mounted the strange horse and went forth with her on that adventure.

And this is where the first story begins.

I LO I the man, whose Muse whilome did maske,
As time her taught, in lowly Shepheards weeds,
Am now enforst a far vnfitter taske,
For trumpets sterne to chaunge mine Oaten reeds,
And sing of Knights and Ladies gentle deeds;
Whose prayses hauing slept in silence long,
Me, all too meane, the sacred Muse areeds
To blazon broad emongst her learned throng:
Fierce warres and faithfull loues shall moralize my song.

II Helpe then, O holy Virgin chiefe of nine,
Thy weaker Nouice to performe thy will,
Lay forth out of thine euerlasting scryne
The antique rolles, which there lye hidden still,
Of Faerie knights and fairest *Tanaquill*,
Whom that most noble Briton Prince so long
Sought through the world, and suffered so much ill,
That I must rue his vndeserued wrong:
O helpe thou my weake wit, and sharpen my dull tong.

III And thou most dreaded impe of highest *Ioue*,
Faire *Venus* sonne, that with thy cruell dart
At that good knight so cunningly didst roue,
That glorious fire it kindled in his hart,
Lay now thy deadly Heben bow apart,
And with thy mother milde come to mine ayde:
Come both, and with you bring triumphant *Mart*,
In loues and gentle iollities arrayd,
After his murdrous spoiles and bloudy rage allayd.

IV And with them eke, O Goddesse heauenly bright,
Mirrour of grace and Maiestie diuine,
Great Lady of the greatest Isle, whose light
Like *Phoebus* lampe throughout the world doth shine,
Shed thy faire beames into my feeble eyne,
And raise my thoughts too humble and too vile,
To thinke of that true glorious type of thine,
The argument of mine afflicted stile:
The which to heare, vouchsafe, O dearest dred a-while.

Lo, I, the man whose Muse was formerly inspired to write peaceful, pastoral poetry, am now forced to undertake a far more difficult task: to swap the gentle reed pipes of rustic verse for the stern trumpets that sing of the gentle deeds of knights and ladies, whose praises have been sleeping in a long silence. The sacred Muse advises me, unworthy as I am, to blazon broad amongst her learned throng. Therefore, these fierce wars and faithful loves shall instruct through my song.

Help then, O holy virgin, chief of the nine muses. Lay forth your ancient scrolls which are hidden in the everlasting casket. Tell the stories of the Faerie knights and of the fairest Tanaquill, for whom that most noble Briton, Prince Arthur, sought so long through all the world, and for whom he suffered so much, that I must mourn his undeserved wrongs. O help my weak wit, and sharpen my dull tongue.

Cupid, most cunning child of highest Jove and fair Venus, whose cruel dart shot at that noble knight and kindled that glorious fire in his heart, lay aside your deadly wooden bow now, and with your mild mother, come to my aid. Come, both, and bring triumphant Mars, the god of war, with you. After his murderous spoils and bloody rage is allayed, let us now arrange loves and gentle jollities.

And with them also, O Faerie Queene, heavenly bright, mirror of grace and divine majesty, great lady of the greatest isle, whose light, like the lamp of Phoebus, shines throughout the world, shed your fair beams into my feeble eyes, and raise my too humble and vile thoughts to think of that true glorious image of yours, and hear the subject of my lowly pen. Grant me this a while, Gloriana, O dearest formidable one.

INTRODUCTION, AND NOTES ON CANTO I

Introduction to Canto I:

While enjoying this fast-moving story, it is important to keep in mind that *The Faerie Queene* also reflects the political climate of the era. The five-year reign of Queen Mary, known for her harsh and bloody treatment of Protestants, and King Phillip II of Spain's recent attempt to invade England with the Armada, were still fresh in the minds of Protestants, like Spenser. Therefore, the story's characters and their actions often reflect Spenser's criticism of Roman Catholicism and his defense of Elizabethan Protestantism. When Spenser submitted his manuscript to Sir Walter Raleigh, he included an introductory letter explaining the background to the story, and it is included in this prose version. Canto I then begins with the traditional calling on the nine Muses: a convention in ancient literature, and here Spenser imitates Virgil's opening to the Aeneid.

Canto: means 'song' in Italian, and is a poetic name for 'chapter' in a long poem.

Faerie Queene: also Gloriana and Tanaquill, is Queen Elizabeth I. Edmund Spenser was a great admirer and supporter.

Redcross Knight: is the hero of Book I, in which he represents England's patron, **Saint George**, as well as a Christian in search of holiness. He Redcrosse represents the individual Christian, on the search for Holiness, is armed with faith in Christ: the shield with the red cross. His armor includes both the physical armor, and the armor described by Paul in Ephesians 6:10-18.

George: means 'farmer' in Greek, and is Redcross's real name.

Faerie: Spenser's Faeries are heroic and human-sized, and are not to be confused with the diminutive winged beings in children's stories from early 17th century onwards. In Book II, Canto X, of *The Faerie Queene*, Sir Guyon reads a history of the Faeries, telling how Prometheus fashions a man named Elfe who finds a lovely woman named Fay in the garden of Adonis. Elfe and Fay begin the race that rules Faerieland.

Elf: Again, not the cute, little, pointy-eared creatures. The etymology of the word 'elf' can be traced back to the word: white, with PIE root *alb*. Elf was a popular component in Anglo-Saxon names, but the only 'Elfin' name still in use today is Alfred. Albion is the oldest known name for England, possibly named because of the White Cliffs of Dover, so Elf might refer to an indigenous English person, but many other theories exist.

Una: Her name means "one:" the One Truth (of the Protestant/Anglican church).

The Dwarf: symbolizes reason and prudence. Reason is useful, but must be guided by Truth.

The lamb: a symbol of purity that appears in earlier paintings of the legend of St George, and would have been instantly recognized by Spenser's first readers.

Error: a monster, half-serpent, half-woman, who embodies the problem of *erring*: travelling off the path. Error represents greed and the Roman church.

The Wandering Wood: a metaphor for "wandering off the path" and being led astray.

Archimago: is a sorcerer who symbolizes religious hypocrisy, the deceptions of the Jesuits, and King Phillip II of Spain.

Morpheus: god of sleep.

The word "seeming:" Spenser frequently uses the word 'seeming' to suggest that 'not all is as it seems.'

CANTO I

REDCROSS BATTLES ERROR

The Patron of true Holinesse,
Foule Errour doth defeate:
Hypocrisie him to entrappe,
Doth to his home entreate.

I A Gentle Knight was pricking on the plaine,
Y cladd in mightie armes and siluer shielde,
Wherein old dints of deepe wounds did remaine,
The cruell markes of many' a bloudy fielde;
Yet armes till that time did he neuer wield:
His angry steede did chide his foming bitt,
As much disdayning to the curbe to yield:
Full iolly knight he seemd, and faire did sitt,
As one for knightly giusts and fierce encounters fitt.

II But on his brest a bloodie Crosse he bore,
The deare remembrance of his dying Lord,
For whose sweete sake that glorious badge he wore,
And dead as liuing euer him ador'd:
Vpon his shield the like was also scor'd,
For soueraine hope, which in his helpe he had:
Right faithfull true he was in deede and word,
But of his cheere did seeme too solemne sad;
Yet nothing did he dread, but euer was ydrad.

III Vpon a great aduenture he was bond,
That greatest *Gloriana* to him gaue,
That greatest Glorious Queene of *Faerie* lond,
To winne him worship, and her grace to haue,
Which of all earthly things he most did craue;
And euer as he rode, his hart did earne
To proue his puissance in battell braue
Vpon his foe, and his new force to learne;
Vpon his foe, a Dragon horrible and stearne.

IV A louely Ladie rode him faire beside,
Vpon a lowly Asse more white then snow,
Yet she much whiter, but the same did hide
Vnder a vele, that wimpled was full low,
And ouer all a blacke stole she did throw,
As one that inly mournd: so was she sad,
And heauie sat vpon her palfrey slow:
Seemed in heart some hidden care she had,
And by her in a line a milke white lambe she lad.

V So pure and innocent, as that same lambe,
She was in life and euery vertuous lore,
And by descent from Royall lynage came
Of ancient Kings and Queenes, that had of yore
Their scepters stretcht from East to Westerne shore,
And all the world in their subiection held;
Till that infernall feend with foule vprore
Forwasted all their land, and them expeld
Whom to auenge, she had this Knight from far compeld.

The patron of true holiness defeats foul Error, but Hypocrisy entraps Redcross and leads him to his home.

THE GENTLE KNIGHT WAS RIDING HIS HORSE ACROSS THE PLAIN. CLAD IN mighty armor, he held a silver shield, wherein old dents of deep wounds remained: the cruel marks of many a bloody field. Yet, until that time, he had never wielded arms. His angry steed gnashed at his foaming bit, disdaining the reins that curbed him. Such a gallant knight he seemed, fairly fit for knightly jousts and fierce encounters.

On his breast, he bore a red cross symbol, the dear remembrance of his dying Lord. For the knight adored Him, and he wore that glorious badge for His sweet sake. The same red cross was scored on his shield, hoping for promised sovereign help. Faithfully true in word and deed, though of solemn cheer, he dreaded nothing, but was ever dreaded.

The knight was bound on a great quest that Gloriana, Queene of Faerieland, had granted him. Above all other earthly things, he craved to win her honor and grace. So ever on, as he rode, his heart yearned to prove his might in brave battle upon his foe: a horrible and stern dragon.

The lovely Una rode beside him on a lowly donkey that was whiter than snow. While she was even whiter, she veiled her fair face under the folds of a wimple, and cloaked herself under a long black stole, as one who inwardly mourned. She sat sadly and heavily upon her slow palfrey, and it seemed she had some hidden care in her heart. On a lead beside her, she led a milk white lamb, 5 and like the lamb, she was as fair, pure, and virtuous in every lore. She came from a royal lineage of ancient kings and queens whose scepters stretched from east to western shores. And until that infernal fiend with foul uproar laid all their land to waste, and expelled them from it, they had held all the world in their subjection. And now Una had accepted this knight from afar, and his offer to avenge.

VI Behind her farre away a Dwarfe did lag,
That lasie seemd in being euer last,
Or wearied with bearing of her bag
Of needments at his backe. Thus as they past,
The day with cloudes was suddeine ouercast,
And angry *Ioue* an hideous storme of raine
Did poure into his Lemans lap so fast,
That euery wight to shrowd it did constrain,
And this faire couple eke to shroud themselves were fain.

VII Enforst to seeke some couert nigh at hand,
A shadie groue not far away they spide,
That promist ayde the tempest to withstand:
Whose loftie trees yclad with sommers pride,
Did spred so broad, that heauens light did hide,
Not perceable with power of any starre:
And all within were pathes and alleies wide,
With footing worne, and leading inward farre:
Faire harbour that them seemes; so in they entred ar.

VIII And foorth they passe, with pleasure forward led,
Ioying to heare the birdes sweete harmony,
Which therein shrouded from the tempest dred,
Seemd in their song to scorne the cruell sky.
Much can they prayse the trees so straight and hy,
The sayling Pine, the Cedar proud and tall,
The vine-prop Elme, the Poplar neuer dry,
The builder Oake, sole king of forrests all,
The Aspine good for staues, the Cypresse funerall.

IX The Laurell, meed of mightie Conquerours
And Poets sage, the Firre that weepeth still,
The Willow worne of forlorne Paramours,
The Eugh obedient to the benders will,
The Birch for shaftes, the Sallow for the mill,
The Mirrhe sweete bleeding in the bitter wound,
The warlike Beech, the Ash for nothing ill,
The fruitfull Oliue, and the Platane round,
The caruer Holme, the Maple seeldom inward sound.

X Led with delight, they thus beguile the way,
Vntill the blustring storme is ouerblowne;
When weening to returne, whence they did stray,
They cannot finde that path, which first was showne,
But wander too and fro in wayes vnknowne,
Furthest from end then, when they neerest weene,
That makes them doubt, their wits be not their owne:
So many pathes, so many turnings seene,
That which of them to take, in diuerse doubt they been.

6 Lagging far behind them, came the dwarf. Always last, he seemed lazy or wearied from bearing her bag of necessities on his back.

Thus, as they passed by, the day became suddenly overcast, and angry Jove poured out a hideous rainstorm that came from his beloved Leman's[1] lap. The rain came down so fast that every living thing ran for shelter, including this fair couple and their page. Forced to seek some cover close at hand, they noticed a shady grove not far away, that promised to help them withstand the tempest. The lofty trees were clad with summer's pride and spread so broad that their branches hid the light of heaven, and allowed no star to pierce by night. Within the grove, many worn paths and wide alleys led far inward, and it seemed like a fair shelter.

So they entered, led by the pleasure of hearing the joyful sweet harmony of the birds, who were also sheltering from the tempest, seeming to scorn the cruel sky with their song. And much is there to praise of these trees so straight and high: the sailing-ship Pine, the proud and tall Cedar, the vine-prop Elm, the never-dry Poplar, the builder Oak; sole king of all forests, the Aspen; good for staves, and the Cypress; funerals. The Laurel; prize of mighty conquerors and sage poets, the Fir that still weeps resin, the sad Willow, worn by forlorn lovers, the obedient Yew; bending to the will, the Birch for shaft, the Sallow for the mill, the Myrrh, sweet bleeding in bitter wound, the warlike Beech Tree, the Ash for nothing ill, the fruitful Olive, the Plane Tree, the carver Holly, and the Maple that is seldom inwardly sound: all were honored with glorious birdsong.

10 Led with delight, they thus whiled away their time until the blustering storm had blown over. But when they sought to return from whence they strayed, they could not find the path in which they came. So they wandered to and fro on unfamiliar trails to no avail, doubtful of their own wits. So many paths, so many turnings were seen, but all left them in doubt about which to take.

XI At last resoluing forward still to fare,
Till that some end they finde or in or out,
That path they take, that beaten seemd most bare,
And like to lead the labyrinth about;
Which when by tract they hunted had throughout,
At length it brought them to a hollow caue,
Amid the thickest woods. The Champion stout
Eftsoones dismounted from his courser braue,
And to the Dwarfe a while his needlesse spere he gaue.

XII Be well aware, quoth then that Ladie milde,
Least suddaine mischiefe ye too rash prouoke:
The danger hid, the place vnknowne and wilde,
Breedes dreadfull doubts: Oft fire is without smoke,
And perill without show: therefore your stroke
Sir knight with-hold, till further triall made.
Ah Ladie (said he) shame were to reuoke
The forward footing for an hidden shade:
Vertue giues her selfe light, through darkenesse for to wade.

XIII Yea but (quoth she) the perill of this place
I better wot then you, though now too late
To wish you backe returne with foule disgrace,
Yet wisedome warnes, whilest foot is in the gate,
To stay the steppe, ere forced to retrate.
This is the wandring wood, this *Errours den*,
A monster vile, whom God and man does hate:
Therefore I read beware. Fly fly (quoth then
The fearefull Dwarfe:) this is no place for liuing men.

XIV But full of fire and greedy hardiment,
The youthfull knight could not for ought be staide,
But forth vnto the darksome hole he went,
And looked in: his glistring armor made
A litle glooming light, much like a shade,
By which he saw the vgly monster plaine,
Halfe like a serpent horribly displaide,
But th'other halfe did womans shape retaine,
Most lothsom, filthie, foule, and full of vile disdaine.

XV And as she lay vpon the durtie ground,
Her huge long taile her den all ouerspred,
Yet was in knots and many boughtes vpwound,
Pointed with mortall sting. Of her there bred
A thousand yong ones, which she dayly fed,
Sucking vpon her poisonous dugs, each one
Of sundry shapes, yet all ill fauored:
Soone as that vncouth light vpon them shone,
Into her mouth they crept, and suddain all were gone.

11 Resolving to fare onward until they found a way out, they decided to take the path that seemed most beaten, and therefore most likely to lead from this labyrinth. At length, it brought them to a dark hollow cave amid the thickest woods. Undaunted, the brave knight dismounted from his horse, and handed his unneeded lance to the dwarf for safe keeping.

"Be well aware," warned that mild lady, "lest you provoke some sudden mischief by being rash. Since this place is wild and unknown, and danger is hidden, it breeds dreadful doubts. Often, there is fire without smoke, and peril without show. Therefore, withhold your strike, Sir knight, until further enquiry is made."

"Ah, lady," replied the knight, "it would be a shame to have to turn back because of a hidden shadow. Instead, we must progress. Virtue gives her own light to wade through darkness."

"Yes, but I know the peril of this place better than you," she said. "Though you have already committed to proceed, wisdom warns us to stop while our foot is still at the gate, before we are forced to retreat. This is the wandering wood where men go astray, and this is Error's den. She is a vile monster, hated by God and man. Therefore, I warn: Beware! Fly, fly!"

And the fearful dwarf added: "This is no place for living men."

But full of fire and puffed up with pride, the youthful knight would not stay for anything, and went forth into the darksome hole to explore. His glistering armor created just enough gloomy light to reveal an ugly monster, half serpent and half woman. **15** Filthy, foul, and full of vile disdain, she lay upon the dirty ground with her huge tail, partly spread out, partly coiled and knotted, and pointed with a venomous sting. Scampering about the monster's body, there bred a thousand ill-favored young ones of sundry shapes, that she fed with her ugly poisonous breasts.

As soon as that mysterious light settled upon them, the brood crept into the monster's mouth and were suddenly gone.

XVI Their dam vpstart, out of her den effraide,
And rushed forth, hurling her hideous taile
About her cursed head, whose folds displaid
Were stretcht now forth at length without entraile.
She lookt about, and seeing one in mayle
Armed to point, sought backe to turne againe;
For light she hated as the deadly bale,
Ay wont in desert darknesse to remaine,
Where plain none might her see, nor she see any plaine.

XVII Which when the valiant Elfe perceiu'd, he lept
As Lyon fierce vpon the flying pray,
And with his trenchand blade her boldly kept
From turning backe, and forced her to stay:
Therewith enrag'd she loudly gan to bray,
And turning fierce, her speckled taile aduaunst,
Threatning her angry sting, him to dismay:
Who nought aghast, his mightie hand enhaunst:
The stroke down from her head vnto her shoulder glaunst.

XVIII Much daunted with that dint, her sence was dazd,
Yet kindling rage, her selfe she gathered round,
And all attonce her beastly body raizd
With doubled forces high aboue the ground:
Tho wrapping vp her wrethed sterne arownd,
Lept fierce vpon his shield, and her huge traine
All suddenly about his body wound,
That hand or foot to stirr he stroue in vaine:
God helpe the man so wrapt in *Errours* endlesse traine.

XIX His Lady sad to see his sore constraint,
Cride out, Now now Sir knight, shew what ye bee,
Add faith vnto your force, and be not faint:
Strangle her, else she sure will strangle thee.
That when he heard, in great perplexitie,
His gall did grate for griefe and high disdaine,
And knitting all his force got one hand free,
Wherewith he grypt her gorge with so great paine,
That soone to loose her wicked bands did her constraine.

XX Therewith she spewd out of her filthy maw
A floud of poyson horrible and blacke,
Full of great lumpes of flesh and gobbets raw,
Which stunck so vildly, that it forst him slacke
His grasping hold, and from her turne him backe:
Her vomit full of bookes and papers was,
With loathly frogs and toades, which eyes did lacke,
And creeping sought way in the weedy gras:
Her filthy parbreake all the place defiled has.

16 Alarmed, the monster hurled her hideous, uncoiled tail about her cursed head, and rushed forth out of her den. But when she spied one in chainmail and arms, she sought to turn back. For she hated the light and only wanted to remain in her familiar darkness, unseen and unseeing.

When the valiant Elf perceived this, he leapt fiercely upon the fleeing prey like a lion. With his sharpened blade, he boldly kept her from turning back, and forced her to stay and engage in fight. Enraged, she began to roar loudly, turning fierce and advancing her speckled tail, threatening the alarmed knight with her sting. But the knight, unaffected, raised his mighty hand and smashed the sword upon her head and shoulder.

Much daunted by that blow, her sense was dazed. Yet, kindling rage, she gathered herself around, and all at once, raised her beastly body with doubled forces high above the ground. Then, amassing her wretched tail, the monster leapt fiercely at the shield and suddenly swung the huge train, twisting it around the knight's body, so that he could move neither hand nor foot.

God help the man so wrapped up in Error's endless train!

His lady was sad to see his perilous constraint, and she cried out, "Now! Now! Sir knight, show what you are. Add faith unto your strength and be not faint. Strangle her, else she will strangle you!"

20 When the now entangled knight heard this, he grated with grief and high disdain. Then, combining all his force, he freed one hand, and grabbed the monster's throat with so much strength, she was forced to loosen her wicked bands. But, then, out of her filthy mouth she spewed forth a flood of horrible poison, black lumps of flesh, and raw gobbets, and it stank so vilely that it forced Redcross to slacken his grasp and turn his back. The vomit was full of books and papers, and crawling with loathly frogs and eyeless toads, which slunk away into the weedy grass, defiling the entire place.

XXI As when old father *Nilus* gins to swell
With timely pride aboue the *Aegyptian* vale,
His fattie waues do fertile slime outwell,
And ouerflow each plaine and lowly dale:
But when his later spring gins to auale,
Huge heapes of mudd he leaues, wherein there breed
Ten thousand kindes of creatures, partly male
And partly female of his fruitfull seed;
Such vgly monstrous shapes elswhere may no man reed.

XXII The same so sore annoyed has the knight,
That welnigh choked with the deadly stinke,
His forces faile, ne can no longer fight.
Whose corage when the feend perceiu'd to shrinke,
She poured forth out of her hellish sinke
Her fruitfull cursed spawne of serpents small,
Deformed monsters, fowle, and blacke as inke,
Which swarming all about his legs did crall,
And him encombred sore, but could not hurt at all.

XXIII As gentle Shepheard in sweete euentide,
When ruddy *Phoebus* gins to welke in west,
High on an hill, his flocke to vewen wide,
Markes which do byte their hasty supper best;
A cloud of combrous gnattes do him molest,
All striuing to infixe their feeble stings,
That from their noyance he no where can rest,
But with his clownish hands their tender wings
He brusheth oft, and oft doth mar their murmurings.

XXIV Thus ill bestedd, and fearefull more of shame,
Then of the certaine perill he stood in,
Halfe furious vnto his foe he came,
Resolv'd in minde all suddenly to win,
Or soone to lose, before he once would lin;
And strooke at her with more then manly force,
That from her body full of filthie sin
He raft her hatefull head without remorse;
A streame of cole black bloud forth gushed from her corse.

XXV Her scattred brood, soone as their Parent deare
They saw so rudely falling to the ground,
Groning full deadly, all with troublous feare,
Gathred themselues about her body round,
Weening their wonted entrance to haue found
At her wide mouth: but being there withstood
They flocked all about her bleeding wound,
And sucked vp their dying mothers blood,
Making her death their life, and eke her hurt their good.

21 When old father Nile begins to swell with seasonal pride above the Egyptian valley, his thick waves pour out fertile slime and overflow each plain and lowly dale. But when spring comes, he retreats and leaves huge heaps of mud, breeding ten thousand kinds of creatures, partly male and partly female [2] Such ugly monstrous shapes as these, and this monster, may no man see elsewhere!

This same sore sight nearly choked the knight with deadly stench, his forces failing so he could no longer fight. When the fiend perceived his courage shrinking, she poured forth, out of her stomach, a mass of fruitful cursed spawn of small serpents. Swarming all around his ankles, black as ink, the foul deformed critters slithered up his legs and all over him, riling but not harming him.

Like a gentle shepherd, sitting high on a hill observing his sheep munch their grass to check their health, while ruddy Phoebus begins to set in the west, he is suddenly attacked by an aggressive cloud of gnats, all striving to infix their feeble stings, but since he can't leave his post, he has no respite from their annoyance, and all he can do is brush them off with clumsy hands, marring their tender wings and murmurings.

Thus, ill situated, with a similar pest, and more fearful of shame than of certain peril, Redcross came unto his foe half furious, but now resolved to win or lose the fight without stopping once. Without remorse, he struck at the monster with more than manly force so that he chopped her hateful head from her filthy sinful body. A stream of coal-black blood gushed from the corpse.

25 Her scattered offspring, dashing in every direction, groaned with deadly troubled fear when they saw their dear parent so rudely falling to the ground. They gathered themselves around her body expecting to find their usual entrance at her wide mouth. Finding it blocked, they all flocked about the monster's bleeding wound and sucked up their dying mother's blood, making her death their life, and her hurt their good.

XXVI That detestable sight him much amazde,
To see th'vnkindly Impes of heauen accurst,
Deuoure their dam; on whom while so he gazd,
Hauing all satisfide their bloudy thurst,
Their bellies swolne he saw with fulnesse burst,
And bowels gushing forth: well worthy end
Of such as drunke her life, the which them nurst;
Now needeth him no lenger labour spend,
His foes haue slaine themselues, with whom he should contend.

XXVII His Ladie seeing all, that chaunst, from farre
Approcht in hast to greet his victorie,
And said, Faire knight, borne vnder happy starre,
Who see your vanquisht foes before you lye:
Well worthy be you of that Armorie,
Wherein ye haue great glory wonne this day,
And prooud your strength on a strong enimie,
Your first aduenture: many such I pray,
And henceforth euer wish, that like succeed it may.

XXVIII Then mounted he vpon his Steede againe,
And with the Lady backward sought to wend;
That path he kept, which beaten was most plaine,
Ne euer would to any by-way bend,
But still did follow one vnto the end,
The which at last out of the wood them brought.
So forward on his way (with God to frend)
He passed forth, and new aduenture sought;
Long way he traueiled, before he heard of ought.

XXIX At length they chaunst to meet vpon the way
An aged Sire, in long blacke weedes yclad,
His feete all bare, his beard all hoarie gray,
And by his belt his booke he hanging had;
Sober he seemde, and very sagely sad,
And to the ground his eyes were lowly bent,
Simple in shew, and voyde of malice bad,
And all the way he prayed, as he went,
And often knockt his brest, as one that did repent.

XXX He faire the knight saluted, louting low,
Who faire him quited, as that courteous was:
And after asked him, if he did know
Of straunge aduentures, which abroad did pas.
Ah my deare Sonne (quoth he) how should, alas,
Silly old man, that liues in hidden cell,
Bidding his beades all day for his trespas,
Tydings of warre and worldly trouble tell?
With holy father sits not with such things to mell.

26 The knight was appalled at the detestable sight of those cursed imps devouring the dam. Worse still, when they had satisfied their bloody thirst, their swollen bellies burst and their bowels gushed forth. Well worthy end for those who were nursed by, and drank, Error's life!

And now the knight wasted no more effort there, since his foes had slain themselves.

His lady, having seen all that happened from afar, approached in haste to greet his victory, and said, "Fair knight, born under a happy star, who sees his vanquished foes lie before him, you are well worthy of your armor, wherein you have won great glory this day, and proven your strength on a strong enemy. While this was your first test, I pray that henceforth you may continue to succeed likewise, in that which is yet to come."

Mounted upon their steeds once more, the knight, his lady, and the dwarf, sought to turn back. They kept to one path that was most plainly worn from use, and decided to follow until they came to the end, rather than turn off on by-ways and other diversions.

At last, it brought them out of the wood and into the bright sunlight. So forward, on their way, with God as friend, they roamed, seeking a new adventure. And long they travelled before they heard of any.

AT LENGTH, THEY CHANCED TO MEET AN OLD MAN UPON THE WAY. HE WAS dressed in long black clothes, his feet were bare, his beard old and gray, and a holy book was hanging on his belt. With his eyes lowly bent to the ground, he seemed serious and sagely sad. Simple in appearance and seemingly void of bad malice, he prayed all the way as he went, often beating his breast as one did to repent.

30 When he saw the fair knight, he greeted him and bowed low, while Redcross kindly returned his courtesies. Then the knight asked the old man if he knew of any strange adventures which had passed abroad.

"Ah my dear son," he said, "how should I, alas, simple old man who lives in a hidden cell, praying his rosary beads all day for his trespasses, know of tidings of wars and worldly trouble? A holy father does not meddle in such things.

XXXI But if of daunger which hereby doth dwell,
And homebred euill ye desire to heare,
Of a straunge man I can you tidings tell,
That wasteth all this countrey farre and neare.
Of such (said he) I chiefly do inquere,
And shall you well reward to shew the place,
In which that wicked wight his dayes doth weare:
For to all knighthood it is foule disgrace,
That such a cursed creature liues so long a space.

XXXII Far hence (quoth he) in wastfull wildernesse
His dwelling is, by which no liuing wight
May euer passe, but thorough great distresse.
Now (sayd the Lady) draweth toward night,
And well I wote, that of your later fight
Ye all forwearied be: for what so strong,
But wanting rest will also want of might?
The Sunne that measures heauen all day long,
At night doth baite his steedes the *Ocean* waues emong.

XXXIII Then with the Sunne take Sir, your timely rest,
And with new day new worke at once begin:
Vntroubled night they say giues counsell best.
Right well Sir knight ye haue aduised bin,
(Quoth then that aged man;) the way to win
Is wisely to aduise: now day is spent;
Therefore with me ye may take vp your In
For this same night. The knight was well content:
So with that godly father to his home they went.

XXXIV A little lowly Hermitage it was,
Downe in a dale, hard by a forests side,
Far from resort of people, that did pas
In trauell to and froe: a little wyde
There was an holy Chappell edifyde,
Wherein the Hermite dewly wont to say
His holy things each morne and euentyde:
Thereby a Christall streame did gently play,
Which from a sacred fountaine welled forth alway.

XXXV Arriued there, the little house they fill,
Ne looke for entertainement, where none was:
Rest is their feast, and all things at their will;
The noblest mind the best contentment has.
With faire discourse the euening so they pas:
For that old man of pleasing wordes had store,
And well could file his tongue as smooth as glas;
He told of Saintes and Popes, and euermore
He strowd an *Aue-Mary* after and before.

31 But, if you desire to hear of dangers closer to home, and of homebred evil, I can tell you tidings of a strange man that lays waste to all this country, far and near."

"Of such," said Redcross, "I chiefly do inquire, and shall well reward you if you can show me the place in which that wicked creature spends his days. For, to all knighthood, it is foul disgrace that such cursed creatures should live so long."

The old man pointed ahead, "Far hence, in wasteful wilderness is his dwelling. But no living creature can pass through without great distress."

"But now," said the lady, "night draws near and I well know that you are wearied from your recent fight. For doesn't strength also need rest? Even the sun that measures heaven all day long, feeds his horses among the ocean waves at night. With the sun then, sir, take your timely rest, and with a new day, new work can begin. An untroubled night, they say, gives best counsel."

"Right well have you been advised, Sir knight," said the old man. "And the way to win is to heed wise advice. Now the day is spent. Therefore, you may take up lodgings with me for this same night."

The knight was well content. So, they all went with that godly father to his home.

It was a lowly little hermitage, down in a dale, hard by the forest's side, but far away from where people usually pass, travelling to and fro. A little way off, stood a holy chapel building, wherein the hermit would duly say his holy prayers each morning and evening. Next to it, a crystal stream gently played, and a sacred fountain ever welled forth.

35 Once they arrived, they filled the tiny humble hermitage. None looked for entertainment where there was none. Rest was their feast, and all things at their will. For the noblest mind can entertain itself and has the best contentment, and they passed the evening in fair discussion. For that old man of pleasing words had plenty to say, and could file his tongue as smooth as glass. He told of saints and popes, while scattering a Hail Mary before and after his speeches.

XXXVI The drouping Night thus creepeth on them fast,
And the sad humour loading their eye liddes,
As messenger of *Morpheus* on them cast
Sweet slombring deaw, the which to sleepe them biddes.
Vnto their lodgings then his guestes he riddes:
Where when all drownd in deadly sleepe he findes,
He to his study goes, and there amiddes
His Magick bookes and artes of sundry kindes,
He seekes out mighty charmes, to trouble sleepy minds.

XXXVII Then choosing out few wordes most horrible,
(Let none them read) thereof did verses frame,
With which and other spelles like terrible,
He bad awake blacke *Plutoes* griesly Dame,
And cursed heauen, and spake reprochfull shame
Of highest God, the Lord of life and light;
A bold bad man, that dar'd to call by name
Great *Gorgon*, Prince of darknesse and dead night,
At which *Cocytus* quakes, and *Styx* is put to flight.

XXXVIII And forth he cald out of deepe darknesse dred
Legions of Sprights, the which like little flyes
Fluttring about his euer damned hed,
A-waite whereto their seruice he applyes,
To aide his friends, or fray his enimies:
Of those he chose out two, the falsest twoo,
And fittest for to forge true-seeming lyes;
The one of them he gaue a message too,
The other by him selfe staide other worke to doo.

XXXIX He making speedy way through spersed ayre,
And through the world of waters wide and deepe,
To *Morpheus* house doth hastily repaire.
Amid the bowels of the earth full steepe,
And low, where dawning day doth neuer peepe,
His dwelling is; there *Tethys* his wet bed
Doth euer wash, and *Cynthia* still doth steepe
In siluer deaw his euer-drouping hed,
Whiles sad Night ouer him her mantle black doth spred

XL Whose double gates he findeth locked fast,
The one faire fram'd of burnisht Yuory,
The other all with siluer ouercast;
And wakefull dogges before them farre do lye,
Watching to banish Care their enimy,
Who oft is wont to trouble gentle Sleepe.
By them the Sprite doth passe in quietly,
And vnto *Morpheus* comes, whom drowned deepe
In drowsie fit he findes: of nothing he takes keepe.

36 The drooping night crept on them fast, the gloomy air made their eyelids heavy, and the messenger of Morpheus cast sweet slumbering dew on them.

The old man showed his guests their beds, and when they were all drowned in deep sleep, he slunk to his study. There, amidst his magic books and arts of similar kind, he sought out mighty charms to trouble sleepy minds. Then, choosing from a few most horrible words, he framed verses and other terrible spells with which he commanded Persephone, Pluto's dark grisly dame, to awaken. At the same time, he cursed heaven and spoke reproachful shame of highest God, the Lord of light and life. He was such a bold bad man that he even dared to call the Great Demogorgon, by name. Yet even the River Cocytus quakes, and The Styx is put to flight, at the mention of this prince of darkness.

And now, out of the deep dreaded darkness, the old man called forth legions of sprites. Like little flies, they fluttered about his ever-damned head, waiting to hear where their services might be applied. Will it be to aid his friends, or frighten his foes? Of those sprites, he chose two: the two falsest and fittest, to forge true-seeming lies. To one he gave a message, while the other stayed by with other work to do.

The messenger sprite sped away through the air, then through the world of wide and deep waters, straight down into the bowels of the earth, where the light of day never peeps, until he came to Morpheus's house. There, Tethys, the goddess of oceans, ever washed Morpheus' bed, and Cynthia, the moon, immersed his ever-drooping head in silver dew, while sad night spread her black mantle over him.

40 Finally, the sprite arrived at the portly gates. One of the doors was framed in polished ivory, for false dreams, and the other, plated in silver, for true. But both he found locked fast. Watchdogs lay before them, safeguarding against Care and Worry, that are often wanting to trouble gentle sleep. By them, and up and over the gates, the sprite buzzed in quietly and came unto Morpheus, whom he found drowned in a deep drowsy fit, heeding nothing.

XLI And more, to lulle him in his slumber soft,
A trickling streame from high rocke tumbling downe
And euer-drizling raine vpon the loft,
Mixt with a murmuring winde, much like the sowne
Of swarming Bees, did cast him in a swowne:
No other noyse, nor peoples troublous cryes,
As still are wont t'annoy the walled towne,
Might there be heard: but carelesse Quiet lyes,
Wrapt in eternall silence farre from enimyes.

XLII The messenger approching to him spake,
But his wast wordes returnd to him in vaine:
So sound he slept, that nought mought him awake.
Then rudely he him thrust, and pusht with paine,
Whereat he gan to stretch: but he againe
Shooke him so hard, that forced him to speake.
As one then in a dreame, whose dryer braine
Is tost with troubled sights and fancies weake,
He mumbled soft, but would not all his silence breake.

XLIII The Sprite then gan more boldly him to wake,
And threatned vnto him the dreaded name
Of *Hecate*: whereat he gan to quake,
And lifting vp his lompish head, with blame
Halfe angry asked him, for what he came.
Hither (quoth he) me *Archimago* sent,
He that the stubborne Sprites can wisely tame,
He bids thee to him send for his intent
A fit false dreame, that can delude the sleepers sent.

XLIV The God obayde, and calling forth straight way
A diuerse dreame out of his prison darke,
Deliuered it to him, and downe did lay
His heauie head, deuoide of carefull carke,
Whose sences all were straight benumbd and starke.
He backe returning by the Yuorie dore,
Remounted vp as light as chearefull Larke,
And on his litle winges the dreame he bore
In hast vnto his Lord, where he him left afore.

XLV Who all this while with charmes and hidden artes,
Had made a Lady of that other Spright,
And fram'd of liquid ayre her tender partes
So liuely, and so like in all mens sight,
That weaker sence it could haue rauisht quight:
The maker selfe for all his wondrous witt,
Was nigh beguiled with so goodly sight:
Her all in white he clad, and ouer it
Cast a black stole, most like to seeme for *Vna* fit.

41 A gentle waterfall trickled down from a high rock, further lulling Morpheus in soft slumber, while the ever-drizzling rain upon the loft, mixed with a murmuring wind, sounding like swarming bees, cast him in a swoon. No other noise or people's troublesome cries, that usually annoy those in busy walled towns, could be heard. Only Quiet, free from care, lay wrapped in eternal silence, far from enemies.

Approaching slumbering Morpheus, the sprite then spoke the message into his ear. But his wasted words returned to him in vain, for Morpheus slept too soundly. The sprite then jabbed him sharply in the ribs and gave him a rude shove, but Morpheus only stretched for a moment, before resuming his torpor. Again, the sprite shook him so hard, that he was finally forced to lift his head and address his tormenter. As one in a dream, whose dull, muddled brain is tossed with troubled sights and weak fancies, Morpheus softly mumbled and dozed off again. Growing impatient, the sprite began to wake him more boldly and threatened him with the dreaded name of Hecate, goddess of the underworld. At that, he began to quake and lift his lumpish head.

"What do you want?" snapped Morpheus.

"Archimago sent me hither," said the sprite. "He, who the untamable sprites can skillfully tame. And he bids you send him a suitable false dream to delude a sleeper's sense."

The god obeyed and immediately called forth a distressing, distracting dream that came straight out of his dark prison, and delivered it to the sprite. Once again, Morpheus lay down his heavy head. His senses were numb, stark, and devoid of cares.

45The sprite returned by the ivory door of false dreams, and remounted as light as a cheerful lark. On his little wings he bore the dream, which he brought in haste to his lord in his study.

In the meantime, Archimago had been busy with his charms and occult arts, and had turned that other sprite into a lady. He framed her tender parts with bright, feminine air that was so lifelike, and so resembling life itself, that a weaker man's sense would have been ravished. The maker himself, for all his wondrous wit, was nearly tempted with such a beautiful sight. Lastly, he clad her in the same white dress and black stole as Una.

XLVI Now when that ydle dreame was to him brought,
Vnto that Elfin knight he bad him fly,
Where he slept soundly void of euill thought,
And with false shewes abuse his fantasy,
In sort as he him schooled priuily:
And that new creature borne without her dew,
Full of the makers guile, with vsage sly
He taught to imitate that Lady trew,
Whose semblance she did carrie vnder feigned hew.

XLVII Thus well instructed, to their worke they hast,
And comming where the knight in slomber lay,
The one vpon his hardy head him plast,
And made him dreame of loues and lustfull play,
That nigh his manly hart did melt away,
Bathed in wanton blis and wicked ioy:
Then seemed him his Lady by him lay,
And to him playnd, how that false winged boy,
Her chast hart had subdewd, to learne Dame pleasures toy.

XLVIII And she her selfe of beautie soueraigne Queene,
Faire *Venus* seemde vnto his bed to bring
Her, whom he waking euermore did weene,
To be the chastest flowre, that ay did spring
On earthly braunch, the daughter of a king,
Now a loose Leman to vile seruice bound:
And eke the *Graces* seemed all to sing,
   Hymen iô Hymen, dauncing all around,
Whilst freshest *Flora* her with Yuie girlond crownd.

XLIX In this great passion of vnwonted lust,
Or wonted feare of doing ought amis,
He started vp, as seeming to mistrust,
Some secret ill, or hidden foe of his:
Lo there before his face his Lady is,
Vnder blake stole hyding her bayted hooke,
And as halfe blushing offred him to kis,
With gentle blandishment and louely looke,
Most like that virgin true, which for her knight him took.

L All cleane dismayd to see so vncouth sight,
And halfe enraged at her shamelesse guise,
He thought haue slaine her in his fierce despight:
But hasty heat tempring with sufferance wise,
He stayde his hand, and gan himselfe aduise
To proue his sense, and tempt her faigned truth.
Wringing her hands in wemens pitteous wise,
Tho can she weepe, to stirre vp gentle ruth,
Both for her noble blood, and for her tender youth.

46 Now, when that frivolous dream was brought to Archimago, he bade the sprite fly unto the Elfin knight, who was now sleeping soundly, void of all evil thought. There, he was to deceive the knight's dreams with false images in the way Archimago had already secretly coached him. Next, Archimago coached the other sprite to imitate the true lady. Born unnaturally, and full of her maker's guile, that sprite was now identical to Una.

Thus, well instructed, the wicked sprites hastened to their work. Arriving where the knight lay in slumber, the first sprite placed a dream upon his hardy head, and made him dream of loves and lustful play. Bathed in wanton bliss and wicked joy, it nearly melted his heart away. Then it seemed his lady lay beside him, complaining how that false winged Cupid had subdued her chaste heart to become his pleasure toy. And it seemed that fair Venus herself brought her unto his bed. Yet he had thought her to be the most chaste flower that ever sprang on earthly branch. Daughter of a king, she was now but a loose Leman lover, bound to vile service. Then the handmaids to Venus seemed all to sing, *Hymen io Hymen*[3], dancing all around, whilst freshest Flora crowned her with an ivy garland.

Disturbed by this unwanted lust, and afraid of doing wrong, the knight leapt out of bed. He seemed to suspect some secret ill or hidden foe in this. But, Lo, there before his eyes was his lady, wrapped in her black stole, hiding her baited hook. Half blushing, she offered to kiss him with gentle enticing words and lovely look, seeming just like that true maiden who took him for her knight.

50 Completely dismayed to see such a vulgar sight, and half enraged at her shameless manner, he thought to slay her in fierce fury. But hasty heat is tempered with suffering wisdom, and he stayed his hand. Then he began to advise himself to prove his senses, and test for truth. But the false Una was wringing her hands in pitiful ways, weeping to stir up gentle sympathy for her noble blood and tender youth.

LI And said, Ah Sir, my liege Lord and my loue,
Shall I accuse the hidden cruell fate,
And mightie causes wrought in heauen aboue,
Or the blind God, that doth me thus amate,
For hoped loue to winne me certaine hate?
Yet thus perforce he bids me do, or die.
Die is my dew: yet rew my wretched state
You, whom my hard auenging destinie
Hath made iudge of my life or death indifferently.

LII Your owne deare sake forst me at first to leaue
My Fathers kingdome,--There she stopt with teares;
Her swollen hart her speach seemd to bereaue,
And then againe begun, My weaker yeares
Captiu'd to fortune and frayle worldly feares,
Fly to your faith for succour and sure ayde:
Let me not dye in languor and long teares.
Why Dame (quoth he) what hath ye thus dismayd?
What frayes ye, that were wont to comfort me affrayd?

LIII Loue of your selfe, she said, and deare constraint
Lets me not sleepe, but wast the wearie night
In secret anguish and vnpittied plaint,
Whiles you in carelesse sleepe are drowned quight.
Her doubtfull words made that redoubted knight
Suspect her truth: yet since no' vntruth he knew,
Her fawning loue with foule disdainefull spight
He would not shend, but said, Deare dame I rew,
That for my sake vnknowne such griefe vnto you grew.

LIV Assure your selfe, it fell not all to ground;
For all so deare as life is to my hart,
I deeme your loue, and hold me to you bound;
Ne let vaine feares procure your needlesse smart,
Where cause is none, but to your rest depart.
Not all content, yet seemd she to appease
Her mournefull plaintes, beguiled of her art,
And fed with words, that could not chuse but please,
So slyding softly forth, she turnd as to her ease.

LV Long after lay he musing at her mood,
Much grieu'd to thinke that gentle Dame so light,
For whose defence he was to shed his blood.
At last dull wearinesse of former fight
Hauing yrockt a sleepe his irkesome spright,
That troublous dreame gan freshly tosse his braine,
With bowres, and beds, and Ladies deare delight:
But when he saw his labour all was vaine,
With that misformed spright he backe returnd againe

---

51 The false Una sighed, "Ah sir, my liege lord and my love. Shall I accuse the hidden cruel fate and mighty causes formed in heaven above? Or the blind god Cupid who dismays me, bringing me certain hate when I hoped to win love? Yet thus, by force, love enticed me to do or die. And dying is now my due, since you reject my wretched state: you whom my hard-avenging destiny has made indifferent judge of my life or death. Your own dear sake forced me at first to leave my father's kingdom …."

There she stopped with false tears, making her speech appear to bereave her swollen heart, before continuing, "My weaker years are captive to fortune and frail worldly fears, flee to your faith for help. Let me not die in woeful plight and long tears."

"Why, lady," said the perplexed knight, "what has dismayed you? What frightens you, when you are the brave one who has so far been offering comfort and wisdom to *me*?"

"Love of you," she sighed, "and dear restraint stops me sleeping. It wastes the weary night in secret anguish and unanswered need, while you are quite drowned in careless sleep."

Her doubtful words made that wary knight suspect her truth, yet he could find no untruth in what she said.

He decided not to scold her fawning love with foul disdainful spite, and replied instead: "Dear lady, I regret that for my sake you suffered such grief. Assure yourself that your love is not wasted. For I deem your love as dear as life is to my heart, and hold you bound to me. Do not let vain fears cause needless pain where cause is none, but depart to your rest."

Beguiled by magic, and fed with a script, the pouting sprite could not choose but to obey, and pretending her mournful plaints had been appeased, the false Una returned to bed.

55 LONG AFTER, THE KNIGHT LAY MUSING AT HER MOOD, MUCH GRIEVED TO think that gentle dame was so easy and fickle. Yet it was for her defense he was to shed his blood. At last dull weariness from the former fight rocked his disturbed spirit to sleep. But that troublesome dream began to freshly toss in his brain, with bowers and beds and dear delightful ladies. When the dream sprite saw that his labor was all in vain, he returned to Archimago with that other malformed sprite to make new plans.

1 *Leman: goddess lover*
2 *The ancients believed in Spontaneous Generation*
3 *A wedding song*

NOTES ON CANTO II

Sansfoy: is French for "without faith," and his brothers are: Sansloy and Sansjoy: without law and without joy. They represent the three stages of loss of faith: first, without faith, then without law, and finally without joy.

Saracen: Muslim, but interchangeably with heathen and pagan. Medieval Europe had endured a long history of clashes with Muslim invaders from the 8th century onwards, so Saracens are often featured as the bad guys in stories of this era. However, they don't necessarily represent a religion or a culture, but are symbols of faithlessness or 'an unbeliever.'

Duessa: Double nature. Duessa is a witch disguised as a noble maiden. She represents the false church of Rome masquerading as true religion, as well as Mary Queen of Scots.

Fidessa: Faithful. This is Duessa's false name, especially created to mislead.

Fradubio: Doubt. *Reader challenge*: what do you think is the first step Fradubio takes that leads to his downfall?

Fraelissa: Frail: Fraelissa was too frail to ward off evil.

Talking Trees: similar myths are found in Ovid's Metamorphoses, Virgil's Aeneid, and Dante's Inferno.

CANTO II

REDCROSS AND UNA PART WAYS

The guilefull great Enchaunter parts
The Redcrosse Knight from Truth:
Into whose stead faire falshood steps,
And workes him wofull ruth.

I BY this the Northerne wagoner had set
His seuenfold teme behind the stedfast starre,
That was in Ocean waues yet neuer wet,
But firme is fixt, and sendeth light from farre
To all, that in the wide deepe wandring arre:
And chearefull Chaunticlere with his note shrill
Had warned once, that Phoebus fiery carre
In hast was climbing vp the Easterne hill,
Full enuious that night so long his roome did fill.

II When those accursed messengers of hell,
That feigning dreame, and that faire-forged Spright
Came to their wicked maister, and gan tell
Their bootelesse paines, and ill succeeding night:
Who all in rage to see his skilfull might
Deluded so, gan threaten hellish paine
And sad Proserpines wrath, them to affright.
But when he saw his threatning was but vaine,
He cast about, and searcht his baleful bookes againe.

III Eftsoones he tooke that miscreated faire,
And that false other Spright, on whom he spred
A seeming body of the subtile aire,
Like a young Squire, in loues and lusty-hed
His wanton dayes that euer loosely led,
Without regard of armes and dreaded fight:
Those two he tooke, and in a secret bed,
Couered with darknesse and misdeeming night,
Them both together laid, to ioy in vaine delight.

IV Forthwith he runnes with feigned faithfull hast
Vnto his guest, who after troublous sights
And dreames, gan now to take more sound repast,
Whom suddenly he wakes with fearefull frights,
As one aghast with feends or damned sprights,
And to him cals, Rise rise vnhappy Swaine,
That here wex old in sleepe, whiles wicked wights
Haue knit themselues in Venus shamefull chaine;
Come see, where your false Lady doth her honour staine.

V All in amaze he suddenly vp start
With sword in hand, and with the old man went;
Who soone him brought into a secret part,
Where that false couple were full closely ment
In wanton lust and lewd embracement:
Which when he saw, he burnt with gealous fire,
The eye of reason was with rage yblent,
And would haue slaine them in his furious ir
But hardly was restreined of that aged sire.

*The great guileful enchanter parts the Redcross knight from truth,
into whose stead steps fair falsehood, and works him
woeful mischief and ruin.*

IN THE NIGHT SKY, THE NORTHERN WAGONER HAD SET HIS SEVENFOLD TEAM behind the Pole Star. Sending light from afar to all that are in the wide, deep wandering, the firm and fixed Big Dipper always seemed to set in ocean waves, yet never sink.

With his shrill note, the cheerful rooster, Chanticleer, had already warned that Phoebus's fiery chariot was climbing up the eastern hill in haste, envious that night had filled his room so long.

MEANWHILE, THOSE ACCURSED MESSENGERS OF HELL: THAT DREAM-FAKER AND the falsely-fair sprite, came to their wicked master. There, they began to tell of their ineffective plans, and of the ill succeeding night. Enraged to hear his skillful power had failed, Archimago began to threaten and frighten them with hellish pain and sad Proserpina's wrath. But when he realized his threats were in vain, he cast about, and searched his dreadful books again.

Soon he took that sprite he had already turned into a false Una, and turned the fake-dream sprite into a debonair young squire. He created him as a lusty-headed lover, who spent his wanton days wherever they loosely led, without regard for arms or brave battle. Then he took those two, put them into a secret bed, and covered it with darkness and misleading night. Next, he bade them lie together to enjoy vain delight.

Forthwith, he ran to his guest with faked faithful haste. The knight, after tossing and turning with troublesome dreams, had just begun to sleep more soundly. But Archimago suddenly shook him awake with fearful fright, as one aghast with fiends and damned sprites.

He called to the knight, "Rise, rise, unhappy youth, who here grows old in sleep while wicked creatures have knit themselves in Venus's shameful chain. Come see, where your false lady stains her honor."

5 Amazed, Redcross leapt out of bed, sword in hand. The old man then led him to a secret room where that false couple was closely joined in wanton lust and lewd embrace. When Redcross saw this sight, he burned with jealous fire and was blinded in his eye of reason. He would have slain them in his furious ire, had he not been restrained, with some difficulty, by that old man.

VI Returning to his bed in torment great,
And bitter anguish of his guiltie sight,
He could not rest, but did his stout heart eat,
And wast his inward gall with deepe despight,
Yrkesome of life, and too long lingring night.
At last faire Hesperus in highest skie
Had spent his lampe, and brought forth dawning light,
Then vp he rose, and clad him hastily;
The Dwarfe him brought his steed: so both away do fly.

VII Now when the rosy-fingred Morning faire,
Weary of aged Tithones saffron bed,
Had spred her purple robe through deawy aire,
And the high hils Titan discouered,
The royall virgin shooke off drowsy-hed,
And rising forth out of her baser bowre,
Lookt for her knight, who far away was fled,
And for her Dwarfe, that wont to wait each houre;
Then gan she waile and weepe, to see that woefull stowre.

VIII And after him she rode with so much speede
As her slow beast could make; but all in vaine:
For him so far had borne his light-foot steede,
Pricked with wrath and fiery fierce disdaine,
That him to follow was but fruitlesse paine;
Yet she her weary limbes would neuer rest,
But euery hill and dale, each wood and plaine
Did search, sore grieued in her gentle brest,
He so vngently left her, whom she loued best.

IX But subtill Archimago, when his guests
He saw diuided into double parts,
And Vna wandring in woods and forrests,
Th'end of his drift, he praisd his diuelish arts,
That had such might ouer true meaning harts;
Yet rests not so, but other meanes doth make,
How he may worke vnto her further smarts:
For her he hated as the hissing snake,
And in her many troubles did most pleasure take.

X He then deuisde himselfe how to disguise;
For by his mightie science he could take
As many formes and shapes in seeming wise,
As euer Proteus to himselfe could make:
Sometime a fowle, sometime a fish in lake,
Now like a foxe, now like a dragon fell,
That of himselfe he oft for feare would quake,
And oft would flie away. O who can tell
The hidden power of herbes, and might of Magicke spell?

6 Returning to bed in great torment and bitter anguish, he could not rest. His brave heart was now consumed by deep spite, irksome of life, and too long in lingering night.

Finally, fair Hesperus, last star in the highest sky, had spent his lamp and brought forth the dawning light. Then up rose the knight and hastily clad himself. The dwarf brought his steed, and they both flew away.

THEN WHEN THE ROSY-FINGERED GODDESS OF THE DAWN, FAIR AURORA, WEARY of old Tithones saffron bed, had spread her purple robe through dewy air, and Titan had revealed the high hills, Una was shaking off her drowsy head. Rising forth from her humble bed, she began to look for her knight. But he was already far away. Next, she frantically sought the dwarf who usually waited on her every hour, but he too was gone. Then she began to wail and weep, to see that woeful situation, and not wanting to waste another moment, she rode after him as fast as she could. But her donkey was slow, and it was all in vain. For Redcross, spurred with wrath and fierce fiery disdain, had already travelled far on his light-footed steed, and it was fruitless to follow.

Thenceforth, she decided, she would never rest her weary limbs until she had searched every hill and dale, each wood and plain. For she so grieved why he, whom she loved best, left her so urgently, and in such an ungentlemanly manner.

Meanwhile, when cunning Archimago saw his guests divided and going off in different directions, he rubbed his bony hands with glee to realize that his plot had been successful. With Una now wandering alone in woods and forests, he praised his devilish arts that had such power over truth-seeking hearts. Yet he did not rest, but started to make new plans to cause her further pains. For he hated her as a hissing snake, and took great pleasure in her troubles. **10** He then devised how he might create a disguise. With his mighty science, he could already take on many forms and shapes: sometimes like the sea-god, Proteus, sometimes a fowl, sometimes a fish in a lake, now like a fox. Other times he could change himself into a dreadful dragon, and find himself so frightening, he would quake for fear and fly away! O, who can tell the hidden power of herbs and mighty magic spells?

XI But now seemde best, the person to put on
Of that good knight, his late beguiled guest:
In mighty armes he was yclad anon,
And siluer shield vpon his coward brest
A bloudy crosse, and on his crauen crest
A bounch of haires discolourd diuersly:
Full iolly knight he seemde, and well addrest,
And when he sate vpon his courser free,
Saint George himself ye would haue deemed him to be.

XII But he the knight, whose semblaunt he did beare,
The true Saint George was wandred far away,
Still flying from his thoughts and gealous feare;
Will was his guide, and griefe led him astray.
At last him chaunst to meete vpon the way
A faithlesse Sarazin all arm'd to point,
In whose great shield was writ with letters gay
Sans foy: full large of limbe and euery ioint
He was, and cared not for God or man a point.

XIII He had a faire companion of his way,
A goodly Lady clad in scarlot red,
Purfled with gold and pearle of rich assay,
And like a Persian mitre on her hed
She wore, with crownes and owches garnished,
The which her lauish louers to her gaue;
Her wanton palfrey all was ouerspred
With tinsell trappings, wouen like a waue,
Whose bridle rung with golden bels and bosses braue.

XIV With faire disport and courting dalliaunce
She intertainde her louer all the way:
But when she saw the knight his speare aduaunce,
She soone left off her mirth and wanton play,
And bad her knight addresse him to the fray:
His foe was nigh at hand. He prickt with pride
And hope to winne his Ladies heart that day,
Forth spurred fast: adowne his coursers side
The red bloud trickling staind the way, as he did ride.

XV The knight of the Redcrosse when him he spide,
Spurring so hote with rage dispiteous,
Gan fairely couch his speare, and towards ride:
Soone meete they both, both fell and furious,
That daunted with their forces hideous,
Their steeds do stagger, and amazed stand,
And eke themselues too rudely rigorous,
Astonied with the stroke of their owne hand,
Do backe rebut, and each to other yeeldeth land.

11 But now, he thought to himself, the best disguise would be to put on that of the good knight: his recent beguiled guest. Soon, Archimago was clad in mighty arms, complete with silver shield. On his cowardly chest, he displayed a red cross, and on his gutless head he wore a wig. Well attired, he now seemed just like the jolly knight, and when he sat upon his lively steed, you would have thought he were Saint George himself.

BUT THE KNIGHT, WHOSE SEMBLANCE HE BORE, THE TRUE SAINT GEORGE, HAD already wandered far away, fleeing from his thoughts and jealous fear. Willfulness was his guide, and wrath led him astray.

At length, he chanced to meet a faithless Saracen upon the way. He was fully armed, and on his shield, the name "Sans Foy" was written in gay letters. Though large in limb and joint, he cared not one iota for God or man.

Next to the Saracen rode a seemingly good lady, clad in scarlet red. She was adorned with gold and pearl, and other rich worth. On her head, she wore a Persian tiara crowned with garnished jewels, which had been given to her by previous lavish lovers. Her wanton palfrey was covered with tinsel trimmings and ripples of precious cloth, and its bridle rang with golden bells and studs. She entertained her lover with flirtations and fair frivolity.

But when she saw Redcross appear with his lance ready, she immediately left off her mirth and wanton play, and bade her knight challenge him, for he was a foe. Sansfoy was pricked with pride and hoped to win his lady's heart that day. So he advanced towards Redcross, spurring his horse so hard that blood trickled all the way.

15 When Redcross noticed him spurring so hot with unmerciful rage, he began to level his lance and ride towards him. Soon they met, both deadly and furious, daunted by each others' hideous forces. Their steeds staggered and stood amazed. Too rough and rigorous, and stunned by their own hand, they retreated for a moment to catch their breath.

XVI As when two rams stird with ambitious pride,
Fight for the rule of the rich fleeced flocke,
Their horned fronts so fierce on either side
Do meete, that with the terrour of the shocke
Astonied both, stand sencelesse as a blocke,
Forgetfull of the hanging victory:
So stood these twaine, vnmoued as a rocke,
Both staring fierce, and holding idely
The broken reliques of their former cruelty.

XVII The Sarazin sore daunted with the buffe
Snatcheth his sword, and fiercely to him flies;
Who well it wards, and quyteth cuff with cuff:
Each others equall puissaunce enuies,
And through their iron sides with cruell spies
Does seeke to perce: repining courage yields
No foote to foe. The flashing fier flies
As from a forge out of their burning shields,
And streames of purple bloud new dies the verdant fields.

XVIII Curse on that Crosse (quoth then the Sarazin)
That keepes thy body from the bitter fit;
Dead long ygoe I wote thou haddest bin,
Had not that charme from thee forwarned it:
But yet I warne thee now assured sitt,
And hide thy head. Therewith vpon his crest
With rigour so outrageous he smitt,
That a large share it hewd out of the rest,
And glauncing downe his shield, from blame him fairely blest.

XIX Who thereat wondrous wroth, the sleeping spark
Of natiue vertue gan eftsoones reuiue,
And at his haughtie helmet making mark,
So hugely stroke, that it the steele did riue,
And cleft his head. He tumbling downe aliue,
With bloudy mouth his mother earth did kis,
Greeting his graue: his grudging ghost did striue
With the fraile flesh; at last it flitted is,
Whither the soules do fly of men, that liue amis.

XX The Lady when she saw her champion fall,
Like the old ruines of a broken towre,
Staid not to waile his woefull funerall,
But from him fled away with all her powre;
Who after her as hastily gan scowre,
Bidding the Dwarfe with him to bring away
The Sarazins shield, signe of the conqueroure.
Her soone he ouertooke, and bad to stay,
For present cause was none of dread her to dismay.

16 When two rams are stirred with ambitious pride, and fight for the rule of the rich fleeced flock, their fierce horned heads meet each other. But with the terror of the shock, they both stand back, astonished and senseless as blocks. Likewise, forgetful of the dangling victory, so stood the two knights, vainly holding their now shattered lances, still as rocks, staring fiercely at each other.

Sore daunted by the blow, the Saracen snatched his sword and fiercely flew at the other knight. Redcross blocked the blade well, and they traded blow for blow. Exchanging cruel glances, each sought to rival the other in equal power, each sought to pierce the side of the other with their iron, and each envied the other's courage. Out of their burning shields, flashing fire flew as from a forge, while streams of purple blood now dyed the verdant fields.

"Curse on that cross that keeps your body from the bitter tune of death!" roared the Saracen. "You would have been dead long ago, had that charm not prevented it. But I warn you now, so sit firm and watch your head."

Therewith, the Saracen struck Redcross on the head with such outrageous rigor that he chopped out a chunk of helmet. But Redcross, glancing down at the shield, realized the sign was keeping him from harm and blessing him fairly. Then, the sleeping spark of natural courage began to revive, and with a burst of wondrous wrath, Redcross returned the blow with such a huge stroke that it split the steel of his foe's lofty helmet, and gashed his head. Down tumbled the Saracen, kissing his mother earth with bloody mouth and greeting the grave, yet still alive. His grudging ghost strove with its frail flesh, but at last it flew whither the souls of men who live wrongly fly.

20 When the lady saw her champion fall like the ruins of a broken tower, she did not stay to wail his woeful death. Instead, she fled far from him with all her might. After bidding the dwarf to retrieve the Saracen's shield as a trophy, Redcross rode hastily after her. He soon caught up and bade her stay with him, for there was nothing to fear.

XXI She turning backe with ruefull countenaunce,
Cride, Mercy mercy Sir vouchsafe to show
On silly Dame, subiect to hard mischaunce,
And to your mighty will. Her humblesse low
In so ritch weedes and seeming glorious show,
Did much emmoue his stout hero"icke heart,
And said, Deare dame, your suddein ouerthrow
Much rueth me; but now put feare apart,
And tell, both who ye be, and who that tooke your part.

XXII Melting in teares, then gan she thus lament;
The wretched woman, whom vnhappy howre
Hath now made thrall to your commandement,
Before that angry heauens list to lowre,
And fortune false betraide me to your powre,
Was, (O what now auaileth that I was!)
Borne the sole daughter of an Emperour,
He that the wide West vnder his rule has,
And high hath set his throne, where Tiberis doth pas.

XXIII He in the first flowre of my freshest age,
Betrothed me vnto the onely haire
Of a most mighty king, most rich and sage;
Was neuer Prince so faithfull and so faire,
Was neuer Prince so meeke and debonaire;
But ere my hoped day of spousall shone,
My dearest Lord fell from high honours staire,
Into the hands of his accursed fone,
And cruelly was slaine, that shall I euer mone.

XXIV His blessed body spoild of liuely breath,
Was afterward, I know not how, conuaid
And fro me hid: of whose most innocent death
When tidings came to me vnhappy maid,
O how great sorrow my sad soule assaid.
Then forth I went his woefull corse to find,
And many yeares throughout the world I straid,
A virgin widow, whose deepe wounded mind
With loue, long time did languish as the striken hind.

XXV At last it chaunced this proud Sarazin
To meete me wandring, who perforce me led
With him away, but yet could neuer win
The Fort, that Ladies hold in soueraigne dread.
There lies he now with foule dishonour dead,
Who whiles he liu'de, was called proud Sans foy,
The eldest of three brethren, all three bred
Of one bad sire, whose youngest is Sans ioy,
And twixt them both was borne the bloudy bold Sans loy.

---

21 Turning away with a forlorn expression, she cried, "Mercy, sir, promise to show mercy on this helpless lady, victim of misfortune, now submitting to your mighty will."

Her humble bows while dressed in such rich clothing and other glorious adornments, greatly moved his brave heroic heart.

He said, "Dear lady, your sudden misfortune saddens me. But now put your fears aside and tell me who you are, and who was your knight?"

Melting with tears, she began to thus lament, "This wretched woman, whom this unhappy hour has made subject to your authority was, before the angry heavens wished to lower me, and false fortune betrayed me to your power—O what little value now to what I was!—born the sole daughter of an emperor.[1]

"My father, he that has the wide west[2] under his rule, had set his high throne in Rome where flows the Tiber River. In the first flower of my freshest age, he betrothed me unto the only heir of a most rich, sage and mighty king. Never was there a prince so faithful and fair. Never was there a prince so meek and debonair. But, just before my promised wedding day shone, my dearest lord fell from high honor's stair into the hands of his accursed foes, and was cruelly slain. That, I shall ever moan. His blessed body, robbed of the breath of life, was afterward—I know not how—taken and hidden from me. Then, when tidings of his most innocent death came to me, unhappy maid, O how great the sorrow that tested my soul. Then forth I went to find his woeful body, and for many years now, I have strayed throughout the world. I, virgin widow, whose mind is deeply wounded with love, have long languished like the stricken deer.

25 "At last, it chanced that this proud Saracen met me wandering, and he forced me to go with him. But he could never win that private fortress that ladies hold in sovereign dread. And now there he lies, dead with foul dishonor who, when he lived, was called Sansfoy. He was the eldest of three brothers, all three bred of one bad sire. The youngest is Sansjoy, and between the two was born the bloody and bold Sansloy.

XXVI In this sad plight, friendlesse, vnfortunate,
Now miserable I Fidessa dwell,
Crauing of you in pitty of my state,
To do none ill, if please ye not do well.
He in great passion all this while did dwell,
More busying his quicke eyes, her face to view,
Then his dull eares, to heare what she did tell;
And said, Faire Lady hart of flint would rew
The vndeserued woes and sorrowes, which ye shew.

XXVII Henceforth in safe assuraunce may ye rest,
Hauing both found a new friend you to aid,
And lost an old foe, that did you molest:
Better new friend then an old foe is said.
With chaunge of cheare the seeming simple maid
Let fall her eyen, as shamefast to the earth,
And yeelding soft, in that she nought gain-said,
So forth they rode, he feining seemely merth,
And she coy lookes: so dainty they say maketh derth.

XXVIII Long time they thus together traueiled,
Till weary of their way, they came at last,
Where grew two goodly trees, that faire did spred
Their armes abroad, with gray mosse ouercast,
And their greene leaues trembling with euery blast,
Made a calme shadow far in compasse round:
The fearefull Shepheard often there aghast
Vnder them neuer sat, ne wont there sound
His mery oaten pipe, but shund th'vnlucky ground.

XXIX But this good knight soone as he them can spie,
For the coole shade him thither hastly got:
For golden Phoebus now ymounted hie,
From fiery wheeles of his faire chariot
Hurled his beame so scorching cruell hot,
That liuing creature mote it not abide;
And his new Lady it endured not.
There they alight, in hope themselues to hide
From the fierce heat, and rest their weary limbs a tide.

XXX Faire seemely pleasaunce each to other makes,
With goodly purposes there as they sit:
And in his falsed fancy he her takes
To be the fairest wight, that liued yit;
Which to expresse, he bends his gentle wit,
And thinking of those braunches greene to frame
A girlond for her dainty forehead fit,
He pluckt a bough; out of whose rift there came
Small drops of gory bloud, that trickled downe the same.

26 In this sad, friendless, unfortunate, and now miserable plight, I, Fidessa, do dwell. So I implore you, in my state of pity, that if you are not willing to help me, do me no harm."

Meanwhile, Redcross had been dwelling on her in great interest, mostly busying his quick eyes with her unveiled face, than his dull ears with her words.

Then he said, "Fair lady, even a heart of flint would break with the undeserved woes and sorrows you tell. Henceforth you may rest in safe assurance, having found both a new friend to aid you, and lost an old foe who mistreated you. As it is said: better a new friend, than an old foe."

With a change of cheer, the seeming simple maid let her eyes fall to the earth in humility, softly yielding and agreeing.

So forth they rode: he faking cheerfulness, while she: coy looks. Dainty looks and playing coy, they say, makes the wooer more eager to woo.

They travelled together like this until, weary, they arrived at a place where two large trees grew. Their fair branches spread broadly with gray overhanging moss. Their green leaves trembled with every gust of wind, and a calm shadow encompassed the whole area around it. But the shepherd was afraid of those trees, and would neither sit under them, nor play his merry reed pipe there. Instead, he shunned the unlucky ground.

But as soon as the good knight saw the trees, he sought them for their cool shade. For golden Phoebus was now mounted high, and the fiery wheels of his fair chariot hurled his beam, so scorching and cruelly hot, that no living creature might abide. And his new lady could not endure it either. So they dismounted in hope to shelter themselves from the fierce heat, and rest their weary limbs for a while.

30 As they were sitting in the cool, they made pleasant conversation together, and in his false fantasy, Redcross took Fidessa to be the fairest creature who ever yet lived. To express his admiration for her, he decided to fashion a green garland for her dainty head, so he broke off a bough. But out of the crack there came small drops of clotted blood, that trickled down.

XXXI Therewith a piteous yelling voyce was heard,
Crying, O spare with guilty hands to teare
My tender sides in this rough rynd embard,
But fly, ah fly far hence away, for feare
Least to you hap, that happened to me heare,
And to this wretched Lady, my deare loue,
O too deare loue, loue bought with death too deare.
Astond he stood, and vp his haire did houe,
And with that suddein horror could no member moue.

XXXII At last whenas the dreadfull passion
Was ouerpast, and manhood well awake,
Yet musing at the straunge occasion,
And doubting much his sence, he thus bespake;
What voyce of damned Ghost from Limbo lake,
Or guilefull spright wandring in empty aire,
Both which fraile men do oftentimes mistake,
Sends to my doubtfull eares these speaches rare,
And ruefull plaints, me bidding guiltlesse bloud to spare?

XXXIII Then groning deepe, Nor damned Ghost, (quoth he,)
Nor guilefull sprite, to thee these wordes doth speake,
But once a man Fradubio, now a tree,
Wretched man, wretched tree; whose nature weake,
A cruell witch her cursed will to wreake,
Hath thus transformd, and plast in open plaines,
Where Boreas doth blow full bitter bleake,
And scorching Sunne does dry my secret vaines:
For though a tree I seeme, yet cold and heat me paines.

XXXIV Say on Fradubio then, or man, or tree,
Quoth then the knight, by whose mischieuous arts
Art thou misshaped thus, as now I see?
He oft finds med'cine, who his griefe imparts;
But double griefs afflict concealing harts,
As raging flames who striueth to suppresse.
The author then (said he) of all my smarts,
Is one Duessa a false sorceresse,
That many errant knights hath brought to wretchednesse.

XXXV In prime of youthly yeares, when corage hot
The fire of loue and ioy of cheualree
First kindled in my brest, it was my lot
To loue this gentle Lady, whom ye see,
Now not a Lady, but a seeming tree;
With whom as once I rode accompanyde,
Me chaunced of a knight encountred bee,
That had a like faire Lady by his syde,
Like a faire Lady, but did fowle Duessa hyde.

31 Therewith, a pitiful yelling voice was heard, crying, "O spare with guilty hands to tear my tender sides in this rough manner, while I am entrapped in bark. But flee, oh flee far hence away for fear, lest the same thing happen to you, as happened to me and this wretched lady here. My dear love, O too dear love, because love bought with death is too dear."

Astonished, Redcross stood there frozen, his hair prickling on the back of his neck for sudden horror. At last, when he had recovered himself, and regained his bravery, he marveled over such a strange wonder.

Although still doubting his senses, the knight spoke to the voice, "What voice of damned ghost from Limbo's lake, or cunning sprite wandering in the empty air, both of which mislead frail men, sends to my doubtful ears these strange speeches and rueful pleas, bidding me to spare guiltless blood?"

Then, groaning deep, the voice from the tree replied, "Neither damned ghost nor cunning sprite speaks these words to you, but one man whose nature was weak: Fradubio, now a tree, wretched man, wretched tree. A cruel witch inflicted her cursed will, and has thus transformed me. She then placed the trees in open plains where the Northern Boreas blows full and bitterly bleak, and the scorching sun dries my secret veins. For though I seem a tree, I still feel the cold and heat."

"Tell on, Fradubio then, or man, or tree," urged the knight. "By whose mischievous arts are you misshapen thus, as I see you now? He who imparts his grief often finds a remedy. But he who strives to suppress raging flames: double griefs will afflict concealing hearts."

The voice then answered, "The author, then, of all my pains is one Duessa: a false sorceress who has brought many errant knights to wretchedness. **35** In the prime of my youthful years, when hot courage first kindled love and the joy of chivalry in my breast, it was my fate to love this gentle lady whom you see. Now not a lady, but a seeming tree. I used to accompany her, and one day, we chanced upon a knight who rode with a similar fair lady by his side. But this was really the foul Duessa, disguised as a fair lady.

XXXVI Whose forged beauty he did take in hand,
All other Dames to haue exceeded farre;
I in defence of mine did likewise stand,
Mine, that did then shine as the Morning starre:
So both to battell fierce arraunged arre,
In which his harder fortune was to fall
Vnder my speare: such is the dye of warre:
His Lady left as a prise martiall,
Did yield her comely person, to be at my call.

XXXVII So doubly lou'd of Ladies vnlike faire,
Th'one seeming such, the other such indeede,
One day in doubt I cast for to compare,
Whether in beauties glorie did exceede;
A Rosy girlond was the victors meede:
Both seemde to win, and both seemde won to bee,
So hard the discord was to be agreede.
Frælissa was as faire, as faire mote bee,
And euer false Duessa seemde as faire as shee.

XXXVIII The wicked witch now seeing all this while
The doubtfull ballaunce equally to sway,
What not by right, she cast to win by guile,
And by her hellish science raisd streightway
A foggy mist, that ouercast the day,
And a dull blast, that breathing on her face,
Dimmed her former beauties shining ray,
And with foule vgly forme did her disgrace:
Then was she faire alone, when none was faire in place.

XXXIX Then cride she out, Fye, fye, deformed wight,
Whose borrowed beautie now appeareth plaine
To haue before bewitched all mens sight;
O leaue her soone, or let her soone be slaine.
Her loathly visage viewing with disdaine,
Eftsoones I thought her such, as she me told,
And would haue kild her; but with faigned paine,
The false witch did my wrathfull hand with-hold;
So left her, where she now is turnd to treen mould.

XL Thensforth I tooke Duessa for my Dame,
And in the witch vnweeting ioyd long time,
Ne euer wist, but that she was the same,
Till on a day (that day is euery Prime,
When Witches wont do penance for their crime)
I chaunst to see her in her proper hew,
Bathing her selfe in origane and thyme:
A filthy foule old woman I did vew,
That euer to haue toucht her, I did deadly rew.

36 The knight wanted me to agree that Duessa's forged beauty exceeded that of all other ladies, but I stood by my own fair lady, who then shone like the morning star. So we arranged and fought a fierce battle, in which his harder fortune was to fall under my lance. Such is the fate of war. His lady was then left as a prize of war, and she yielded her attractive person to be at my call.

"And so, I was loved by two incomparable fair ladies: one seeming such, the other such indeed. One day, in doubt, I decided to subject them to a beauty contest, to judge whether one exceeded in beauty's glory. A rosary bead garland would be the winner's prize. But both seemed to win, and both seemed keen to win. So hard was the decision. Fraelissa, though frail, was as fair as fair might be, and ever false Duessa seemed as fair as she.

"The wicked witch, now seeing the doubtful balance swaying equally, and not to her liking, decided to win by cunning. By her hellish science, she raised a foggy mist that confused and overcast the day, and a dull wind that breathed on Fraelissa's face. The breeze dimmed her former beauty's shining ray and marred her with foul ugly form. Then Duessa was the fairest of them all, when no other was fair in her place.

"Then Duessa cried out at her, 'Fie, fie, deformed creature, whose borrowed beauty now appears plain, and who before bewitched all men's sight. O leave her soon, or let her soon be slain.' Looking at Fraelissa's loathly visage with disdain, I soon began to see as she saw, and in my state of doubt I agreed with Duessa,. And I would have killed Fraelissa if that false witch, with faked distress, had not withheld my wrathful hand. So I left my true lady, where she is now turned into a tree.

40 "Thenceforth, I took Duessa for my lady and enjoyed that witch unknowingly for a long time. I took her to be as she appeared, and did not suspect anything until, one day, in springtime, when witches are accustomed to do penance for their crimes. Whilst she bathed in an oregano and thyme bath, I chanced to see her in her true form. There I saw such a filthy, foul, old woman, that to have touched her I deadly regretted.

XLI Her neather partes misshapen, monstruous,
Were hidd in water, that I could not see,
But they did seeme more foule and hideous,
Then womans shape man would beleeue to bee.
Thensforth from her most beastly companie
I gan refraine, in minde to slip away,
Soone as appeard safe opportunitie:
For danger great, if not assur'd decay
I saw before mine eyes, if I were knowne to stray.

XLII The diuelish hag by chaunges of my cheare
Perceiu'd my thought, and drownd in sleepie night,
With wicked herbes and ointments did besmeare
My bodie all, through charmes and magicke might,
That all my senses were bereaued quight:
Then brought she me into this desert waste,
And by my wretched louers side me pight,
Where now enclosd in wooden wals full faste,
Banisht from liuing wights, our wearie dayes we waste.

XLIII But how long time, said then the Elfin knight,
Are you in this misformed house to dwell?
We may not chaunge (quoth he) this euil plight,
Till we be bathed in a liuing well;
That is the terme prescribed by the spell.
O how, said he, mote I that well out find,
That may restore you to your wonted well?
Time and suffised fates to former kynd
Shall vs restore, none else from hence may vs vnbynd.

XLIV The false Duessa, now Fidessa hight,
Heard how in vaine Fradubio did lament,
And knew well all was true. But the good knight
Full of sad feare and ghastly dreriment,
When all this speech the liuing tree had spent,
The bleeding bough did thrust into the ground,
That from the bloud he might be innocent,
And with fresh clay did close the wooden wound:
Then turning to his Lady, dead with feare her found.

XLV Her seeming dead he found with feigned feare,
As all vnweeting of that well she knew,
And paynd himselfe with busie care to reare
Her out of carelesse swowne. Her eylids blew
And dimmed sight with pale and deadly hew
At last she vp gan lift: with trembling cheare
Her vp he tooke, too simple and too trew,
And oft her kist. At length all passed feare,
He set her on her steede, and forward forth did beare.

41 Her nether parts were misshapen and monstrous, and hidden in water so I could not see clearly. But they did seem more foul and hideous than a woman's normal shape. Then I began to avoid her most beastly company, and I had in mind to slip away as soon as a safe opportunity appeared. For I saw before mine eyes that, if I were known to stray, the danger would be great: if not assured death. The devilish hag noticed the changes in my mood and perceived my thought. Drowned in a deep sleep one night, she smeared all my body with wicked herbs and ointments, and through charms and magic powers she stunted all my senses. Next, she brought me here into this desert waste, and planted me by my wretched lover's side, where now I am enclosed in unyielding wooden walls. Banished from living creatures, we waste our weary days."

"But how long," asked the Elfin knight, "are you doomed to live in this malformed house?"

"We cannot change this evil plight till we are bathed in a living well: the Well of Life. That is the term prescribed by the spell," replied Fradubio.

"O how might I find that well so that I may restore you to your true self?" asked the good knight.

"Time and the fulfillment of destiny shall restore us to our former kind. None else from hence may unbind us," came the voice from the tree.

The false Duessa, now named Fidessa, heard how Fradubio lamented in vain, and she knew very well that all was true. But the good knight, full of sad fear when the ghastly story came to an end, took the bleeding bough and thrust it into the ground, so that he might be innocent of the blood he accidentally spilled. Then, with some fresh clay, he closed the wooden wound.

Next, he turned to his lady, and found her looking dead with fear. **45** Faking a swoon from phony fear, she had pretended to be unaware of all that she well knew. Her eyelids were blue, her sight dimmed, and her complexion pale and deathlike. Redcross pained himself busily trying to revive her, and at last she began to lift her head. With uneasy and trembling cheer, he took her up, too simple and too true, and kissed her many times, unaware. At length, all the fear passed, and he set her on her steed, and forward forth they departed.

1   emperor *suggests head of the Catholic Church in Rome*

2   The wide west *suggests the Western, Catholic church, as opposed to Una's parents' kingdom that stretched from the East to the West: the universal church.*

NOTES ON CANTO III

Lion: Natural Law. The lion naturally aids Una. However, it is no match for Sansloy ("without the law of God"), who operates outside the domain of divine law.

Abessa: means nun. She is deaf to hearing the truth, and **Corceca**: blind devotion and superstition. They represent monasticism, which is a feature of the Catholic Church, and in Spenser's time, monasteries were often accused of taking donations to the poor for themselves. The women stand for a criticism of monasteries that are ignorant of the needs of the world, as they live in seclusion. Corceca's regime of fasting, ashes, sackcloth and hundreds of Hail Mary's is a critique of Catholicism's practices.

Kirkrapine: the name means 'church-robber.' He not only robs churches to gain money, but he uses that money to pay Abessa for prostitution services.

CANTO III

UNA AND THE LION

Forsaken Truth long seekes her loue,
And makes the Lyon mylde,
Marres blind Deuotions mart, and fals
In hand of leachour vylde.

I Nought there vnder heau'ns wilde hollownesse,
That moues more deare compassion of mind,
Then beautie brought t'vnworthy wretchednesse
Through enuies snares or fortunes freakes vnkind:
I, whether lately through her brightnesse blind,
Or through alleageance and fast fealtie,
Which I do owe vnto all woman kind,
Feele my heart perst with so great agonie,
When such I see, that all for pittie I could die.

II And now it is empassioned so deepe,
For fairest *Vnaes* sake, of whom I sing,
  That my fraile eyes these lines with teares do steepe,
To thinke how she through guilefull handeling,
Though true as touch, though daughter of a king,
Though faire as euer liuing wight was faire,
Though nor in word nor deede ill meriting,
Is from her knight diuorced in despaire
And her due loues deriu'd to that vile witches share.

III Yet she most faithfull Ladie all this while
Forsaken, wofull, solitarie mayd
Farre from all peoples prease, as in exile,
In wildernesse and wastfull deserts strayd,
To seeke her knight; who subtilly betrayd
Through that late vision, which th'Enchaunter wrought,
Had her abandond. She of nought affrayd,
Through woods and wastnesse wide him daily sought;
Yet wished tydings none of him vnto her brought.

IV One day nigh wearie of the yrkesome way,
From her vnhastie beast she did alight,
And on the grasse her daintie limbes did lay
In secret shadow, farre from all mens sight:
From her faire head her fillet she vndight,
And laid her stole aside. Her angels face
As the great eye of heauen shyned bright,
And made a sunshine in the shadie place;
Did neuer mortall eye behold such heauenly grace.

V It fortuned out of the thickest wood
A ramping Lyon rushed suddainly,
Hunting full greedie after saluage blood;
Soone as the royall virgin he did spy,
With gaping mouth at her ran greedily,
To haue attonce deuour'd her tender corse:
But to the pray when as he drew more ny,
His bloudie rage asswaged with remorse,
And with the sight amazd, forgat his furious forse

Forsaken truth long seeks her love, tames the lion, mars
blind Devotion's trade, and falls into the hands of a wild lecher.

NOTHING UNDER HEAVEN'S WILD EXPANSE MOVES DEAR COMPASSION OF MIND more than beauty brought to undeserved wretchedness through envy's snares, or fortune's unkind whims. Whether lately, through beauty's blind brightness, or through allegiance and firm faith, which I owe unto all womankind, I feel my heart pierced with great agony, when such I see.

And now my impassioned pity is so deep for fairest Una's sake, of whom I sing, that I soak these lines with tears from my frail eyes. To think how she, by cunning handling, though proven to be true, though daughter of a king, though fair as ever living creature was fair, though deserving of no ill in word or deed, is separated from her knight in despair, and her due love has been diverted to that vile witch. Through that recent vision wrought by the enchanter, her knight had abandoned her. Yet Una, most faithful lady all this time, forsaken, woeful, solitary maid, far from human company, as in exile, in wilderness and desolate deserts she strayed, seeking him. She was afraid of nothing, for there is no fear in love, and through woods and wide wilderness she sought him daily. Yet, while she wished for news of his whereabouts, she found none.

ONE DAY, WEARY OF THE TIRESOME WANDERINGS, SHE DISMOUNTED FROM HER sluggish donkey, and laid her dainty limbs on the grass in a hidden shadow, far from all men's sight. She took off her head covering and laid her cloak aside. Her angelic face shone like the sun, brightening that shady place, and no mortal eye ever beheld such heavenly grace.

5 It fortuned that, out of the thickest wood, a raging lion suddenly rushed into the clearing, ravenous for savage blood. As soon he saw the royal maid, he greedily ran at her with gaping mouth, craving to devour her tender body. But as he drew nearer to the prey, his bloody rage was calmed with pity, and with amazed sight, he forgot his furious force.

VI In stead thereof he kist her wearie feet,
And lickt her lilly hands with fawning tong,
As he her wronged innocence did weet.
O how can beautie maister the most strong,
And simple truth subdue auenging wrong?
Whose yeelded pride and proud submission,
Still dreading death, when she had marked long,
Her hart gan melt in great compassion,
And drizling teares did shed for pure affection.

VII The Lyon Lord of euerie beast in field,
Quoth she, his princely puissance doth abate,
And mightie proud to humble weake does yield,
Forgetfull of the hungry rage, which late
Him prickt, in pittie of my sad estate:
But he my Lyon, and my noble Lord,
How does he find in cruell hart to hate
Her that him lou'd, and euer most adord,
As the God of my life? why hath he me abhord?

VIII Redounding teares did choke th'end of her plaint,
Which softly ecchoed from the neighbour wood;
And sad to see her sorrowfull constraint
The kingly beast vpon her gazing stood;
With pittie calmd, downe fell his angry mood.
At last in close hart shutting vp her paine,
Arose the virgin borne of heauenly brood,
And to her snowy Palfrey got againe,
To seeke her strayed Champion, if she might attaine.

IX The Lyon would not leaue her desolate,
But with her went along, as a strong gard
Of her chast person, and a faithfull mate
Of her sad troubles and misfortunes hard:
Still when she slept, he kept both watch and ward,
And when she wakt, he waited diligent,
With humble seruice to her will prepard:
From her faire eyes he tooke commaundement,
And euer by her lookes conceiued her intent.

X Long she thus traueiled through deserts wyde,
By which she thought her wandring knight shold pas,
Yet neuer shew of liuing wight espyde;
Till that at length she found the troden gras,
In which the tract of peoples footing was,
Vnder the steepe foot of a mountaine hore;
The same she followes, till at last she has
A damzell spyde slow footing her before,
That on her shoulders sad a pot of water bore.

6 Instead, he kissed her weary feet and licked her lily hands with fawning tongue, as if he knew of her wronged innocence. O how is it that beauty can master the strongest, and simple truth subdue vengeance? Una's heart, while still dreading death, began to melt in great compassion at the lion's yielded pride and proud submission, and she drizzled tears for pure affection.

"The lion is lord of every beast in the field," said Una. "His princely power abates and yields from mighty-proud to humble-weak. Forgetful of his hungry rate, which recently drove him to me, he feels pity for my sad state. Therefore, why does my true lion and noble lord hate me with his cruel heart, though I loved and ever most adored him, as the God of my life? Why has Redcross abandoned me?"

Increasing tears choked the end of her plaint which softly echoed from the surrounding woods, and sad to see her sorrowful distress, the kingly beast stood gazing upon her. The pity he felt further calmed his angry mood. At last, putting her sadness aside, the maiden of heavenly ancestry arose, and with her snowy donkey, wandered off to seek her champion who had gone astray.

The lion would not leave her desolate, but strode along with her, as a strong guard to her chaste person, and as a faithful mate in her sad troubles and hard misfortunes. When she was sleeping, he kept both watch and ward, and when she was awake, he waited diligently on her with humble service. From her fair eyes he took commands, and by her looks he understood her intentions.

10 LONG SHE THUS TRAVELLED AND TOILED THROUGH WIDE DESERTS, BY WHICH she thought her wandering knight might pass. Yet there was no sign of any living creature. At length, under the steep foot of a gray mountain, she found some trodden grass indicating tracks of human footsteps. She followed it until, at last, she saw a damsel walking slowly, bearing a heavy pot of water on her shoulders.

XI To whom approching she to her gan call,
To weet, if dwelling place were nigh at hand;
But the rude wench her answer'd nought at all,
She could not heare, nor speake, nor vnderstand;
Till seeing by her side the Lyon stand,
With suddaine feare her pitcher downe she threw,
And fled away: for neuer in that land
Face of faire Ladie she before did vew,
And that dread Lyons looke her cast in deadly hew.

XII Full fast she fled, ne euer lookt behynd,
As if her life vpon the wager lay,
And home she came, whereas her mother blynd
Sate in eternall night: nought could she say,
But suddaine catching hold, did her dismay
With quaking hands, and other signs of feare:
Who full of ghastly fright and cold affray,
Gan shut the dore. By this arriued there
Dame *Vna*, wearie Dame, and entrance did requere.

XIII Which when none yeelded, her vnruly Page
With his rude clawes the wicket open rent,
And let her in; where of his cruell rage
Nigh dead with feare, and faint astonishment,
She found them both in darkesome corner pent;
Where that old woman day and night did pray
Vpon her beades deuoutly penitent;
Nine hundred *Pater nosters* euery day,
And thrise nine hundred *Aues* she was wont to say.

XIV And to augment her painefull pennance more,
Thrise euery weeke in ashes she did sit,
And next her wrinkled skin rough sackcloth wore,
And thrise three times did fast from any bit:
But now for feare her beads she did forget.
Whose needlesse dread for to remoue away,
Faire *Vna* framed words and count›nance fit:
Which hardly doen, at length she gan them pray,
That in their cotage small, that night she rest her may.

XV The day is spent, and commeth drowsie night,
When euery creature shrowded is in sleepe;
Sad *Vna* downe her laies in wearie plight,
And at her feet the Lyon watch doth keepe:
In stead of rest, she does lament, and weepe
For the late losse of her deare loued knight,
And sighes, and grones, and euermore does steepe
Her tender brest in bitter teares all night,
All night she thinks too long, and often lookes for light.

11 Una called to her, asking if she knew of any houses nearby where she could stay. But the rude wench did not answer: for she could neither hear, nor speak, nor understand. And when she saw the lion standing by Una, she dropped her pitcher and fled in fright. For, while she had never seen a lady of such fair a face in that land, the dread of the lion turned the wench white as a ghost. She fled at full speed, as if her very life was on the line, not looking back once. Breathless, she ran inside her home and clung to her mother, who was blind, and sad in eternal night. The wench could say nothing, but by the manner in which she caught hold of her mother, with quaking hands and other signs of fear, she soon understood. Full of ghastly fright and cold terror, she began to bolt up the door. But Una had already arrived at this same door, weary, knocking, and pleading to enter.

When no one answered, Una's unruly lion-page tore open the front door with his rough claws and let her in. Una found the mother and daughter cowering in a darksome corner, afraid of the lion's violent rage, nearly dead with fear and faint astonishment. There, the devoutly penitent old woman prayed her Pater Nosters day and night, as well as her usual three times nine hundred Ave Marias. Thrice weekly, she would sit in ashes and wear rough sackcloth next to her wrinkled skin to increase her painful penance.[1] And thrice weekly, she would fast from all food. But, cowering now in the same corner, she had, out of fear, forgotten to pray the beads that might remove this unfounded dread. Now, however, fair Una spoke gently and smiled warmly, trying to reassure them. With their fears somewhat relieved, she began, at length, to ask them if she might rest there, though their cottage was small.

15 The day was over and the drowsy night arrived as every creature was shrouded in sleep. Sad Una lay down in weary plight, with the lion keeping watch at her feet. Instead of rest, though, she lamented and wept for the recent loss of her dear loved knight. She sighed and groaned, and evermore steeped her tender breast in bitter tears. All night, she thought too long, and often looked for light.

XVI Now when *Aldeboran* was mounted hie
Aboue the shynie *Cassiopeias* chaire,
And all in deadly sleepe did drowned lie,
One knocked at the dore, and in would fare;
He knocked fast, and often curst, and sware,
That readie entrance was not at his call:
For on his backe a heauy load he bare
Of nightly stelths and pillage seuerall,
Which he had got abroad by purchase criminall.

XVII He was to weete a stout and sturdie thiefe,
Wont to robbe Churches of their ornaments,
And poore mens boxes of their due reliefe,
Which giuen was to them for good intents;
The holy Saints of their rich vestiments
He did disrobe, when all men carelesse slept,
And spoild the Priests of their habiliments,
Whiles none the holy things in safety kept;
Then he by cunning sleights in at the window crept.

XVIII And all that he by right or wrong could find,
Vnto this house he brought, and did bestow
Vpon the daughter of this woman blind,
   Abessa daughter of *Corceca* slow,
With whom he whoredome vsd, that few did know,
And fed her fat with feast of offerings,
And plentie, which in all the land did grow;
Ne spared he to giue her gold and rings:
And now he to her brought part of his stolen things.

XIX Thus long the dore with rage and threats he bet,
Yet of those fearefull women none durst rize,
The Lyon frayed them, him in to let:
He would no longer stay him to aduize,
But open breakes the dore in furious wize,
And entring is; when that disdainfull beast
Encountring fierce, him suddaine doth surprize,
And seizing cruell clawes on trembling brest,
Vnder his Lordly foot him proudly hath supprest.

XX Him booteth not resist, nor succour call,
His bleeding hart is in the vengers hand,
Who streight him rent in thousand peeces small,
And quite dismembred hath: the thirstie land
Drunke vp his life; his corse left on the strand.
His fearefull friends weare out the wofull night,
Ne dare to weepe, nor seeme to vnderstand
The heauie hap, which on them is alight,
Affraid, least to themselues the like mishappen might.

16 But when the star, Aldeboran, was mounted high above the shiny constellation of Cassiopeia, and all was drowned in deadly sleep, there came a loud knock at the door. It was Kirkrapine, the church robber, with his latest haul. He knocked again vigorously, and then cursed and swore that the door was not opened. On his back, he wore a heavy load that was full of his nightly thefts and diverse pillages. He was known as a bold and ruthless thief, accustomed to robbing churches of their ornaments and alms boxes full of donations for the poor, which had been given with good intent. While all men slept, he stole the rich vestments of the holy saints, and the clothing belonging to the priests. None of these holy things were kept locked up, so all he had to do was climb in a window with cunning dexterity, and take it all without a trace.

All that he could find, by right or wrong, he brought unto this house and gave it to the daughter of this blind woman, Abessa, daughter of slow Corceca, to pay for her prostitution services. He fed her fat with a feast of church offerings, and plenty of that which grew on the land, as well as adorned her with gold and rings. Now he stood at the door, bringing her part of his stolen things.

Thus, he beat at the door with rage and threats. But those fearful women dared not rise to let him in, because the lion frightened them. Finally, he kicked down the door in a furious way, and entering, he encountered that indignant beast, who suddenly surprised him. Leaping on the plunderer with cruel claws, the fearsome beast seized him by his trembling chest and overpowered him under his lordly foot.

20It was no use to resist or call for help. His bleeding heart was in the avenger's hand who immediately ripped him into a thousand small pieces. The thirsty land drunk up his life, and his corpse was left on the ground.

Meanwhile, his fearful friends wore out the woeful night, quaking in a corner. They dared not weep, or seek to understand the grave event that had befallen them. Terrified, they hid, lest the same happen to them.

XXI Now when broad day the world discouered has,
Vp *Vna* rose, vp rose the Lyon eke,
And on their former iourney forward pas,
In wayes vnknowne, her wandring knight to seeke,
With paines farre passing that long wandring *Greeke*,
That for his loue refused deitie;
Such were the labours of this Lady meeke,
Still seeking him, that from her still did flie,
Then furthest from her hope, when most she weened nie.

XXII Soone as she parted thence, the fearefull twaine,
That blind old woman and her daughter deare
Came forth, and finding *Kirkrapine* there slaine,
For anguish great they gan to rend their heare,
And beat their brests, and naked flesh to teare.
And when they both had wept and wayld their fill,
Then forth they ranne like two amazed deare,
Halfe mad through malice, and reuenging will,
To follow her, that was the causer of their ill.

XXIII Whom ouertaking, they gan loudly bray,
With hollow howling, and lamenting cry,
Shamefully at her rayling all the way,
And her accusing of dishonesty,
That was the flowre of faith and chastity;
And still amidst her rayling, she did pray,
That plagues, and mischiefs, and long misery
Might fall on her, and follow all the way,
And that in endlesse error she might euer stray.

XXIV But when she saw her prayers nought preuaile,
She backe returned with some labour lost;
And in the way as she did weepe and waile,
A knight her met in mighty armes embost,
Yet knight was not for all his bragging bost,
But subtill *Archimag*, that *Vna* sought
By traynes into new troubles to haue tost:
Of that old woman tydings he besought,
If that of such a Ladie she could tellen ought.

XXV Therewith she gan her passion to renew,
And cry, and curse, and raile, and rend her heare,
Saying, that harlot she too lately knew,
That causd her shed so many a bitter teare,
And so forth told the story of her feare:
Much seemed he to mone her haplesse chaunce,
And after for that Ladie did inquere;
Which being taught, he forward gan aduaunce
His fair enchaunted steed, and eke his charmed launce.

21 When broad daylight had rediscovered the world, up rose Una and the lion. Soon, they continued forward on their former journey to seek her wandering knight. With pain far surpassing that long wandering Odysseus, who refused Calypso for his true love in Ithaca, Una persevered. Such were that labors of this meek lady, still seeking him who fled from her. And when she most thought he was nearby, he was furthest from her hope.

Soon after Una and the lion left the house, the blind woman and her deaf daughter came out of hiding and found Kirkrapine slain just next to the door. With great anguish, they began to rend their hair, beat their breasts, and tear their naked flesh. And when they had both wept and wailed their fill, they ran after Una like two panic-stricken deer. Half mad with malice, half with avenging will, they were intent on pursuing the cause of their ill.

When they finally caught up with Una, they began to yell loudly with hollow howling and lamenting cry, railing shamefully at her all the way. They even accused that flower of faith and chastity with indecency. Amidst her railing, Corceca prayed that plagues, misfortunes, and long misery might fall on her, and follow all the way, and that she might stray in endless error.

But when she saw that her prayers did not prevail, she turned back towards home, having wasted her time and labor. And on her way, as she wept and wailed, she met a knight adorned in mighty arms. Yet the knight was not as his gallant appearance seemed, but crafty Archimago in disguise, and he was busy seeking Una so that, through guile, he could toss her into new troubles. He therefore stopped that old woman and asked her if she had come across someone who matched her description.

25 Therewith, she began to renew her passion, and to cry, curse, rail and rend her hair, telling him that this was the very same harlot she had just encountered, who had caused her to shed many a bitter tear. Then she told the false knight what had become of Kirkrapine. Archimago falsely lamented with her over her misfortunes, then enquired after the current location of that lady. The old woman pointed out the direction, and he advanced forward on his fair enchanted steed, with his charmed lance.

XXVI Ere long he came, where *Vna* traueild slow,
And that wilde Champion wayting her besyde:
Whom seeing such, for dread he durst not show
Himselfe too nigh at hand, but turned wyde
Vnto an hill; from whence when she him spyde,
By his like seeming shield, her knight by name
She weend it was, and towards him gan ryde:
Approching nigh, she wist it was the same,
And with faire fearefull humblesse towards him shee came.

XXVII And weeping said, Ah my long lacked Lord,
Where haue ye bene thus long out of my sight?
Much feared I to haue bene quite abhord,
Or ought haue done, that ye displeasen might,
That should as death vnto my deare hart light:
For since mine eye your ioyous sight did mis,
My chearefull day is turnd to chearelesse night,
And eke my night of death the shadow is;
But welcome now my light, and shining lampe of blis.

XXVIII He thereto meeting said, My dearest Dame,
Farre be it from your thought, and fro my will,
To thinke that knighthood I so much should shame,
As you to leaue, that haue me loued still,
And chose in Faery court of meere goodwill,
Where noblest knights were to be found on earth:
The earth shall sooner leaue her kindly skill
To bring forth fruit, and make eternall derth,
Then I leaue you, my liefe, yborne of heauenly berth.

XXIX And sooth to say, why I left you so long,
Was for to seeke aduenture in strange place,
Where *Archimago* said a felon strong
To many knights did daily worke disgrace;
But knight he now shall neuer more deface:
Good cause of mine excuse; that mote ye please
Well to accept, and euermore embrace
My faithfull seruice, that by land and seas
Haue vowd you to defend. Now then your plaint appease.

XXX His louely words her seemd due recompence
Of all her passed paines: one louing howre
For many yeares of sorrow can dispence:
A dram of sweet is worth a pound of sowre:
She has forgot, how many a wofull stowre
For him she late endur'd; she speakes no more
Of past: true is, that true loue hath no powre
To looken backe; his eyes be fixt before.
Before her stands her knight, for whom she toyld so sore.

---

26 Soon he came across Una, wandering solemnly with that wild protective champion beside her. When Archimago spied the lion, he dared not show himself too near, for dread, but turned wide unto a hill. From where he stood, and by his shield, Una thought she had found her Redcross. Approaching near, she believed it was he, and with fair fearful humbleness, she began to ride towards him.

With tears in her eyes, Una said, "Ah, my long-needed lord, where have you been so long out of my sight? Much have I feared to have been quite abandoned, and long have I wondered if I had done anything that might have displeased you, that should land like death unto my loving heart. For since I have missed your joyous sight, my cheerful day has been turned to cheerless night and shadow of death. But welcome now my light and shining lamp of bliss."

Responding with similar pleasantries, the false knight replied, "My dearest lady, far be it from your thought and from my will that I should shame knighthood by deserting the one who still loved me. I am the untested knight who was chosen in the Faerie court, on pure goodwill, where the noblest knights on earth were to be found. The earth shall sooner end her natural skills to bring forth fruit, and create eternal famines, than I should leave you, my beloved, born of heavenly birth. And it is true to say that, the reason I left you so long, was to seek adventures in a strange place. Archimago said there was a strong criminal about who did daily work to disgrace many knights. But now he has been dealt with, and shall never more deface any knight. I hope you excuse this good cause of mine and that you will be pleased to accept and ever more embrace my faithful service, by land and sea, having vowed to defend you. Now let your plaint be appeased."

30 His loving words seemed due recompense for all her passed pains. For one loving hour can make amends for many years of sorrow, as a dram of sweet is worth a pound of sour. Una soon forgot how many a woeful danger she had recently endured for him, and she spoke no more of the past. True love does not look back, but fixes his eyes forward. And now, before her stood her knight, for whom she toiled so sore.

XXXI Much like, as when the beaten marinere,
That long hath wandred in the *Ocean* wide,
Oft soust in swelling *Tethys* saltish teare,
And long time hauing tand his tawney hide
With blustring breath of heauen, that none can bide,
And scorching flames of fierce *Orions* hound,
Soone as the port from farre he has espide,
His chearefull whistle merrily doth sound,
And *Nereus* crownes with cups; his mates him pledg around.

XXXII Such ioy made *Vna*, when her knight she found;
And eke th'enchaunter ioyous seemd no lesse,
Then the glad marchant, that does vew from ground
His ship farre come from watrie wildernesse,
He hurles out vowes, and *Neptune* oft doth blesse:
So forth they past, and all the way they spent
Discoursing of her dreadfull late distresse,
In which he askt her, what the Lyon ment:
Who told her all that fell in iourney as she went.

XXXIII They had not ridden farre, when they might see
One pricking towards them with hastie heat,
Full strongly armd, and on a courser free,
That through his fiercenesse fomed all with sweat,
And the sharpe yron did for anger eat,
When his hot ryder spurd his chauffed side;
His looke was sterne, and seemed still to threat
Cruell reuenge, which he in hart did hyde,
And on his shield *Sans loy* in bloudie lines was dyde.

XXXIV When nigh he drew vnto this gentle payre
And saw the Red-crosse, which the knight did beare,
He burnt in fire, and gan eftsoones prepare
Himselfe to battell with his couched speare.
Loth was that other, and did faint through feare,
To taste th'vntryed dint of deadly steele;
But yet his Lady did so well him cheare,
That hope of new good hap he gan to feele;
So bent his speare, and spurnd his horse with yron heele.

XXXV But that proud Paynim forward came so fierce,
And full of wrath, that with his sharp-head speare
Through vainely crossed shield he quite did pierce,
And had his staggering steede not shrunke for feare,
Through shield and bodie eke he should him beare:
Yet so great was the puissance of his push,
That from his saddle quite he did him beare:
He tombling rudely downe to ground did rush,
And from his gored wound a well of bloud did gush.

31 When the weather-beaten mariner, having long wandered the ocean wide, often soaked in Tethys' salty ocean spray, his tawny skin endlessly tanned with the blustering breath of heaven that none can endure, and scorched in flames of fierce Orion's hound of the hottest months, spies the port from far, he merrily sounds his cheerful whistle. Then all the sailors drink a round to the sea-god, Nereus. Such was the joy Una felt when she found her knight.

The enchanter also seemed as joyous. Like the glad merchant on shore who sees that his ship has come safely far across the watery wilderness, he hurls out prayers and continuous blessings to Neptune.

So forth they ventured, and all the way, they passed the time discussing her dreadful recent distress. He asked her warily about the lion, and she told of all that had befallen her, and how the lion was now her guard.

The false knight, Una, and the lion, had not ridden far when they saw another knight riding towards them with hasty heat. He was fully armored and on a noble horse that, through fierceness, foamed with sweat and gnashed at the iron bit, while his fervent rider spurred his chaffed sides. The knight's look was stern and seemed to threaten a cruel revenge that was hidden in his heart. On his shield, the name, 'Sans Loy,' was dyed in bloody lines.

When he had drawn near the gentle pair, and noticed the red cross on the false knight's shield, he burned in fire, leveled his lance, and began to prepare himself to do battle. The false knight, though, was reluctant and almost fainted through fear, having never before tasted the blows of deadly steel. But his lady, Una, did so well to cheer him that he began to feel that luck might be on his side. So he bent his lance and spurred his horse forward.

35 But that proud pagan galloped forward so fiercely, and so full of wrath, that the sharp-headed lance pierced straight through Archimago's shield, that bore the cross in vain. Had his staggering horse not backed away in fear, the lance would have pierced through Archimago's body as well. Yet so great was the power of this force, that it sent the false knight tumbling roughly out of his saddle and onto the ground, where a well of blood gushed from his gored wound.

XXXVI Dismounting lightly from his loftie steed,
He to him lept, in mind to reaue his life,
And proudly said, Lo there the worthie meed
Of him, that slew *Sansfoy* with bloudie knife;
Henceforth his ghost freed from repining strife,
In peace may passen ouer *Lethe* lake,
When morning altars purgd with enemies life,
The blacke infernall *Furies* doen aslake:
Life from *Sansfoy* thou tookst, *Sansloy* shall from thee take.

XXXVII Therewith in haste his helmet gan vnlace,
Till *Vna* cride, O hold that heauie hand,
Deare Sir, what euer that thou be in place:
Enough is, that thy foe doth vanquisht stand
Now at thy mercy: Mercie not withstand:
For he is one the truest knight aliue,
Though conquered now he lie on lowly land,
And whilest him fortune fauourd, faire did thriue
In bloudie field: therefore of life him not depriue.

XXXVIII Her piteous words might not abate his rage,
But rudely rending vp his helmet, would
Haue slaine him straight: but when he sees his age,
And hoarie head of *Archimago* old,
His hastie hand he doth amazed hold,
And halfe ashamed, wondred at the sight:
For the old man well knew he, though vntold,
In charmes and magicke to haue wondrous might,
Ne euer wont in field, ne in round lists to fight.

XXXIX And said, Why *Archimago*, lucklesse syre,
What doe I see? what hard mishap is this,
That hath thee hither brought to taste mine yre?
Or thine the fault, or mine the error is,
In stead of foe to wound my friend amis?
He answered nought, but in a traunce still lay,
And on those guilefull dazed eyes of his
The cloud of death did sit. Which doen away,
He left him lying so, ne would no lenger stay.

XL But to the virgin comes, who all this while
Amased stands, her selfe so mockt to see
By him, who has the guerdon of his guile,
For so misfeigning her true knight to bee:
Yet is she now in more perplexitie,
Left in the hand of that same Paynim bold,
From whom her booteth not at all to flie;
Who by her cleanly garment catching hold,
Her from her Palfrey pluckt, her visage to behold.

---

36 Dismounting quickly from his lofty horse, Sansloy leapt to the sham knight, ready to end his life.

Indicating the false red cross shield, Sansloy said, "Lo, there is the worthy trophy of him who slew Sansfoy with bloody knife. Henceforth his ghost, now freed from vexation, may finally pass in peace over the river Lethe, once the black infernal Furies have satisfied themselves with enemy blood on the mourning altars. You took the life of Sansfoy, now Sansloy will take yours!"

Then he began to unlace Archimago's helmet, until Una cried, "O hold that heavy hand, dear sir! Isn't it enough for your rank, that your foe lies here vanquished, now at your mercy? For he is the one truest of knights alive, and although conquered now, and lying on the lowly ground, whilst fortune favored him, he thrived in bloody field. Therefore, do not deprive him of life!"

Her pitiful words hardly abated his rage, and ripping the false knight's helmet from his head, he would have slain him immediately. But when Sansloy discovered gray haired Archimago instead, he withheld his hasty hand in amazement, half ashamed, wondering at the sight. For he knew the old man well, and that he had wondrous might in charms and magic. And he also knew he was unaccustomed to battlefield or tournament.

Astonished, Sansloy said, "Why Archimago, luckless sire, what do I see? What hard mishap is this, that has brought you hither to taste my anger? Is it your fault, or my error that, instead of wounding a foe, I am mistaking a friend?"

Archimago didn't answer. Instead, he lay still and staring, as in a trance, and on his cunning dazed eyes lay the cloud of death. But Sansloy was keen to move on, so left him lying thus.

40But the maiden, who had been watching all this time, sat there on her donkey amazed at how deceived she had been. Lying on the ground, Archimago had received the just reward for his deceit in pretending to be her true knight. Yet she was now even more distressed, and left in the hand of that bold pagan, from whom it was of no avail to flee. For he grabbed her by her cloak of purity, and dragged her off her donkey to gaze upon her face.

XLI But her fierce seruant full of kingly awe
And high disdaine, whenas his soueraine Dame
So rudely handled by her foe he sawe,
With gaping iawes full greedy at him came,
And ramping on his shield, did weene the same
Haue reft away with his sharpe rending clawes:
But he was stout, and lust did now inflame
His corage more, that from his griping pawes
He hath his shield redeem'd, and forth his sword he drawes.

XLII O then too weake and feeble was the forse
Of saluage beast, his puissance to withstand:
For he was strong, and of so mightie corse,
As euer wielded speare in warlike hand,
And feates of armes did wisely vnderstand.
Eftsoones he perced through his chaufed chest
With thrilling point of deadly yron brand,
And launcht his Lordly hart: with death opprest
He roar'd aloud, whiles life forsooke his stubborne brest.

XLIII Who now is left to keepe the forlorne maid
From raging spoile of lawlesse victors will?
Her faithfull gard remou'd, her hope dismaid,
Her selfe a yeelded pray to saue or spill.
He now Lord of the field, his pride to fill,
With foule reproches, and disdainfull spight
Her vildly entertaines, and will or nill,
Beares her away vpon his courser light:
Her prayers nought preuaile, his rage is more of might.

XLIV And all the way, with great lamenting paine,
And piteous plaints she filleth his dull eares,
That stony hart could riuen haue in twaine,
And all the way she wets with flowing teares:
But he enrag›d with rancor, nothing heares.
Her seruile beast yet would not leaue her so,
But followes her farre off, ne ought he feares,
To be partaker of her wandring woe,
More mild in beastly kind, then that her beastly foe.

41But when her fierce servant, the lion, full of kingly awe and indignation, saw how rudely she was handled by her foe, he came at him with gaping greedy jaws. Rearing up on Sansloy's shield he tried to wrench it from him, with sharp rending claws. But Sansloy was bold, and lust now inflamed him, so he gained more courage and snatched the shield back from the lion's gripping paws. Then he drew forth his sword.

O, then too weak and feeble was the force of savage beast against Sansloy's might. For Sansloy was strong, adept in the feats of arms, and one of the mightiest men ever to wield a lance in warlike hand. So, he soon pierced the lion's angered chest with his deadly sword, and lanced his lordly heart. With death oppressing him, he roared loudly, then life departed his untamable breast.

Who is left to guard the forlorn maid, now spoil of this lawless victor's evil will? Her faithful guard removed, her hope dismayed, she waited as the surrendered prey for him to spare or spoil her life. Now lord of the field, his pride filled, with foul reproaches and spiteful disdain, he approached her vilely. Unheeding of her pleas, he snatched her up, and bore her away upon his horse, whether she liked it or not.

And all the way, lamenting painfully, she filled his dull and unhearing ears with such pitiful pleas and tears, that even a heart of stone might have broken. But he, enraged with malice, heard nothing.

MEANWHILE, HER SNOW-WHITE DONKEY WOULD NOT LEAVE HER, BUT FOLLOWED, unafraid, from a distance. Willing companion in her wandering woe, the gentle animal was milder in animal nature than her beastly foe.

---

1 *Penance: the Greek 'Metanoia' (repentance, or more literally "with mind"), was translated into Latin as 'paenitentia' by Jerome in 405AD, and later as "do penance" in the early English Bibles (Wycliffe and Douay-Rheims Catholic Bible). No such word exists in the NT, though the word continued to be used in Christian contexts. The mistranslation, that affected theology for 1000 years, was corrected by Tyndale, and he was executed for it.*

NOTES ON CANTO IV

House of Pride: It looks impressive, but is built on poor foundations. The gate is wide and the path there is broad, alluding to Matt 7:13-14 *"Enter through the narrow gate. For wide is the gate and broad is the road that leads to destruction, and many enter through it. But small is the gate and narrow the road that leads to life, and only a few find it."*
Malvenu: is the porter at the Castle of Pride, and his name is French for "badly come."
The Queen: Lucifera: Pride: the 'queen' of the Seven Deadly Sins. Pride was the sin of Satan that caused his fall from Heaven, and the Queen of Pride is associated with Lucifer by her name.
Idleness, Gluttony, Lechery, Avarice, Envy, and Wrath: With Lucifera (Pride), the counsellors complete the Seven Deadly Sins. Each of these counselors suffers from the disease thought to have been caused by its specific sin, which was a Medieval belief.

CANTO IV

THE CASTLE OF PRIDE

To sinfull house of Pride, Duessa
guides the faithfull knight,
Where brothers death to wreak Sansioy
doth chalenge him to fight.

I Young knight, what euer that dost armes professe,
And through long labours huntest after fame,
Beware of fraud, beware of ficklenesse,
In choice, and change of thy deare loued Dame,
Least thou of her beleeue too lightly blame,
And rash misweening doe thy hart remoue:
For vnto knight there is no greater shame,
Then lightnesse and inconstancie in loue;
That doth this *Redcrosse* knights ensample plainly proue.

II Who after that he had faire *Vna* lorne,
Through light misdeeming of her loialtie,
And false *Duessa* in her sted had borne,
Called *Fidess'*, and so supposd to bee;
Long with her traueild, till at last they see
A goodly building, brauely garnished,
The house of mightie Prince it seemd to bee:
And towards it a broad high way that led,
All bare through peoples feet, which thither traueiled.

III Great troupes of people traueild thitherward
Both day and night, of each degree and place,
But few returned, hauing scaped hard,
With balefull beggerie, or foule disgrace,
Which euer after in most wretched case,
Like loathsome lazars, by the hedges lay.
Thither *Duessa* bad him bend his pace:
For she is wearie of the toilesome way,
And also nigh consumed is the lingring day.

IV A stately Pallace built of squared bricke,
Which cunningly was without morter laid,
Whose wals were high, but nothing strong, nor thick,
And golden foile all ouer them displaid,
That purest skye with brightnesse they dismaid:
High lifted vp were many loftie towres,
And goodly galleries farre ouer laid,
Full of faire windowes, and delightfull bowres;
And on the top a Diall told the timely howres.

V It was a goodly heape for to behould,
And spake the praises of the workmans wit;
But full great pittie, that so faire a mould
Did on so weake foundation euer sit:
For on a sandie hill, that still did flit,
And fall away, it mounted was full hie,
That euery breath of heauen shaked it:
And all the hinder parts, that few could spie,
Were ruinous and old, but painted cunningly.

Duessa guides the faithful knight to the sinful house of Pride,
where Sansjoy challenges him to avenge his brother's death.

YOUNG KNIGHT, WHO MAKES BATTLE HIS PROFESSION, AND THROUGH LONG labors hunts after fame, beware of fraud, beware of faithlessness, beware of fickleness in choice, and remove rash misunderstanding from your heart, lest you blame your dear lady too lightly. For unto knights there is no greater shame than lightness and inconstancy in love, which the example of this Redcross knight plainly proves. Misjudging Una's loyalty, he had left her forlorn, and taken the false Duessa as his lady instead. She had claimed her name was Fidessa, deceiving him into thinking she was a lady of faith.

REDCROSS, DUESSA AND THE DWARF TRAVELLED ALL DAY UNTIL AT LAST THEY glimpsed a lofty castle towering in the distance. Boldly arrayed, it seemed like the palace of a mighty prince. A wide gate and a broad way led towards it, worn out by footsteps of the multitudes who had already thither travelled. Day and night, great troupes of people of every kind and place travelled hitherward. But few returned, having barely escaped. Instead, they ended up like loathsome lepers, ever after lying by the hedges in wretched beggary or foul disgrace. Thither Duessa bade the knight turn, and quicken his footsteps. For she was weary of toilsome travel, and concerned that the day was nearly through.

The stately palace was hewn with square bricks, cunningly laid without mortar, so that the misleading walls were high, but not solid or strong. The walls were gilded in gold so dazzling, that their garish glow even conquered the purest sky. Many lofty towers rose above them, with vast galleries full of glittering bay windows and delightful bowers. Higher still, a clock tolled the ominous hours.

5 It was a magnificent castle to behold, and spoke the praises of the workman's skill. But what a great pity that such a fair structure sat upon so weak a foundation. For it was built on such an unstable sandy hill, that every breeze from heaven shook it, and its hidden ruins were cunningly painted over to make it look new.

VI Arriued there they passed in forth right;
For still to all the gates stood open wide,
Yet charge of them was to a Porter hight
Cald *Maluenú*, who entrance none denide:
Thence to the hall, which was on euery side
With rich array and costly arras dight:
Infinite sorts of people did abide
There waiting long, to win the wished sight
Of her, that was the Lady of that Pallace bright.

VII By them they passe, all gazing on them round,
And to the Presence mount; whose glorious vew
Their frayle amazed senses did confound:
In liuing Princes court none euer knew
Such endlesse richesse, and so sumptuous shew;
Ne *Persia* selfe, the nourse of pompous pride
Like euer saw. And there a noble crew
Of Lordes and Ladies stood on euery side
Which with their presence faire, the place much beautifide.

VIII High aboue all a cloth of State was spred,
And a rich throne, as bright as sunny day,
On which there sate most braue embellished
With royall robes and gorgeous array,
A mayden Queene, that shone as *Titans* ray,
In glistring gold, and peerelesse pretious stone:
Yet her bright blazing beautie did assay
To dim the brightnesse of her glorious throne,
As enuying her selfe, that too exceeding shone.

IX Exceeding shone, like *Phoebus* fairest childe,
That did presume his fathers firie wayne,
And flaming mouthes of steedes vnwonted wilde
Through highest heauen with weaker hand to rayne;
Proud of such glory and aduancement vaine,
While flashing beames do daze his feeble eyen,
He leaues the welkin way most beaten plaine,
And rapt with whirling wheeles, inflames the skyen,
With fire not made to burne, but fairely for to shyne.

X So proud she shyned in her Princely state,
Looking to heauen; for earth she did disdayne,
And sitting high; for lowly she did hate:
Lo vnderneath her scornefull feete, was layne
A dreadfull Dragon with an hideous trayne,
And in her hand she held a mirrhour bright,
Wherein her face she often vewed fayne,
And in her selfe-lou'd semblance tooke delight;
For she was wondrous faire, as any liuing wight.

6 Arriving there, the three travelers passed straight through the entrance, for the gates stood wide open. Malvenu, the entrusted porter who guarded the gate, denied none an entrance. Leaving their horses with the dwarf, Redcross and Duessa made their way down the hall, which was decorated with rich array, and every wall was adorned with lavish tapestries. A diverse crowd of people waited patiently there, hoping to win the wished sight of the queen of that bright palace.

With everyone gazing at them on all sides, Redcross and Duessa made their way through the crowds, and arrived at the throne room entrance. Here, the glorious view confounded frail senses even more, for never had such endless riches, and so sumptuous a show in a prince's court, been seen before. Not even Persia herself, the nurse and nourisher of pompous pride, ever saw such a sight. Standing on every side, a noble crew of Lords and Ladies beautified the place with their fair presence. An emblem flag was spread as a canopy above the richest throne where, beautifully adorned in royal robes and gorgeous array, sat the maiden queen. The throne shone like a Titan's ray in glistering gold and peerless precious stone. Yet the queen's blazing beauty strove to dim the brightness of her glorious throne, that she believed envied her: she who shone too exceedingly.

Too exceedingly she shone. Just like Phoebus's fairest child Phaeton, who wanted to drive his father's fiery chariot through the highest heaven, with its wild, flaming mouthed horses, she also disdained the earth. Phaeton's weaker reining hand, full of pride and vanity, flashing beams dazzling his feeble eyes, left the beaten path of the sun, and instead, inflamed the constellations with fire not made to burn, but to shine.

Likewise, the queen shone in the pride of her princely state, looking to heaven. **10** Despising all humility, she was seated high, and underneath her scornful feet lay a dreadful dragon with a hideous tail. In her hand, she held a bright mirror, wherein she frequently gazed upon herself, taking great delight in her self-loved image. For she was wondrously fair, as any living creature.

XI Of griesly *Pluto* she the daughter was,
And sad *Proserpina* the Queene of hell;
Yet did she thinke her pearelesse wroth to pas
That parentage, with pride so did she swell,
And thundring *Ioue*, that high in heauen doth dwell,
And wield the world, she claymed for her syre,
Or if that any else did *Ioue* excell:
For to the highest she did still aspyre,
Or if ought higher were then that, did it desyre.

XII And proud *Lucifera* men did her call,
That made her selfe a Queene, and crownd to be,
Yet rightfull kingdome she had none at all,
Ne heritage of natiue soueraintie,
But did vsurpe with wrong and tyrannie
Vpon the scepter, which she now did hold:
Ne ruld her Realmes with lawes, but pollicie,
And strong aduizement of six wisards old,
That with their counsels bad her kingdome did vphold.

XIII Soone as the Elfin knight in presence came,
And false *Duessa* seeming Lady faire,
A gentle Husher, *Vanitie* by name
Made rowme, and passage for them did prepaire:
So goodly brought them to the lowest staire
Of her high throne, where they on humble knee
Making obeyssance, did the cause declare,
Why they were come, her royall state to see,
To proue the wide report of her great Maiestee.

XIV With loftie eyes, halfe loth to looke so low,
She thanked them in her disdainefull wise,
Ne other grace vouchsafed them to show
Of Princesse worthy, scarse them bad arise.
Her Lordes and Ladies all this while deuise
Themselues to setten forth to straungers sight:
Some frounce their curled haire in courtly guise,
Some prancke their ruffes, and others trimly dight
Their gay attire: each others greater pride does spight.

XV Goodly they all that knight do entertaine,
Right glad with him to haue increast their crew:
But to *Duess'* each one himselfe did paine
All kindnesse and faire courtesie to shew;
For in that court whylome her well they knew:
Yet the stout Faerie mongst the middest crowd
Thought all their glorie vaine in knightly vew,
And that great Princesse too exceeding prowd,
That to strange knight no better countenance allowd.

---

11 Yet, as the daughter of grisly Pluto and sad Proserpina, she was also the Queen of Hell, and so swollen with pride, that she fancied her peerless wrath surpassed that of her parents. What is more, since thundering Jove dwelt higher in heaven and ruled the world, she claimed *he* was her sire, and if there had been anything excelling him, she desired that instead. Such was her desire to aspire. Men called her proud Lucifera, and she had crowned herself queen. Yet she had no rightful kingdom, or heritage of any native sovereignty at all. Instead, upon that scepter she now held, she ruled with error and tyranny. Her realms were not ruled with laws, but her own policies, and the firm advice of six old wizards, upholding her kingdom with their bad counsels.

As soon as the Elfin knight arrived, along with the false Duessa, seemingly a fair lady, a gentle usher named Vanity made a passage to the queen for them. He graciously guided them to the lowest stair of the queen's high throne, where they paid their respects on humble knee. Then they declared why they had come, explaining that it was to see her royal state and prove the wide report of her great majesty. With lofty eyes, half loath to look so low, she thanked them in her disdainful way, hardly offering any other grace that would be worthy of a princess, even to tell them to arise from their bowing.

Meanwhile, her Lords and Ladies strutted about, arranging and braiding their curled hair in courtly guise or flaunting their ruffles, while others adorned their gay attire, envying each other's greater pride. **15** Happy to have increased their crew, they entertained that knight well. They also took great pains to show all kindness and fair courtesy to Duessa, for she was already well known in that court.

Yet, even in the thickest crowd, the stout Faerie, Redcross, in knightly view, thought all their glory was vain, and found the great princess excessively proud and ill mannered.

XVI Suddein vpriseth from her stately place
The royall Dame, and for her coche doth call:
All hurtlen forth, and she with Princely pace,
As faire *Aurora* in her purple pall,
Out of the East the dawning day doth call:
So forth she comes: her brightnesse brode doth blaze;
The heapes of people thronging in the hall,
Do ride each other, vpon her to gaze:
Her glorious glitterand light doth all mens eyes amaze.

XVII So forth she comes, and to her coche does clyme,
Adorned all with gold, and girlonds gay,
That seemd as fresh as *Flora* in her prime,
And stroue to match, in royall rich array,
Great *Junoes* golden chaire, the which they say
The Gods stand gazing on, when she does ride
To *Joves* high house through heauens bras-paued way
Drawne of faire Pecocks, that excell in pride,
And full of *Argus* eyes their tailes dispredden wide.

XVIII But this was drawne of six vnequall beasts,
On which her six sage Counsellours did ryde,
Taught to obay their bestiall beheasts,
With like conditions to their kinds applyde:
Of which the first, that all the rest did guyde,
Was sluggish *Idlenesse* the nourse of sin;
Vpon a slouthfull Asse he chose to ryde,
Arayd in habit blacke, and amis thin,
Like to an holy Monck, the seruice to begin.

XIX And in his hand his Portesse still he bare,
That much was worne, but therein little red,
For of deuotion he had little care,
Still drownd in sleepe, and most of his dayes ded;
Scarse could he once vphold his heauie hed,
To looken, whether it were night or day:
May seeme the wayne was very euill led,
When such an one had guiding of the way,
That knew not, whether right he went, or else astray.

XX From worldy cares himselfe he did esloyne,
And greatly shunned manly exercise,
From euery worke he chalenged essoyne,
For contemplation sake: yet otherwise,
His life he led in lawlesse riotise;
By which he grew to grieuous malady;
For in his lustlesse limbs through euill guise
A shaking feuer raignd continually:
Such one was *Idlenesse*, first of this company.

16 Presently, the royal dame rose from her throne and called for her coach. As fair as Aurora in her crimson robe, rising from the east and calling for the dawning day, she emerged with blazing brightness. The multitudes thronging in the hall strained to rise above each other, hoping to catch a glimpse, for her glorious glitter and light dazzled all men's eyes.

So forth she came, and climbed into her coach, adorned with gold and gay garlands that seemed as fresh as the Roman goddess Flora in her prime. In royal rich array, the proud queen strove to match great Juno's golden chariot, which they say the gods stand gazing upon.

When Juno rides to Jove's high house through heaven's brass-paved way, she is drawn by fair peacocks that excel in pride, their colorful tails spread wide, full of Argus eyes. [1]

But this coach was drawn by six different beasts, each ridden by one of her six sage counselors. Having long obeyed their bestial commands, the counselors were matched with beasts most like their natures.

The first was sluggish *Idleness*, known as the nurse of sin, and he guided the rest. He chose to ride upon a slothful donkey, and he was arrayed in a black habit and monk's hood, looking like a holy monk about to begin a procession. In his hand, he held a prayer book, worn but little read, for he cared little for devotion. Ever drowned in sleep, he could barely hold up his heavy head to see if it were night or day. With such a person guiding the way, who did not know right from astray, the coach seemed very badly led. **20** He withdrew himself from worldly cares for the sake of contemplation, shunning manly exercise, and any kind of work. Otherwise, the life he led was lawless and riotous, and from this he grew a grievous malady. For, in his listless limbs through evil ways of living, a shaking fever reigned continually. Such was the first of this company: Idleness.

XXI And by his side rode loathsome *Gluttony*,
Deformed creature, on a filthie swyne,
His belly was vp-blowne with luxury,
And eke with fatnesse swollen were his eyne,
And like a Crane his necke was long and fyne,
With which he swallowd vp excessiue feast,
For want whereof poore people oft did pyne;
And all the way, most like a brutish beast,
He spued vp his gorge, that all did him deteast.

XXII In greene vine leaues he was right fitly clad;
For other clothes he could not weare for heat,
And on his head an yuie girland had,
From vnder which fast trickled downe the sweat:
Still as he rode, he somewhat still did eat,
And in his hand did beare a bouzing can,
Of which he supt so oft, that on his seat
His dronken corse he scarse vpholden can,
In shape and life more like a monster, then a man.

XXIII Vnfit he was for any worldy thing,
And eke vnhable once to stirre or go,
Not meet to be of counsell to a king,
Whose mind in meat and drinke was drowned so,
That from his friend he seldome knew his fo:
Full of diseases was his carcas blew,
And a dry dropsie through his flesh did flow:
Which by misdiet daily greater grew:
Such one was *Gluttony*, the second of that crew.

XXIV And next to him rode lustfull *Lechery*,
Vpon a bearded Goat, whose rugged haire,
And whally eyes (the signe of gelosy,)
Was like the person selfe, whom he did beare:
Who rough, and blacke, and filthy did appeare,
Vnseemely man to please faire Ladies eye;
Yet he of Ladies oft was loued deare,
When fairer faces were bid standen by:
O who does know the bent of womens fantasy?

XXV In a greene gowne he clothed was full faire,
Which vnderneath did hide his filthinesse,
And in his hand a burning hart he bare,
Full of vaine follies, and new fanglenesse:
For he was false, and fraught with ficklenesse,
And learned had to loue with secret lookes,
And well could daunce, and sing with ruefulnesse,
And fortunes tell, and read in louing bookes,
And thousand other wayes, to bait his fleshly hookes.

21 By his side, rode loathsome *Gluttony*, a deformed creature riding on a filthy swine. His belly was enlarged with luxury, and even his eyes were swollen with fat. His neck, though, was long and scrawny like a crane, and with it, he swallowed up excessive feast, depriving the poor and leaving them to starve. He was such a brutish, bulimic beast that he even spewed up anything he disliked. He was, like Bacchus, most fitly clad in green vine leaves, for other clothes he could not wear for heat. On his head, he wore an ivy garland, and sweat trickled down his puffy face. Even as he rode, he continued to stuff food in his mouth with one hand, while guzzling on the beer can in the other. He could scarcely hold up his drunken body: a shape and life more like a monster, than a man, and his mind was so drowned in meat and drink, that he couldn't tell friend from foe. His body was blue, and swollen with edema, while his excessive thirst increased daily from such a bad diet. Unable to stir or walk, he was unfit for any worldly thing, let alone counsel to a king. Such one was Gluttony, the second of that crew.

And next to him rode lustful *Lechery* upon a bearded goat, whose shaggy, rugged hair, and jealous, glaring, green eyes, resembled the person he bore upon his back. Rough, shadowy and crude, this man's appearance did not seem likely to attract fair ladies' eyes. Yet the ladies often loved him more than fairer folk, who were told to stand aside. *Oh, who knows the inclination of a woman's fancy?*

25 Lechery was dressed in a green gown which hid his lewdness underneath. In his hand, he held a burning heart, full of vain follies and love of latest fashions. For he was false, and fraught with fickleness, and had learned how to love with secret looks, dance with clever steps, and sing with mournful tunes. He could tell fortunes, read love-poetry, and bait his fleshy hooks in a thousand ways.

XXVI Inconstant man, that loued all he saw,
And lusted after all, that he did loue,
Ne would his looser life be tide to law,
But ioyd weake wemens hearts to tempt, and proue
If from their loyall loues he might then moue;
Which lewdnesse fild him with reprochfull paine
Of that fowle euill, which all men reproue,
That rots the marrow, and consumes the braine:
Such one was *Lecherie*, the third of all this traine.

XXVII And greedy *Auarice* by him did ride,
Vpon a Camell loaden all with gold;
Two iron coffers hong on either side,
With precious mettall full, as they might hold,
And in his lap an heape of coine he told;
For of his wicked pelfe his God he made,
And vnto hell him selfe for money sold;
Accursed vsurie was all his trade,
And right and wrong ylike in equall ballaunce waide.

XXVIII His life was nigh vnto deaths doore yplast,
And thred-bare cote, and cobled shoes he ware,
Ne scarse good morsell all his life did tast,
But both from backe and belly still did spare,
To fill his bags, and richesse to compare;
Yet chylde ne kinsman liuing had he none
To leaue them to; but thorough daily care
To get, and nightly feare to lose his owne,
He led a wretched life vnto him selfe vnknowne.

XXIX Most wretched wight, whom nothing might suffise,
Whose greedy lust did lacke in greatest store,
Whose need had end, but no end couetise,
Whose wealth was want, whose plenty made him pore,
Who had enough, yet wished euer more;
A vile disease, and eke in foote and hand
A grieuous gout tormented him full sore,
That well he could not touch, nor go, nor stand:
Such one was *Auarice*, the fourth of this faire band.

XXX And next to him malicious *Enuie* rode,
Vpon a rauenous wolfe, and still did chaw
Betweene his cankred teeth a venemous tode,
That all the poison ran about his chaw;
But inwardly he chawed his owne maw
At neighbours wealth, that made him euer sad;
For death it was, when any good he saw,
And wept, that cause of weeping none he had,
But when he heard of harme, he wexed wondrous glad.

26 Inconstant man, who loved all he saw, and lusted after all that he loved. His loose life was so unprincipled, that he took joy in tempting weak women's hearts, seeking to move their loyal loves to himself. This lewdness causes a certain disease that rots the marrow and consumes the brain. Such was Lechery, the third of the train.

Next came greedy *Avarice*, riding upon a camel[2] laden with gold. Two iron coffers hung on either side, stuffed full of precious metal, and in his lap he counted a pile of coins. For he made a god of his ill-gotten wealth, and sold himself to hell. He made his money in accursed usury, by charging steep interest rates, and mistakenly weighed right and wrong alike in equal balance. Living as though at death's door, he wore a threadbare coat and cobbled shoes. He shunned tasty food, sparing neither his back nor belly, just so he could fill his bags with riches, and acquire more and more. Having neither child, nor living kinsman, there was no one to inherit his vast wealth. Instead, he just filled his empty days with concern over money, and his nights with nightmares about losing it. Most wretched creature, whose greedy lust led to lack, whose need had no end, whose wealth was want, whose plenty made him poor, and whom nothing might satisfy! And though he had enough, ignorant of his own wretchedness, he still wished for ever more, for he who desires most, lacks most. He was tormented by gout: a vile disease of hand and foot. It made him so sore that he could neither touch, nor move, nor stand. Such one was Avarice, the fourth of this fair band.

30 And next to him, upon a ravenous wolf, rode malicious *Envie*. Between his cankered teeth he continually chewed a venomous toad, with poison running down his chin. But inwardly he chewed at the thought of his neighbors' well-being, that made him ever miserable. He was happy when they suffered death, and wept when he had no cause of weeping. Whenever he heard of others being harmed, he became wondrously happy.

XXXI All in a kirtle of discolourd say
He clothed was, ypainted full of eyes;
And in his bosome secretly there lay
An hatefull Snake, the which his taile vptyes
In many folds, and mortall sting implyes.
Still as he rode, he gnasht his teeth, to see
Those heapes of gold with griple Couetyse,
And grudged at the great felicitie
Of proud *Lucifera*, and his owne companie.

XXXII He hated all good workes and vertuous deeds,
And him no lesse, that any like did vse,
And who with gracious bread the hungry feeds,
His almes for want of faith he doth accuse;
So euery good to bad he doth abuse:
And eke the verse of famous Poets witt
He does backebite, and spightfull poison spues
From leprous mouth on all, that euer writt:
Such one vile *Enuie* was, that fift in row did sitt.

XXXIII And him beside rides fierce reuenging *VVrath*,
Vpon a Lion, loth for to be led;
And in his hand a burning brond he hath,
The which he brandisheth about his hed;
His eyes did hurle forth sparkles fiery red,
And stared sterne on all, that him beheld,
As ashes pale of hew and seeming ded;
And on his dagger still his hand he held,
Trembling through hasty rage, when choler in him sweld.

XXXIV His ruffin raiment all was staind with blood,
Which he had spilt, and all to rags yrent,
Through vnaduized rashnesse woxen wood;
For of his hands he had no gouernement,
Ne car'd for bloud in his auengement:
But when the furious fit was ouerpast,
His cruell facts he often would repent;
Yet wilfull man he neuer would forecast,
How many mischieues should ensue his heedlesse hast.

XXXV Full many mischiefes follow cruell *VVrath*;
Abhorred bloudshed, and tumultuous strife,
Vnmanly murder, and vnthrifty scath,
Bitter despight, with rancours rusty knife,
And fretting griefe the enemy of life;
All these, and many euils moe haunt ire,
The swelling Splene, and Frenzy raging rife,
The shaking Palsey, and Saint *Fraunces* fire:
Such one was *VVrath*, the last of this vngodly tire.

31 Envie wore a gown of multi-colored cloth, painted with many envious eyes. Next to his chest lay a secretive, yet hateful, snake, wrapping its sting with its tail bound in many folds. As he rode, he gnashed his teeth with greedy covetousness to see those heaps of gold, and grudged at the great fortune of proud Lucifera, and of his fellow counsellors. He hated all good works and virtuous deeds, never doing any himself. To those who fed the hungry with gracious bread, he accused them of lacking faith, while he abused and twisted every good with bad. As for poets' verses, he would backstab and spew spiteful poison from his leprous mouth at them. Such was vile Envie, seated in the fifth row.

And, upon a lion beside him, rode fierce revenging *Wrath*, unwilling to be led. In his hand, he held a burning torch, which he brandished about his head. His eyes hurled forth fiery red sparks, but he glowered sternly on all who beheld him, like dead pale ashes. In his hand, he gripped his dagger, trembling through hasty rage whenever choler swelled in him. His ruffian clothing was stained with the blood he had spilt, and ripped into rags through the unwise rash actions that made him wild. For he had no control over his hands, nor cared about spilling blood in his cruel vengeances. But when the furious fit was over, he would often repent of his cruel actions. Yet this willful man could never see ahead, and of the many evil consequences that might result from his heedless haste.

35 How many mischiefs will follow cruel Wrath, with his abhorred bloodshed, temper tantrums and tumultuous strife, unmanly murder, wasteful destruction, and costly damage? The enemy of life, he rages in bitter malice with gnawing distress and hatred's bloody knife. All these, and many more evils, haunt Wrath: the swollen spleen, abounding in frenzies. His disease was a skin rash, called St Anthony's Fire. Such one was Wrath, the last of this ungodly procession.

XXXVI And after all, vpon the wagon beame
Rode *Sathan*, with a smarting whip in hand,
With which he forward lasht the laesie teme,
So oft as *Slowth* still in the mire did stand.
Huge routs of people did about them band,
Showting for ioy, and still before their way
A foggy mist had couered all the land;
And vnderneath their feet, all scattered lay
Dead sculsand bones of men, whose life had gone astray.

XXXVII So forth they marchen in this goodly sort,
To take the solace of the open aire,
And in fresh flowring fields themselues to sport;
Emongst the rest rode that false Lady faire,
The fowle *Duessa*, next vnto the chaire
Of proud *Lucifer'*, as one of the traine:
But that good knight would not so nigh repaire,
Him selfe estraunging from their ioyaunce vaine,
Whose fellowship seemd far vnfit for warlike swaine.

XXXVIII So hauing solaced themselues a space
With pleasaunce of the breathing fields yfed
They backe returned to the Princely Place;
Whereas an errant knight in armes ycled,
And heathnish shield, wherein with letters red
Was writ *Sans ioy*, they new arriued find:
Enflam'd with fury and fiers hardy-hed,
He seemd in hart to harbour thoughts vnkind,
And nourish bloudy vengeaunce in his bitter mind.

XXXIX Who when the shamed shield of slaine *Sans foy*
He spide with that same Faery champions page,
Bewraying him, that did of late destroy
His eldest brother, burning all with rage
He to him leapt, and that same enuious gage
Of victors glory from him snatcht away:
But th'Elfin knight, which ought that warlike wage,
Disdaind to loose the meed he wonne in fray,
And him rencountring fierce, reskewd the noble pray.

XL Therewith they gan to hurtlen greedily,
Redoubted battaile ready to darrayne,
And clash their shields, and shake their swords on hy,
That with their sturre they troubled all the traine;
Till that great Queene vpon eternall paine
Of high displeasure, that ensewen might,
Commaunded them their fury to refraine,
And if that either to that shield had right,
In equall lists they should the morrow next it fight.

36 Finally, upon a wagon beam, rode Satan. Smarting whip in hand, he lashed the lazy team ahead, as Sloth was often stuck in the mud. Huge crowds of people surrounded them, shouting for joy. But a foggy mist had covered all the land, and underneath their feet, all scattered about, lay dead skulls and bones of men whose lives had gone astray.

In grand style, this goodly company marched forth, taking solace in the open air, and sporting themselves in fresh flowering fields. Amongst them rode that false fair lady, the foul Duessa, whose chariot came next after proud Lucifera. But that good knight stood his distance, wanting to retreat from this vain festivity, whose fellowship seemed far unfit for warlike youths.

Having solaced themselves a short time with the pleasures of the fragrant fields, the procession returned to the princely palace, where an errant knight, clad in arms, had just arrived. On his heathen-style shield, "Sansjoy" was written in bold red letters. Enflamed with fury and hard headedness, he seemed to harbor unkind thoughts in his heart, and nourish bloody vengeance in his bitter mind.

When Sansjoy spied the shamed shield of slain Sansfoy, carried by that same Faerie champion's page, betraying the fact that he had destroyed his eldest brother, he burned all with rage. He leapt at the dwarf, and snatched that victor's trophy away. But the Elfin knight, who had just arrived in time, did not want to lose the prize he had won in the fray. So he battled him fiercely, rescuing the noble booty. **40** Therewith they rushed at each other, clashing their shields, and shaking their swords on high, ready to settle the claim through deadly battle. The stir troubled the procession, until that great queen commanded them, upon eternal pain, to refrain from their fury, declaring that if either had a right to the shield, they should fight like true knights on equal jousting field tomorrow.

XLI Ah dearest Dame, (quoth then the Paynim bold,)
Pardon the errour of enraged wight,
Whom great griefe made forget the raines to hold
Of reasons rule, to see this recreant knight,
No knight, but treachour full of false despight
And shamefull treason, who through guile hath slayn
The prowest knight, that euer field did fight,
Euen stout *Sans foy* (O who can then refrayn?)
Whose shield he beares renuerst, the more to heape disdayn.

XLII And to augment the glorie of his guile,
His dearest loue the faire *Fidessa* loe
Is there possessed of the traytour vile,
Who reapes the haruest sowen by his foe,
Sowen in bloudy field, and bought with woe:
That brothers hand shall dearely well requight
So be,O Queene, you equall fauour showe.
Him litle answerd th'angry Elfin knight;
He neuer meant with words, but swords to plead his right.

XLIII But threw his gauntlet as a sacred pledge,
His cause in combat the next day to try:
So been they parted both, with harts on edge,
To be aueng'd each on his enimy.
That night they pas in ioy and iollity,
Feasting and courting both in bowre and hall;
For Steward was excessiue *Gluttonie*,
That of his plenty poured forth to all:
Which doen, the Chamberlain *Slowth* did to rest them call.

XLIV Now whenas darkesome night had all displayd
Her coleblacke curtein ouer brightest skye,
The warlike youthes on dayntie couches layd,
Did chace away sweet sleepe from sluggish eye,
To muse on meanes of hoped victory.
But whenas *Morpheus* had with leaden mace
Arrested all that courtly company,
Vp-rose *Duessa* from her resting place,
And to the Paynims lodging comes with silent pace.

XLV Whom broad awake she finds, in troublous fit,
Forecasting, how his foe he might annoy,
And him amoues with speaches seeming fit:
Ah deare *Sans ioy*, next dearest to *Sans foy*,
Cause of my new griefe, cause of my new ioy,
Ioyous, to see his ymage in mine eye,
And greeu'd, to thinke how foe did him destroy,
That was the flowre of grace and cheualrye;
Lo his *Fidessa* to thy secret faith I flye.

41"Ah dearest dame," then said the bold pagan, Sansjoy, "Pardon the error of this enraged creature here, whom great grief made forget to keep the reins on reason's rule. But I saw this cowardly knight, no, not a knight, but a traitor, full of false despite and shameful treason who, through guile, has slain the most skillful knight that ever field did fight: stout Sansfoy—O, who can restrain oneself!—whose shield he bears upside-down, the more to heap disdain. Furthermore, to augment the glory of his guile, Sansfoy's dearest love, the faire Fidessa, lo, is there possessed by that vile traitor who reaps the sown harvest of his foe, sown in bloody field, and bought with woe. That act, this brother's hand shall dearly repay in kind. So be, O queen, you show equal favour."

He did not speak to Redcross, the angry Elfin knight. He never meant to plead his right with words, but with swords. So, he threw down his gauntlet glove as a sacred pledge, and would try his cause in combat the next day. Hearts on edge to be avenged each on his enemy, they parted company.

That night they passed in joy and jollity, feasting and courting both in bower and hall. Since the feasting steward was excessive Gluttony, his plenty poured forth to all. And when done, the chamberlain, Sloth, called them to rest.

Now, as darksome Night had displayed her coal-black curtain over brightest sky, the warlike youths lay on dainty couches, chasing away sweet sleep from their sluggish eye, while musing on means of hoped victory. Meanwhile, when Morpheus had arrested all that courtly company with his leaden mace of sleep, up rose Duessa from her resting place, and crept to the pagan's lodging.

45 She found him broad awake in a troublesome fit, forecasting how he might annoy his foe.

With moving speeches, Duessa began to address him: "Ah dear Sansjoy, next dearest to Sansfoy, cause of my new grief, cause of my new joy, joyous, to see his image in mine eye, but grieved to think how that foe destroyed him, who was the flower of grace and chivalry. Lo, his Fidessa, to your secret faith, I flee."

XLVI With gentle wordes he can her fairely greet,
And bad say on the secret of her hart.
Then sighing soft, I learne that litle sweet
Oft tempred is (quoth she) with muchell smart:
For since my brest was launcht with louely dart
Of deare *Sansfoy*, I neuer ioyed howre,
But in eternall woes my weaker hart
Haue wasted, louing him with all my powre,
And for his sake haue felt full many an heauie stowre.

XLVII At last when perils all I weened past,
And hop'd to reape the crop of all my care,
Into new woes vnweeting I was cast,
By this false faytor, who vnworthy ware
His worthy shield, whom he with guilefull snare
Entrapped slew, and brought to shamefull graue.
Me silly maid away with him he bare,
And euer since hath kept in darksome caue,
For that I would not yeeld, that to *Sans-foy* I gaue.

XLVIII But since faire Sunne hath sperst that lowring clowd,
And to my loathed life now shewes some light,
Vnder your beames I will me safely shrowd,
From dreaded storme of his disdainfull spight:
To you th'inheritance belongs by right
Of brothers prayse, to you eke longs his loue.
Let not his loue, let not his restlesse spright
Be vnreueng'd, that calles to you aboue
From wandring *Stygian* shores, where it doth endlesse moue.

XLIX Thereto said he, Faire Dame be nought dismaid
For sorrowes past; their griefe is with them gone:
Ne yet of present perill be affraid;
For needlesse feare did neuer vantage none,
And helplesse hap it booteth not to mone.
Dead is *Sans-foy*, his vitall paines are past,
Though greeued ghost for vengeance deepe do grone:
He liues, that shall him pay his dewties last,
And guiltie Elfin bloud shall sacrifice in hast.

L O but I feare the fickle freakes (quoth shee)
Of fortune false, and oddes of armes in field.
Why dame (quoth he) what oddes can euer bee,
Where both do fight alike, to win or yield?
Yea but (quoth she) he beares a charmed shield,
And eke enchaunted armes, that none can perce,
Ne none can wound the man, that does them wield.
Charmd or enchaunted (answerd he then ferce)
I no whit reck, ne you the like need to reherce.

46 He greeted her courteously with gentle words, and bade her tell all the secrets of her heart.

Then, sighing softly, she began: "I learned that a little sweetness is often tempered with much pain. For since my breast was pierced with love's arrow of dear Sansfoy, I never enjoyed an hour. But my weaker heart has wasted in eternal woes, loving him with all my power, and having felt many a heavy grief for his sake. At last, when perils I knew were all past, and hoped to reap the crop of all my care, I was cast into new unknown woes by this imposter, who, though unworthy, wore your brother's shield, whom he had guilefully snared, entrapped and slew, and brought to shameful grave.

"Being a helpless maid, he bore me away with him, and has kept me in a darksome cave ever since, because I would not yield that which I promised to Sansfoy. But since the fair sun has dispersed that lowering cloud, and now shows some light to my loathed life, I shall safely shelter myself under your beams, away from the dreaded storm of that Elfin knight's disdainful spite. The inheritance belongs to you by right of brother's praise, and to you, also, belongs his beloved. Let not his love, let not his restless spirit be unavenged. He calls to you above, while ceaselessly wandering Stygian shores, whence he must wait at the River Styx until avenged."

Sansjoy then replied, "Fair Dame, do not be dismayed for sorrows past. Their grief is gone with them. Nor yet be afraid of present peril, for needless fear benefits no one, and fate isn't moved by moaning. Sansfoy is dead, and his vital pains are past. But his grieved ghost groans for deep vengeance. He who still lives shall pay his last debts, and guilty Elfin blood shall be hastily sacrificed."

50 "O but I fear the fickle freaks of false fortune, and the odds of winning," replied Duessa.

"Why Dame," he said, "what advantage can there ever be, where both do fight alike, to win or yield?"

"Yes, but," she said, "he bears a charmed shield, and wears enchanted armor that none can pierce, nor wound the man who wields them."

"Charmed or enchanted," he answered fiercely, "I don't care a whit, nor do you need to warn me.

LI But faire *Fidessa*, sithens fortunes guile,
Or enimies powre hath now captiued you,
Returne from whence ye came, and rest a while
Till morrow next, that I the Elfe subdew,
And with *Sans-foyes* dead dowry you endew.
Ay me, that is a double death (she said)
With proud foes sight my sorrow to renew:
Where euer yet I be, my secrete aid
Shall follow you. So passing forth she him obaid.

51 "But, fair Fidessa, since fortune's guile, or enemy's power, has now captivated you, return from whence you came, and rest until tomorrow. I will subdue the Elf, and endow you with Sansfoy's dead dowry."

"Ay me, that is a double death. My sorrow will renew with the sight of that proud foe," she said. Then in a lower voice, she added: "But, wherever yet I be, my secret aid shall follow you."

So passing forth, she obeyed him.

---

1 *Argus eyes: In memory of the services Argus had rendered her, Juno placed his many eyes on the tail of a peacock*

2 *Camel: Matt 19:24 "it is easier for a camel to go through the eye of a needle than for someone who is rich to enter the kingdom of God."*

NOTES ON CANTO V

Katabasis: means 'going downwards' in Greek. In literature, it refers to an epic descent into the underworld, following the examples in Virgil and Homer.

The Underworld: the Greek mythical otherworld where souls go after death, guarded by **Cerberus**: a gigantic dog.

Pluto: god of Hades: the Underworld.

Daemogorgon: powerful primordial being of the Underworld, whose very name had been taboo.

Avernus: volcanic crater in Italy, believed to be the entrance to the underworld in The Aeneid.

Nebuchadnezzar, King Croesus, King Antiochus, Nimrod, Ninus, Romulus: historic kings.

Ixion, Sisyphus, Tantalus, Tityus, Typhoeus , Theseus, Proserpina, Danaids: characters from ancient Greek and Roman mythology.

Aesculapius: god of medicine in ancient Greek mythology. Zeus killed Asclepius with a thunderbolt because he brought Hippolytus back from the dead.

CANTO V

KATABASIS

The faithfull knight in equall field
subdewes his faithlesse foe,
Whom false Duessa saues, and for
his cure to hell does goe.

I The noble hart, that harbours vertuous thought,
And is with child of glorious great intent,
Can neuer rest, vntill it forth haue brought
Th'eternall brood of glorie excellent:
Such restlesse passion did all night torment
The flaming corage of that Faery knight,
Deuizing, how that doughtie turnament
With greatest honour he atchieuen might;
Still did he wake, and still did watch for dawning light.

II At last the golden Orientall gate
Of greatest heauen gan to open faire,
And *Phoebus* fresh, as bridegrome to his mate,
Came dauncing forth, shaking his deawie haire:
And hurld his glistring beames through gloomy aire.
Which when the wakeful Elfe perceiu'd, streight way
He started vp, and did him selfe prepaire,
In sun-bright armes, and battailous array:
For with that Pagan proud he combat will that day.

III And forth he comes into the commune hall,
Where earely waite him many a gazing eye,
To weet what end to straunger knights may fall.
There many Minstrales maken melody,
To driue away the dull melancholy,
And many Bardes, that to the trembling chord
Can tune their timely voyces cunningly,
And many Chroniclers, that can record
Old loues, and warres for Ladies doen by many a Lord.

IV Soone after comes the cruell Sarazin,
In wouen maile all armed warily,
And sternly lookes at him, who not a pin
Does care for looke of liuing creatures eye.
They bring them wines of *Greece* and *Araby*,
And daintie spices fetcht from furthest *Ynd*,
To kindle heat of corage priuily:
And in the wine a solemne oth they bynd
T'obserue the sacred lawes of armes, that are assynd.

V At last forth comes that far renowmed Queene,
With royall pomp and Princely maiestie;
She is ybrought vnto a paled greene,
And placed vnder stately canapee,
The warlike feates of both those knights to see.
On th'other side in all mens open vew

Duessa placed is, and on a tree
Sans-foy his shield is hangd with bloudy hew
Both those the lawrell girlonds to the victor

The faithful knight subdues his faithless foe in equal field. But Duessa rescues the injured foe, and goes to hell to find his cure.

THE NOBLE HEART THAT HARBORS VIRTUOUS THOUGHT, AND IS EXPECTANT OF glorious great intent, can never rest until it has brought forth the eternal Child of supreme glory.

During the night, such restless passion tormented the flaming courage of that Faerie knight, who lay awake, watching for the dawning light, and planning on how he might achieve greatest honor in that dreaded tournament.

At last, the fair golden gate of the orient began to open, and fresh Phoebus, like a bridegroom, came dancing forth, shaking his dewy hair, and hurling his glistering beams through the gloomy air. When the wakeful Elfin knight perceived the dawn, he arose immediately and began to prepare himself in sun-bright armor and battle-ready array. For he would combat that proud pagan this day.

So forth he came to the communal hall, where waited many an early gazing eye, keen to know what end these stranger knights may fall. Minstrels were busy composing melodies and striving to drive away dull melancholy, while many bards were tuning their voices to the notes and rhythms of the trembling chords. Old chroniclers, experienced in recording old loves, and the many combats fought for ladies, had their pens ready.

Soon after, the fierce Saracen strode in wearing chain-mail armor, his sword ready. He, who cared not a pin for any living creature's eye, looked sternly at Redcross. Meanwhile, the people brought them wines from Greece and Arabia, and precious spices from the furthest India to kindle the heat of inward courage. And with the wine, the knights bound a solemn oath to observe the sacred laws of arms that are assigned in chivalry.

5 At last, with royal pomp and princely majesty, the far renowned queen arrived. She was brought unto a green gated area, and placed under a stately canopy, so that she could clearly see the warlike feats of both those knights. On the other side, Duessa was seated in open view. Next to her, on a tree, hung Sansfoy's shield with bloody hue, and the laurel garland. All of these prizes would go to the victor.

VI A shrilling trompet sownded from on hye,
And vnto battaill bad them selues addresse:
Their shining shieldes about their wrestes they tye,
And burning blades about their heads do blesse,
The instruments of wrath and heauinesse:
With greedy force each other doth assayle,
And strike so fiercely, that they do impresse
Deepe dinted furrowes in the battred mayle;
The yron walles to ward their blowes are weakeand fraile.

VII The Sarazin was stout, and wondrous strong,
And heaped blowes like yron hammers great:
For after bloud and vengeance he did long.
The knight was fiers, and full of youthly heat:
And doubled strokes, like dreaded thunders threat:
For all for prayse and honour he did fight.
Both stricken strike, and beaten both do beat,
That from their shields forth flyeth firie light,
And helmets hewen deepe, shew marks of eithers might.

VIII So th'one for wrong, the other striues for right:
As when a Gryfon seized of his pray,
A Dragon fiers encountreth in his flight,
Through widest ayre making his ydle way,
That would his rightfull rauine rend away:
With hideous horrour both together smight,
And souce so sore, that they the heauens affray:
The wise Southsayer seeing so sad sight,
Th'amazed vulgar tels of warres and mortall fight.

IX So th'one for wrong, the other striues for right,
And each to deadly shame would driue his foe:
The cruell steele so greedily doth bight
In tender flesh, that streames of bloud down flow,
With which the armes, that earst so bright did show,
Into a pure vermillion now are dyde:
Great ruth in all the gazers harts did grow,
Seeing the gored woundes to gape so wyde,
That victory they dare not wish to either side.

X At last the Paynim chaunst to cast his eye,
His suddein eye, flaming with wrathfull fyre,
Vpon his brothers shield, which hong thereby:
Therewith redoubled was his raging yre,
And said, Ah wretched sonne of wofull syre,
Doest thou sit wayling by black *Stygian* lake,
Whilest here thy shield is hangd for victors hyre,
And sluggish german doest thy forces slake,
To after-send his foe, that him may ouertake?

6 A shrill trumpet sounded from on high, and they focused themselves unto knightly battle. After tying their shining shields around their wrists, they blessed their burning swords, ready to brandish these heavy instruments of wrath and grief. With eager force they assailed each other, striking so fiercely that they caused deep dented furrows in their battered chain-mail. These iron walls were too weak and frail to ward their blows.

The Saracen was brave and wondrously strong, and he heaped blows like great iron hammers, for he longed for blood and vengeance. The Elfin knight was brave and full of youthful fervor, and he struck at the Saracen with doubled strokes, like thunder's threat, for he fought for praise and honor. Both struck and both were struck by the blows, and from their shields, fiery light flew forth, while helmets were deeply hewn, showing the marks of the other's might.

One strives for wrong, while the other strives for right.

When a griffin that seizes hold of its prey, and then wanders through the widest air on its unhurried way, encounters a fierce dragon in its flightpath which tries to seize the griffin's rightful prey, they both clash in hideous horror, striking so hard that they frighten heaven itself. The wise soothsayer, seeing so ominous a sight, tells the bewildered peasants that it is a sign for war and mortal fight.

One knight strives for wrong, while the other strives for right. Each wanted to drive his foe to a shameful death. The cruel steel bit their tender flesh so greedily, that streams of blood flowed down, and their armor, that before shone so bright, was now dyed pure vermillion. Meanwhile, great sorrow grew in all the gazers' hearts, seeing the gored wounds gape so wide, that they dared not wish for victory to either side.

10 At last, the pagan chanced to suddenly cast his eye, flaming with wrathful fire, upon his brother's shield which hung nearby. Therewith, he redoubled his raging ire and called out to Sansfoy's spirit, "Ah, wretched son of woeful sire, do you sit wailing at the black Stygian lake, while your shield is hanging up as a victory prize? Sluggish brother, do you slacken your forces to send this foe to hell with you?

XI Goe caytiue Elfe, him quickly ouertake,
And soone redeeme from his long wandring woe;
Goe guiltie ghost, to him my message make,
That I his shield haue quit from dying foe.
Therewith vpon his crest he stroke him so,
That twise he reeled, readie twise to fall;
End of the doubtfull battell deemed tho
The lookers on, and lowd to him gan call
The false *Duessa*, Thine the shield, and I, and all.

XII Soone as the Faerie heard his Ladie speake,
Out of his swowning dreame he gan awake,
And quickning faith, that earst was woxen weake,
The creeping deadly cold away did shake:
Tho mou'd with wrath, and shame, and Ladies sake,
Of all attonce he cast auengd to bee,
And with so'exceeding furie at him strake,
That forced him to stoupe vpon his knee;
Had he not stouped so, he should haue clouen bee.

XIII And to him said, Goe now proud Miscreant,
Thy selfe thy message doe to german deare,
Alone he wandring thee too long doth want:
Goe say, his foe thy shield with his doth beare.
Therewith his heauie hand he high gan reare,
Him to haue slaine; when loe a darkesome clowd
Vpon him fell: he no where doth appeare,
But vanisht is. The Elfe him cals alowd,
But answer none receiues: the darknes him does shrowd.

XIV In haste *Duessa* from her place arose,
And to him running said, O prowest knight,
That euer Ladie to her loue did chose,
Let now abate the terror of your might,
And quench the flame of furious despight,
And bloudie vengeance; lo th'infernall powres
Couering your foe with cloud of deadly night,
Haue borne him hence to *Plutoes* balefull bowres.
The conquest yours, I yours, the shield, and glory yours.

XV Not all so satisfide, with greedie eye
He sought all round about, his thirstie blade
To bath in bloud of faithlesse enemy;
Who all that while lay hid in secret shade:
He standes amazed, how he thence should fade.
At last the trumpets Triumph sound on hie,
And running Heralds humble homage made,
Greeting him goodly with new victorie,
And to him brought the shield, the cause of enmitie.

11 Go, captive Elf, and find him there, and redeem his long wandering woe! Go guilty Redcross knight, and deliver this message to him: that I have recovered his shield from you, dying foe!"

Therewith he struck him on his head so hard, that twice Redcross reeled, twice ready to fall. It seemed the end of the doubtful battle.

The on-lookers began to shout, and the false Duessa cried loudly, "Yours the shield, and I, and all!"

As soon as the Faerie heard his traitorous lady speak such words, he began to awaken from the swooning dream, and reviving faith, that was before waxing weak, shook off the creeping deadly cold. Moved with wrath and shame at what he had just heard, he all at once resolved to be avenged, and struck the Saracen so hard, and with such exceeding fury, that he was forced to sink to his knee, and had he not stooped so low, he would have been split in two.

Then, to him, the Elfin knight said, "Go yourself, proud villain, and deliver your own messages to your brother. Alone he has wandered too long, wanting your company! Tell him that his foe now bears his shield!"

Therewith, he raised his heavy hand to have him slain, when lo, a darksome cloud fell upon him, and suddenly he vanished. The Elf called to him aloud, but received no answer. The darkness shrouded him.

In haste, Duessa arose from her place and came running to him, gushing, "O, most skillful knight, that ever a lady chose to be her love. Let the terror of your might abate, and quench the flame of furious despite and bloody vengeance. Lo, the infernal powers covering your foe with the cloud of deadly night has born him hence to Pluto's miserable lodgings. The conquest is yours, I am yours, the shield, and the glory is yours!"

15 Not all so satisfied, and with eager eye the Elf knight sought all around him, his thirsty blade still eager to bathe in the blood of his faithless enemy, who all the while lay hidden in a secret shade. Finally, the Elfin stood amazed at how he could just vanish. Then the trumpets sounded their triumph on high and running heralds made their humble homage, gallantly greeting him with this new victory, and bringing him the shield, that was the original cause of the dispute.

XVI Wherewith he goeth to that soueraine Queene,
And falling her before on lowly knee,
To her makes present of his seruice seene:
Which she accepts, with thankes, and goodly gree,
Greatly aduauncing his gay cheualree.
So marcheth home, and by her takes the knight,
Whom all the people follow with great glee,
Shouting, and clapping all their hands on hight,
That all the aire it fils, and flyes to heauen bright.

XVII Home is he brought, and laid in sumptuous bed:
Where many skilfull leaches him abide,
To salue his hurts, that yet still freshly bled.
In wine and oyle they wash his woundes wide,
And softly can embalme on euery side.
And all the while, most heauenly melody
About the bed sweet musicke did diuide,
Him to beguile of griefe and agony:
And all the while *Duessa* wept full bitterly.

XVIII As when a wearie traueller that strayes
By muddy shore of broad seuen-mouthed *Nile*,
Vnweeting of the perillous wandring wayes,
Doth meet a cruell craftie Crocodile,
Which in false griefe hyding his harmefull guile,
Doth weepe full sore, and sheddeth tender teares:
The foolish man, that pitties all this while
His mournefull plight, is swallowd vp vnwares,
Forgetfull of his owne, that mindes anothers cares.

XIX So wept *Duessa* vntill euentide,
That shyning lampes in *Ioues* high house were light:
Then forth she rose, ne lenger would abide,
But comes vnto the place, where th'Hethen knight
In slombring swownd nigh voyd of vitall spright,
Lay couer'd with inchaunted cloud all day:
Whom when she found, as she him left in plight,
To wayle his woefull case she would not stay,
But to the easterne coast of heauen makes speedy way.

XX Where griesly *Night*, with visage deadly sad,
That *Phoebus* chearefull face durst neuer vew,
And in a foule blacke pitchie mantle clad,
She findes forth comming from her darkesome mew,
Where she all day did hide her hated hew.
Before the dore her yron charet stood,
Alreadie harnessed for iourney new;
And coleblacke steedes yborne of hellish brood,
That on their rustie bits did champ, as they were wood.

16 Wherewith he presented himself before the sovereign queen, and falling on lowly knee, dedicated his now proven services to her. She, in turn, accepted them with thanks and courteous consent, greatly extolling his gay chivalry.

During the march back to the castle, the queen took the knight by her in the chariot, and they were followed by people shouting with great glee, clapping their hands loudly, and filling the air with joy that flew to bright heaven.

He was brought to the castle and laid in a sumptuous bed, where many skillful doctors attended him, anointing his hurts that still freshly bled. They washed his gaping wounds in wine and oil, and applied soft soothing balms. All the while, the most heavenly melody drifted in the air around the bed to distract him from his pain and grief. Meanwhile, Duessa wept full bitterly.

Just as a weary traveler, who strays by the muddy shores of the broad seven-mouthed Nile, unaware of the perilous wandering ways, is tricked by a cruel, crafty crocodile that fakes his grief while hiding harmful guile, shedding tender tears. The foolish man who forgets his own preservation is suddenly swallowed up by another's cares.

So wept Duessa until evening, when those shining lamps of Jove's high house were lit. Then, resolute, she rose forth and slunk to the hiding place of the heathen Saracen knight.

Slumbering in a swoon ever since, and void of vital spirit, he lay covered with enchanted cloud all day. When she found him in the same state as she left him, she would not stay to wail his woeful case, but made speedy way to the eastern coast of heaven.

20 Meanwhile, gruesome Lady Night, clad in a foul, pitch-black mantle, and with a sad, deadly visage, that Phoebus's cheerful face never dare view, came forth from her darksome den, where she hid her hated hue all day. Before the door, stood her iron chariot with coal-black horses, born of hellish brood, already harnessed for a new journey, gnashing their teeth on rusty bits as if rabid with rage.

XXI Who when she saw *Duessa* sunny bright,
Adornd with gold and iewels shining cleare,
She greatly grew amazed at the sight,
And th'vnacquainted light began to feare:
For neuer did such brightnesse there appeare,
And would haue backe retyred to her caue,
Vntill the witches speech she gan to heare,
Saying, Yet O thou dreaded Dame, I craue
Abide, till I haue told the message, which I haue.

XXII She stayd, and foorth *Duessa* gan proceede,
O thou most auncient Grandmother of all,
More old then *Ioue*, whom thou at first didst breede,
Or that great house of Gods cælestiall,
Which wast begot in *Dæmogorgons* hall,
And sawst the secrets of the world vnmade,
Why suffredst thou thy Nephewes deare to fall
With Elfin sword, most shamefully betrade?
Lo where the stout *Sansioy* doth sleepe in deadly shade.

XXIII And him before, I saw with bitter eyes
The bold *Sansfoy* shrinke vnderneath his speare;
And now the pray of fowles in field he lyes,
Nor wayld of friends, nor laid on groning beare,
That whylome was to me too dearely deare.
O what of Gods then boots it to be borne,
If old *Aveugles* sonnes so euill heare?
Or who shall not great *Nightes* children scorne,
When two of three her Nephews are so fowle forlorne?

XXIV Vp then, vp dreary Dame, of darknesse Queene,
Go gather vp the reliques of thy race,
Or else goe them auenge, and let be seene,
That dreaded *Night* in brightest day hath place,
And can the children of faire light deface.
Her feeling speeches some compassion moued
In hart, and chaunge in that great mothers face:
Yet pittie in her hart was neuer proued
Till then: for euermore she hated, neuer loued.

XXV And said, Deare daughter rightly may I rew
The fall of famous children borne of mee,
And good successes, which their foes ensew:
But who can turne the streame of destinee,
Or breake the chayne of strong necessitee,
Which fast is tyde to *Ioues* eternall seat?
The sonnes of Day he fauoureth, I see,
And by my ruines thinkes to make them great:
To make one great by others losse, is bad excheat.

21 When Night saw sunny bright Duessa, adorned with gold and brightly shining jewels, she grew greatly alarmed at the sight, and began to fear the unacquainted light.

For never did such brightness appear there, and Night would have retired back into her den, if the witch had not then addressed her, saying, "Yet of you, dreaded dame, I crave, wait till I have given you my message."

She stayed, and Duessa began her speech, "O you, most ancient Grandmother of all, older than Jove, whom you first bred, or that great house of celestial gods which was born in Daemogorgon's hall: you who saw the secrets of the world before it was made, why did you allow your dear nephews to fall with Elfin sword, most shamefully betrayed? Lo now brave Sansjoy sleeps in deadly shade, and before him, I beheld with bitter eyes the bold Sansfoy shrink underneath the Elfin's lance. And now he lies in a field: the prey of fowls, not mourned by friends or laid on a funeral bier. He who was formerly so dear to me! O what little good to be born old Blind-Aveugle's sons? Who shall not scorn great Night's children when two of her three nephews are so foully destroyed? Up then, up, dreadful dame, queen of darkness! Go gather up the relics of your dark nephew knights, or else avenge them, and let it be seen that dreaded Night has higher status in brightest day, and can destroy the children of fair light!"

Her emotive speeches moved some compassion in her heart, and change in that great mother's face. Yet pity had never risen in her heart till then, for evermore she hated; never loved.

25 And Night replied: "Dear daughter, rightly may I regret the fall of famous children born of me, and the successes, which their foes ensue. But who can turn the stream of destiny, or break the golden chain of Creation, which is so firmly tied to Jove's eternal seat? He favors the sons of Day, and thinks to make them great with my ruins. But to make one great by another's loss is a bad exchange.

XXVI Yet shall they not escape so freely all;
For some shall pay the price of others guilt:
And he the man that made *Sansfoy* to fall,
Shall with his owne bloud price that he hath spilt.
But what art thou, that telst of Nephews kilt?
I that do seeme not I, *Duessa* am,
(Quoth she) how euer now in garments gilt,
And gorgeous gold arayd I to thee came;
Duessa I, the daughter of Deceipt and Shame.

XXVII Then bowing downe her aged backe, she kist
The wicked witch, saying; In that faire face
The false resemblance of Deceipt, I wist
Did closely lurke; yet so true-seeming grace
It carried, that I scarse in darkesome place
Could it discerne, though I the mother bee
Of falshood, and root of *Duessaes* race.
O welcome child, whom I haue longd to see,
And how haue seene vnwares. Lo now I go with thee.

XXVIII Then to her yron wagon she betakes,
And with her beares the fowle welfauourd witch:
Through mirkesome aire her readie way she makes.
Her twyfold Teme, of which two blacke as pitch,
And two were browne, yet each to each vnlich,
Did softly swim away, ne euer stampe,
Vnlesse she chaunst their stubborne mouths to twitch;
Then foming tarre, their bridles they would champe,
And trampling the fine element, would fiercely rampe.

XXIX So well they sped, that they be come at length
Vnto the place, whereas the Paynim lay,
Deuoid of outward sense, and natiue strength,
Couerd with charmed cloud from vew of day,
And sight of men, since his late luckelesse fray.
His cruell wounds with cruddy bloud congealed,
They binden vp so wisely, as they may,
And handle softly, till they can be healed:
So lay him in her charett, close in night concealed.

XXX And all the while she stood vpon the ground,
The wakefull dogs did neuer cease to bay,
As giuing warning of th'vnwonted sound,
With which her yron wheeles did them affray,
And her darke griesly looke them much dismay;
The messenger of death, the ghastly Owle
With drearie shriekes did also her bewray;
And hungry Wolues continually did howle,
At her abhorred face, so filthy and so fowle.

26 Yet, they shall not escape so freely. For some shall pay the price of others' guilt. And the knight who made Sansfoy fall shall, with his own blood, pay for that which he spilled. But who are you, who tells of my nephews killed?"

Then Duessa replied, "I who do not seem I, Duessa am. Even though I am now arrayed in gilt garments and gorgeous gold, I am Duessa: daughter of Deceit and Shame."

Then bowing down her aged back, Night kissed the wicked witch, saying, "In that fair face I knew the false resemblance of Deceit secretly lurked. Yet it carried such true-seeming grace, that I could scarce discern it in this darksome place, even though I am the mother of falsehood itself, and the root of Duessa's race. O welcome child, whom I have longed to see, and now have seen unawares. Lo, now I go with you."

Then she took herself to her iron chariot, along with the foul, yet beautiful, witch, and in the mirksome air, prepared for the journey. Of her twofold team of assorted horses, two were black as pitch, and two were brown. They seemed to swim softly in the floating mists, and did not stamp their hooves unless she twitched their stubborn mouths with the reins. Then, with foaming tar, they would gnash their bridles, trample the fine air, and rear up fiercely.

Together they sped away until, at length, they came unto the place where the pagan lay, devoid of any outward sense and natural strength. Ever since his late luckless combat, Sansjoy had lain hidden in the charmed cloud, away from the view of day, and sight of men. They skillfully bandaged his cruddy blood-congealed wounds, to protect them softly until they could be healed. Then, in the concealed night, they gently and secretly laid him in the chariot.

30 Meanwhile, wakeful dogs never ceased to bay, as though giving warning, frightened at the unfamiliar sounds of her iron wheels and dark grisly looks. The owl of ill omens, and messenger of death, betrayed her with dreary shrieks, and hungry wolves howled uproariously at the horrid face, so filthy and foul.

XXXI Thence turning backe in silence soft they stole,
And brought the heauie corse with easie pace
To yawning gulfe of deepe *Auernus* hole.
By that same hole an entrance darke and bace
With smoake and sulphure hiding all the place,
Descends to hell: there creature neuer past,
That backe returned without heauenly grace;
But dreadfull *Furies*, which their chaines haue brast,
And damned sprights sent forth to make ill men aghast.

XXXII By that same way the direfull dames doe driue
Their mournefull charet, fild with rusty blood,
And downe to *Plutoes* house are come biliue:
Which passing through, on euery side them stood
The trembling ghosts with sad amazed mood,
Chattring their yron teeth, and staring wide
With stonie eyes; and all the hellish brood
Of feends infernall flockt on euery side,
To gaze on earthly wight, that with the Night durst ride.

XXXIII They pas the bitter waues of *Acheron*,
Where many soules sit wailing woefully,
And come to fiery flood of *Phlegeton*,
Whereas the damned ghosts in torments fry,
And with sharpe shrilling shriekes doe bootlesse cry,
Cursing high *Ioue*, the which them thither sent.
The house of endlesse paine is built thereby,
In which ten thousand sorts of punishment
The cursed creatures doe eternally torment.

XXXIV Before the threshold dreadfull *Cerberus*
His three deformed heads did lay along,
Curled with thousand adders venemous,
And lilled forth his bloudie flaming tong:
At them he gan to reare his bristles strong,
And felly gnarre, vntill dayes enemy
Did him appease; then downe his taile he hong
And suffered them to passen quietly:
For she in hell and heauen had power equally.

XXXV There was *Ixion* turned on a wheele,
For daring tempt the Queene of heauen to sin;
And *Sisyphus* an huge round stone did reele
Against an hill, ne might from labour lin;
There thirstie *Tantalus* hong by the chin;
And *Tityus* fed a vulture on his maw;
　Typhoeus ioynts were stretched on a gin,
　Theseus condemned to endlesse slouth by law,
And fifty sisters water in leake vessels draw.

31 In soft silence, they stole away and brought the heavy body to the yawning gulf of deep Avernus, the dreadful entrance to the underworld. Billowing with smoke and Sulphur, it led the descent into dark and deep hell. No creature ever passed that could return without heavenly grace: except those dreadful furies, having burst their chains, or the damned sprites, sent forth to frighten evil men.

By that same gloomy entrance, the fearful dames now drove their mournful chariot, filled with stained blood. Down to Pluto's house they flew, passing the trembling ghosts on every side, their sad and dazed expressions, chattering iron teeth, and wide-staring stony eyes. The rest of the hellish tribe of infernal fiends flocked on every side to gaze on the earthly creature, who dared to ride with Lady Night.

They passed the bitter waves of the Underworld's River Acheron where many souls sat wailing woefully, and arrived at the fiery flood of Phlegeton, where the damned ghosts fry in torments, crying uselessly with sharp, shrilling shrieks, and cursing high Jove who sent them there. The house of endless pain is built thereby, in which the cursed creatures are eternally tormented with ten thousand sorts of punishment.

Before the threshold, lay the dreadful Cerberus with his three, enormous, deformed heads, with a thousand venomous snakes on each. He lolled his bloody flaming tongue out at them, and reared his strong bristles, snarling fiercely, until Day's enemy, Lady Night, appeased him with a treat. Down went his tail in peace, allowing them to pass quietly. For she had equal power in hell and heaven.

35 They passed by Ixion, who had dared to tempt the queen of heaven, Juno, sentenced to be bound onto an ever-turning wheel, while Sisyphus, the thief who had to push a huge round stone up a hill forever. There was thirsty Tantalus hung by the chin, unable to drink or eat, and Tityus fed a vulture from his liver. Typhoeus' joints were stretched on a rack, Theseus, who tried to kidnap Proserpina, was condemned to endless sloth by law, and the fifty Danaids, having killed their bridegrooms were made to draw water using leaky vessels.

XXXVI They all beholding worldly wights in place,
Leaue off their worke, vnmindfull of their smart,
To gaze on them; who forth by them doe pace,
Till they be come vnto the furthest part:
Where was a Caue ywrought by wondrous art,
Deepe, darke, vneasie, dolefull, comfortlesse,
In which sad *Æsculapius* farre a part
Emprisond was in chaines remedilesse,
For that *Hippolytus* rent corse he did redresse.

XXXVII *Hippolytus* a iolly huntsman was,
That wont in charet chace the foming Bore;
He all his Peeres in beautie did surpas,
But Ladies loue as losse of time forbore:
His wanton stepdame loued him the more,
But when she saw her offred sweets refused
Her loue she turnd to hate, and him before
His father fierce of treason false accused,
And with her gealous termes his open eares abused.

XXXVIII Who all in rage his Sea-god syre besought,
Some cursed vengeance on his sonne to cast:
From surging gulf two monsters straight were brought,
With dread whereof his chasing steedes aghast,
Both charet swift and huntsman ouercast.
His goodly corps on ragged cliffs yrent,
Was quite dismembred, and his members chast
Scattered on euery mountaine, as he went,
That of *Hippolytus* was left no moniment.

XXXIX His cruell stepdame seeing what was donne,
Her wicked dayes with wretched knife did end,
In death auowing th'innocence of her sonne.
Which hearing his rash Syre, began to rend
His haire, and hastie tongue, that did offend:
Tho gathering vp the relicks of his smart
By *Dianes* meanes, who was *Hippolyts* frend,
Them brought to *Æsculape*, that by his art
Did heale them all againe, and ioyned euery part.

XL Such wondrous science in mans wit to raine
When *Ioue* auizd, that could the dead reuiue,
And fates expired could renew againe,
Of endlesse life he might him not depriue,
But vnto hell did thrust him downe aliue,
With flashing thunderbolt ywounded sore:
Where long remaining, he did alwaies striue
Himselfe wilth salues to health for to restore,
And slake the heauenly fire, that raged euermore.

36 Beholding mortal creatures in their realm, they all left off their work, unmindful of their pain, and gazed upon those who marched by.

Finally, they came unto the furthest part, where they found a cave wrought by wondrous art, deep, dark, doleful, uneasy, and comfortless. Here the sad Aesculapius, the god of healing, who displeased Jove by bringing Hippolytus back to life, was isolated and imprisoned in hopeless chains.

Hippolytus was a gallant huntsman who loved to chase the foaming boar. Even though he surpassed all his peers in beauty, he was not interested in ladies' love, preferring to spend his time hunting instead. His stepmother was in love with him, but when he refused her offered sweets of seduction, her love turned to hate. Filled with jealously, she stormed to Poseidon, his fierce father, and falsely accused him of treason

Outraged, Neptune, his sea-god sire, sought to cast some cursed vengeance on his son. Two monster tsunamis were brought up from the surging gulf, chasing Hippolytus, then renting him on ragged cliffs. His dismembered body was scattered on every mountain: the innocent parts separated from the guilty. Finally, there was no trace left of Hippolytus.

His cruel stepmother seeing what had been done, ended her wicked days with a knife, avowing the innocence of her son upon her death. When her father heard of this, he rent his hair and his hasty tongue that had done such damage. Gathering up the relics of his son, with Diane's help, who was also a friend of his mother, Hippolyta, he brought them to Aesculapius, so that he could join every part and heal them again.

40 But when Jove realized that such wondrous skills reigned in this man's abilities, where he could revive the dead, renew expired fates, and control eternal life, he thrust him alive down unto hell, shooting flashing thunderbolts to wound him on the way. There, he has long remained, striving to restore his health with salve, and sooth the heavenly burns that raged evermore.

XLI There auncient Night arriuing, did alight
From her nigh wearie waine, and in her armes
To *Æsculapius* brought the wounded knight:
Whom hauing softly disarayd of armes,
Tho gan to him discouer all his harmes,
Beseeching him with prayer, and with praise,
If either salues, or oyles, or herbes, or charmes
A fordonne wight from dore of death mote raise,
He would at her request prolong her nephews daies.

XLII Ah Dame (quoth he) thou temptest me in vaine,
To dare the thing, which daily yet I rew,
And the old cause of my continued paine
With like attempt to like end to renew.
Is not enough, that thrust from heauen dew
Here endlesse penance for one fault I pay,
But that redoubled crime with vengeance new
Thou biddest me to eeke? Can Night defray
The wrath of thundring *Ioue*, that rules both night and day?

XLIII Not so (quoth she) but sith that heauens king
From hope of heauen hath thee excluded quight,
Why fearest thou, that canst not hope for thing,
And fearest not, that more thee hurten might,
Now in the powre of euerlasting Night?
Goe to then, O thou farre renowmed sonne
Of great *Apollo*, shew thy famous might
In medicine, that else hath to thee wonne
Great paines, and greater praise, both neuer to be donne.

XLIV Her words preuaild: And then the learned leach
His cunning hand gan to his wounds to lay,
And all things else, the which his art did teach:
Which hauing seene, from thence arose away
The mother of dread darknesse, and let stay
   Aueugles sonne there in the leaches cure,
And backe returning tooke her wonted way,
To runne her timely race, whilst *Phoebus* pure
In westerne waues his wearie wagon did recure.

XLV The false *Duessa* leauing noyous Night,
Returnd to stately pallace of dame Pride;
Where when she came, she found the Faery knight
Departed thence, albe his woundes wide
Not throughly heald, vnreadie were to ride.
Good cause he had to hasten thence away;
For on a day his wary Dwarfe had spide,
Where in a dungeon deepe huge numbers lay
Of caytiue wretched thrals, that wayled night and day.

41 The ancient Lady Night arrived at his cave, and dismounting from her now weary horses, carried the wounded knight in her arms to Aesculapius. Having already carefully removed his amour, they began to point out all the wounds, beseeching Aesculapius with prayers and praise, and asking if by either salves, or oils, or herbs, or charms, a doomed creature from the door of death might be raised. Could he prolong her nephew's days?

"Ah dame," he began, sadly, "you tempt me in vain to dare do a thing which I regret daily. My science is the cause of continued pain, and any further attempt to heal the dead will renew it. Is it not enough that I was thrust from heaven here into endless penance to pay for one fault? But you want me to commit again that crime that will bring new vengeance to me? Can Lady Night deflect the wrath of thundering Jove who rules both night and day?"

"No, I cannot," replied Lady Night, "but since that heaven's king has excluded you from the hope of heaven, why do you fear him? For he can not hurt you anymore than he already has, since you are in the power of everlasting Night, who is immortal over all the gods. Come on then, O you, far renowned son of great Apollo, show us your famous might in medicine that has already won you great pains, yet even greater praise, never to be surpassed!"

Her words prevailed, and the learned doctor began to heal the wounds with his cunning hands, and all other things his art had taught him. Having seen this, the mother of Darkness thence arose away, leaving Aveugles's son there in the doctor's cure. Returning, she took her usual way, running her timely race whilst pure Phoebus was restoring his weary wagon in the western waves.

But of further fortunes of Sansjoy? None returned from Hell, without heavenly grace.

45 The false Duessa, leaving noxious Night, returned to the stately palace of Queen Pride. When she arrived, she found the Faerie knight had thence departed, despite unhealed wounds and un-readiness to ride his horse.

But he had good cause to hasten thence away, because his wary Dwarf had discovered a hidden horror. In the deep dungeons, a huge number of captives lay as wretched slaves, wailing day and night.

XLVI A ruefull sight, as could be seene with eie;
Of whom he learned had in secret wise
The hidden cause of their captiuitie,
How mortgaging their liues to *Couetise*,
Through wastfull Pride, and wanton Riotise,
They were by law of that proud Tyrannesse
Prouokt with *VVrath*, and *Enuies* false surmise,
Condemned to that Dongeon mercilesse,
Where they should liue in woe, and die in wretchednesse.

XLVII There was that great proud king of *Babylon*,
That would compell all nations to adore,
And him as onely God to call vpon,
Till through celestiall doome throwne out of dore,
Into an Oxe he was transform'd of yore:
There also was king *Croesus*, that enhaunst
His heart too high through his great riches store;
And proud *Antiochus*, the which aduaunst
His cursed hand gainst God, and on his altars daunst.

XLVIII And them long time before, great *Nimrod* was,
That first the world with sword and fire warrayd;
And after him old *Ninus* farre did pas
In princely pompe, of all the world obayd;
There also was that mightie Monarch layd
Low vnder all, yet aboue all in pride,
That name of natiue syre did fowle vpbrayd,
And would as *Ammons* sonne be magnifide,
Till scornd of God and man a shamefull death he dide.

XLIX All these together in one heape were throwne,
Like carkases of beasts in butchers stall.
And in another corner wide were strowne
The antique ruines of the *Romaines* fall:
Great *Romulus* the Grandsyre of them all,
Proud *Tarquin*, and too lordly *Lentulus*,
Stout *Scipio*, and stubborne *Hanniball*,
Ambitious *Sylla*, and sterne *Marius*,
High *Cæsar*, great *Pompey*, and fierce *Antonius*.

L Amongst these mighty men were wemen mixt,
Proud wemen, vaine, forgetfull of their yoke:
The bold *Semiramis*, whose sides transfixt
With sonnes owne blade, her fowle reproches spoke;
Faire *Sthenoboea*, that her selfe did choke
With wilfull cord, for wanting of her will;
High minded *Cleopatra*, that with stroke
Of Aspes sting her selfe did stoutly kill:
And thousands moe the like, that did that dongeon fill.

46 The dwarf had learned in secret ways the hidden cause of their captivity. They had mortgaged their lives to greed: to selling their souls for worldly gain through wasteful pride and riotous living. They belonged to that proud tyrannical queen by law, provoked to wrath, and envy's false presumptions. Condemned to merciless dungeons—such a rueful sight! –they lived in woe and died in wretchedness. Amongst them, was that proud king of Babylon, Nebuchadnezzar, who would compel all nations to adore him, as though he were the only God to call upon. Then, one day, celestial doom threw him down and transformed him into an ox. There was also King Croesus who lifted his prideful heart too high through a store of great riches, and proud King Antiochus who advanced his cursed hand against God, even dancing on his altars. Long before them, the great Nimrod who built the Tower of Babel, and who was the first to ravage with the sword and fire of war. Then, after him, old Ninus founded Ninevah, and the whole world obeyed him in his princely pomp. Then there was that mighty monarch, Alexander the Great, laid low under all, yet above all in pride. He claimed Jupiter was his father so that he would be magnified in glory, until he was scorned by God and died a shameful death in drink. Once superstars, they were now all thrown together in one heap like the carcasses of beasts in a butcher's stall.

In another corner were strewn the antique ruins of the Romans' fall: great Romulus, the grandfather of them all, proud Tarquin, the last king of Rome, and the too lordly Lentulus, brave Scipio, stubborn Hannibal, ambitious Sylla, stern Marius, high Caesar, great Pompey, and fierce Mark Antony.

50 Amongst these mighty men, were women too: proud women, vain women, and those forgetful of their responsibilities, including bold Semiramis, wife of the founder of Babylon, with knife in her side, testifying to her crime. Fair Sthenoboea who choked herself with a cord for not getting what she wanted. High-minded Cleopatra, who boldly killed herself by a venomous snake, and thousands more of the like filled that dungeon.

LI Besides the endlesse routs of wretched thralles,
Which thither were assembled day by day,
From all the world after their wofull falles,
Through wicked pride, and wasted wealthes decay.
But most of all, which in the Dongeon lay
Fell from high Princes courts, or Ladies bowres,
Where they in idle pompe, or wanton play,
Consumed had their goods, and thriftlesse howres,
And lastly throwne themselues into these heauy stowres.

LII Whose case when as the carefull Dwarfe had tould,
And made ensample of their mournefull sight
Vnto his maister, he no lenger would
There dwell in perill of like painefull plight,
But early rose, and ere that dawning light
Discouered had the world to heauen wyde,
He by a priuie Posterne tooke his flight,
That of no enuious eyes he mote be spyde:
For doubtlesse death ensewd, if any him descryde.

LIII Scarse could he footing find in that fowle way,
For many corses, like a great Lay-stall
Of murdred men which therein strowed lay,
Without remorse, or decent funerall:
Which all through that great Princesse pride did fall
And came to shamefull end. And them beside
Forth ryding vnderneath the castell wall,
A donghill of dead carkases he spide,
The dreadfull spectacle of that sad house of *Pride*.

51 Endless mobs of wretched slaves from all over the world were daily thither assembled, after their woeful falls through wicked pride and wasted wellbeing. But most of all, those who lay in the dungeon had fallen from the high prince's courts or the ladies' chambers, where they consumed their goods in wanton play and wasted hours, eventually throwing themselves down in sorrows.

When the heedful dwarf had told this story, and warned about the mournful sights, the Redcross knight would no longer dwell in such peril. Therefore, as soon as the dawning light had discovered the world to wide heaven, they took their flight by a secret back gate, to slip away unseen by malicious eyes. For he was certain that death ensued if anyone discovered his escape.

53 They could scarcely find a way through that foul path, for many bodies of murdered men lay strewn about like a great rubbish heap, pitiless, and without a decent funeral. Yet they had all fallen through that great queen's pride and came to a shameful end. Riding beside the castle wall, they noticed the dunghill of dead carcasses lying underneath: the dreadful spectacle of that sad house of pride, and they were greatly relieved to get away.

NOTES ON CANTO VI

Fauns and Satyrs: mythological half-human, half-goat creatures, who lived in enchanted forests, and who would help or hinder humans at whim.

Sylvanus: meaning "of the woods" in Latin: the Roman god of woods and fields, and associated with Pan.

Bacchus' merry fruit: wine, and **Bacchus**: the god of wine and farming.

Cybele: earth goddess.

Dryope: princess who became a forest nymph.

Pholoe: lover of Sylvanus/Pan.

Satyrane:—is the son of a human and a satyr (a half-human, half-goat creature). He is "nature's knight," the best a man can be through his own natural abilities, but without the enlightenment of Christianity and God's grace. He is significant in both Book I, III and IV, generally as an aide to the protagonists.

CANTO VI

THE WOODLAND CREATURES

From lawlesse lust by wondrous grace
fayre Vna is releast:
Whom saluage nation does adore,
and learnes her wise beheast.

I AS when a ship, that flyes faire vnder saile,
An hidden rocke escaped hath vnwares,
That lay in waite her wrack for to bewaile,
The Marriner yet halfe amazed stares
At perill past, and yet in doubt ne dares
To ioy at his foole-happie ouersight:
So doubly is distrest twixt ioy and cares
The dreadlesse courage of this Elfin knight,
Hauing escapt so sad ensamples in his sight.

II Yet sad he was that his too hastie speed
The faire *Duess'* had forst him leaue behind;
And yet more sad, that *Vna* his deare dreed
Her truth had staind with treason so vnkind;
Yet crime in her could neuer creature find,
But for his loue, and for her owne selfe sake,
She wandred had from one to other *Ynd*,
Him for to seeke, ne euer would forsake,
Till her vnwares the fierce *Sansloy* did ouertake.

III Who after *Archimagoes* fowle defeat,
Led her away into a forrest wilde,
And turning wrathfull fire to lustfull heat,
With beastly sin thought her to haue defilde,
And made the vassall of his pleasures vilde.
Yet first he cast by treatie, and by traynes,
Her to perswade, that stubborne fort to yilde:
For greater conquest of hard loue he gaynes,
That workes it to his will, then he that it constraines.

IV With fawning wordes he courted her a while,
And looking louely, and oft sighing sore,
Her constant hart did tempt with diuerse guile:
But wordes, and lookes, and sighes she did abhore,
As rocke of Diamond stedfast euermore.
Yet for to feed his fyrie lustfull eye,
He snatcht the vele, that hong her face before;
Then gan her beautie shine, as brightest skye,
And burnt his beastly hart t'efforce her chastitye.

V So when he saw his flatt'ring arts to fayle,
And subtile engines bet from batteree,
With greedy force he gan the fort assayle,
Whereof he weend possessed soone to bee,
And win rich spoile of ransackt chastetee.
Ah heauens, that do this hideous act behold,
And heauenly virgin thus outraged see,
How can ye vengeance iust so long withhold,
And hurle not flashing flames vpon that Paynim

Fair Una is released from lawless lust by wondrous grace.
A savage nation adores her, and learns her wise instruction.

WHEN A SHIP THAT FLIES FAIR UNDER SAIL ESCAPES A HIDDEN ROCK THAT LAY IN wait to wreck her unawares, the mariner stares, still half amazed at the peril now past, while not daring to yet feel joy at this lucky oversight, until he is certain the danger has passed. Likewise, the fearless courage of this Elfin knight was doubly distressed between joy and fear, having barely escaped such a gloomy sight.

Yet he was sad that, with his hasty departure, he had been forced to leave the fair Duessa behind. And yet more sad that Una, whom he most revered, had stained her loyalty with such unexpected treason, even though no transgression existed in her. For she would never forsake her true love, and for that she now wandered, seeking him, from one end of the land to the other, from east to west, throughout the world, until, unaware of the danger, the fierce Sansloy had overtaken her.

AFTER ARCHIMAGO'S FOUL DEFEAT, SANSLOY HAD LED UNA AWAY INTO THE wild forest where, after his wrathful fire had turned to lust, he planned to defile her innocence with beastly sin, and turn her into a slave to his vile pleasures. At first, he tried to seduce her stubborn fort with tricks and treats, because the conquest is greater when won, rather than forced.

So, initially, he courted her with fawning words, loving looks and tender sighs, trying to tempt her constant heart with diverse kinds of cunning, hoping to lead her astray. But she disliked all the words, the looks and the sighs, and stood firm as a rock of diamond. Then, to feed his fiery lustful eye, he snatched off the veil that hung before her face, revealing her shining beauty like the brightest sky. Now his beastly heart burnt more than ever, and he was consumed with thoughts to force himself upon her.

5When he saw all his flattering arts failing, and his subtle tricks rebuffed and proven hopeless, he started to plan out how he would assail her fortress with greedy force. Soon, he would possess her, and win a rich reward of her ransacked chastity.

Ah the heavens! that must behold this hideous act where a heavenly maiden is thus violated. How can you withhold your vengeance and not hurl flashing flames upon that rash pagan?

VI The pitteous maiden carefull comfortlesse,
Does throw out thrilling shriekes, and shrieking cryes,
The last vaine helpe of womens great distresse,
And with loud plaints importuneth the skyes,
That molten starres do drop like weeping eyes;
And *Phoebus* flying so most shamefull sight,
His blushing face in foggy cloud implyes,
And hides for shame. What wit of mortall wight
Can now deuise to quit a thrall from such a plight?

VII Eternall prouidence exceeding thought,
Where none appeares can make her selfe a way:
A wondrous way it for this Lady wrought,
From Lyons clawes to pluck the griped pray.
Her shrill outcryes and shriekes so loud did bray,
That all the woodes and forestes did resownd;
A troupe of *Faunes* and *Satyres* far away
Within the wood were dauncing in a rownd,
Whiles old *Syluanus* slept in shady arber sownd.

VIII Who when they heard that pitteous strained voice,
In hast forsooke their rurall meriment,
And ran towards the far rebownded noyce,
To weet, what wight so loudly did lament.
Vnto the place they come incontinent:
Whom when the raging Sarazin espide,
A rude, misshapen, monstrous rablement,
Whose like he neuer saw, he durst not bide,
But got his ready steed, and fast away gan ride.

IX The wyld woodgods arriued in the place,
There find the virgin dolefull desolate,
With ruffled rayments, and faire blubbred face,
As her outrageous foe had left her late,
And trembling yet through feare of former hate;
All stand amazed at so vncouth sight,
And gin to pittie her vnhappie state,
All stand astonied at her beautie bright,
In their rude eyes vnworthie of so wofull plight.

X She more amaz'd, in double dread doth dwell;
And euery tender part for feare does shake:
As when a greedie Wolfe through hunger fell
A seely Lambe farre from the flocke does take,
Of whom he meanes his bloudie feast to make,
A Lyon spyes fast running towards him,
The innocent pray in hast he does forsake,
Which quit from death yet quakes in euery lim
With chaunge of feare, to see the Lyon looke so grim.

6 The helpless piteous maiden, full of grief, hurled out piercing shrieks and shrieking cries: the last vain help of a woman's great distress. With loud complaints, she begged the skies to drop molten stars like weeping eyes. But Phoebus, flying by such a shameful sight, wrapped his blushing face in a foggy cloud and hid. What mind of mortal creature could now devise a plan to rescue poor Una from such a plight?

But Eternal Providence, so often incomprehensible, can sometimes make herself a way where none seems possible, and like plucking the gripped prey from lion's claws, a wondrous way it made for this lady.

Her shrill cries and shrieks brayed so loudly that all the woods and forests resounded. Far away, a troupe of fauns and satyrs were dancing in a circle, while old Sylvanus, the forest god, was slumbering soundly in a shady arbor, his Pan pipes by his side. Hearing the piteous strained voice, they forsook their rural merriment and ran towards the far echoing noise to find out why a creature would lament so loudly. They tore frantically through the woods, until they came unto the source of the distress. When the raging Saracen beheld such a rough, misshapen, monstrous rabble surrounding him, the likes of which he had never seen before, he dared not stay a moment longer. Terrified, he vaulted on his horse and rode swiftly away.

When the wild wood-gods arrived in that place, just as her vicious foe had left her, they found the doleful and desolate maiden, with her clean clothes ruffled and her fair face sobbing. The fauns and satyrs all stood around her, amazed at such a sight and astonished at her bright beauty, and they began to pity her in her unhappy state.

10 At the sight of these strange creatures, poor Una's fears doubled, and she began to tremble even more in every limb. Just like the feeble lamb whom the greedy wolf snatches, meaning to carry off for a bloody feast, spies a lion running towards him, he forsakes the innocent prey in haste, which, while rescued from death, still quakes in every limb with a new fear: the savage lion. Like a lamb between the wolf and the lion, Una did not know which to fear more.

XI Such fearefull fit assaid her trembling hart,
Ne word to speake, ne ioynt to moue she had:
The saluage nation feele her secret smart,
And read her sorrow in her count'nance sad;
Their frowning forheads with rough hornes yclad,
And rusticke horror all a side doe lay,
And gently grenning, shew a semblance glad
To comfort her, and feare to put away,
Their backward bent knees teach her humbly to obay.

XII The doubtfull Damzell dare not yet commit
Her single person to their barbarous truth,
But still twixt feare and hope amazd does sit,
Late learnd what harme to hastie trust ensu'th,
They in compassion of her tender youth,
And wonder of her beautie soueraine,
Are wonne with pitty and vnwonted ruth,
And all prostrate vpon the lowly plaine,
Do kisse her feete, and fawne on her with count'nance faine.

XIII Their harts she ghesseth by their humble guise,
And yieldes her to extremitie of time;
So from the ground she fearelesse doth arise,
And walketh forth without suspect of crime:
They all as glad, as birdes of ioyous Prime,
Thence lead her forth, about her dauncing round,
Shouting, and singing all a shepheards ryme,
And with greene braunches strowing all the ground,
Do worship her, as Queene, with oliue girlond cround.

XIV And all the way their merry pipes they sound,
That all the woods with doubled Eccho ring,
And with their horned feet do weare the ground,
Leaping like wanton kids in pleasant Spring.
So towards old *Syluanus* they her bring;
Who with the noyse awaked, commeth out,
To weet the cause, his weake steps gouerning,
And aged limbs on Cypresse stadle stout,
And with an yuie twyne his wast is girt about.

XV Far off he wonders, what them makes so glad,
If *Bacchus* merry fruit they did inuent,
Or *Cybeles* franticke rites haue made them mad;
They drawing nigh, vnto their God present
That flowre of faith and beautie excellent.
The God himselfe vewing that mirrhour rare,
Stood long amazd, and burnt in his intent;
His owne faire *Dryope* now he thinkes not faire,
And *Pholoe* fowle, when her to this he doth compaire.

11 Such a fearful fit assailed her trembling heart, that she could neither speak nor move. But the woodland creatures, with their frowning foreheads, rough horns and rugged bristling hair, understood her secret pain and read the sorrow in her sad countenance. They tried to comfort her by putting aside their natural rustic habits, gently grinning at her, showing gladness, and hoping to dispel her fears. And even though their goatish knees bent backwards, they knelt humbly before her.

The doubtful damsel remained wary of their savage honor. Her bewildered, solitary person was still stuck between fear and hope, having recently learned of the harm that results from hasty trust. In compassion of her tender youth, and wondered at her sovereign beauty, won with pity and unaccustomed sympathy, they bowed deeply, kissed her feet, and fawned on her with eager countenance.

Eventually she guessed their hearts by their humble manners, and submitted herself to the needs of the moment. Finally, she bravely rose from the ground and walked forth without suspecting harm. All the fauns and satyrs cheered and applauded, and thence led her forward. Glad as joyous springtime, they danced around her, shouting and singing a shepherd's rhyme. They strewed green branches on the ground, and crowned her with an olive wreath, worshipping her as a queen.

With their merry pipes sounding, so that all the woods rang with a lively, doubled echo, they wore out the ground with their horned feet, leaping like playful kids in pleasant spring. They brought her towards old Sylvanus, whom the clamor had already awakened. Leaning his aged limbs on a stout cypress staff, his robe girdled by an ivy belt, the ancient Roman woodland god shuffled forth to meet them.

15 He had already been wondering what made them so glad, wondering if they had found Bacchus' merry fruit, or if Cybele's frantic rites had made them mad. Drawing near to their leafy god, they presented Una: that flower of faith and supreme beauty. The god viewed that rare image and stood half amazed, burning his gaze intensely. His fair wife Dryope now not so fair, and Pholoe: foul in comparison.

XVI The woodborne people fall before her flat,
And worship her as Goddesse of the wood;
And old *Syluanus* selfe bethinkes not, what
To thinke of wight so faire, but gazing stood,
In doubt to deeme her borne of earthly brood;
Sometimes Dame *Venus* selfe he seemes to see,
But *Venus* neuer had so sober mood;
Sometimes *Diana* he her takes to bee,
But misseth bow, and shaftes, and buskins to her knee.

XVII By vew of her he ginneth to reuiue
His ancient loue, and dearest *Cyparisse*,
And calles to mind his pourtraiture aliue,
How faire he was, and yet not faire to this,
And how he slew with glauncing dart amisse
A gentle Hynd, the which the louely boy
Did loue as life, aboue all worldly blisse;
For griefe whereof the lad n'ould after ioy,
But pynd away in anguish and selfe-wild annoy.

XVIII The wooddy Nymphes, faire *Hamadryades*
Her to behold do thither runne apace,
And all the troupe of light-foot *Naiades*,
Flocke all about to see her louely face:
But when they vewed haue her heauenly grace,
They enuie her in their malitious mind,
And fly away for feare of fowle disgrace:
But all the *Satyres* scorne their woody kind,
And henceforth nothing faire, but her on earth they find.

XIX Glad of such lucke, the luckelesse lucky maid,
Did her content to please their feeble eyes,
And long time with that saluage people staid,
To gather breath in many miseries.
During which time her gentle wit she plyes,
To teach them truth, which worshipt her in vaine,
And made her th'Image of Idolatryes;
But when their bootlesse zeale she did restraine
From her own worship, they her Asse would worship fayn.

XX It fortuned a noble warlike knight
By iust occasion to that forrest came,
To seeke his kindred, and the lignage right,
From whence he tooke his well deserued name:
He had in armes abroad wonne muchell fame,
And fild far landes with glorie of his might,
Plaine, faithfull, true, and enimy of shame,
And euer lou'd to fight for Ladies right,
But in vaine glorious frayes he litle did delight.

16 The wood-born people fell flat before her, worshipping her as goddess of the wood. Meanwhile old Sylvanus, rubbing his hoary chin, did not know what to think about the fair creature, but stood gazing, doubting that she was born of earthly parents. Perhaps she was the daughter of Venus herself, he wondered. Yet Venus never had such a sober mood. Perhaps, then, she was Diana, simply missing a bow, shafts and knee boots.

Gazing upon her, he began to revive his ancient loves. He remembered his dearest Cyparisse, and how he used to look in his youth: how fair he was, and yet not so fair now. He remembered how, as a lovely boy, he had accidently slain a gentle deer with a glancing dart that went amiss. He had loved that deer above all worldly bliss, and thereafter, had shunned joy, pining away in anguish and self-willed grief.

Now the woody nymphs—the fair hamadryads—ran to behold her, along with all the troop of light-footed water naiads, all flocking about to see her lovely face. But once they had inspected her, they began to envy her heavenly grace with their malicious minds, and flew away for fear of foul disgrace. Meanwhile, all the Satyrs scorned their woody kind, having found nothing as fair on earth but her.

Glad of such luck, the luckless, lucky maid contented herself to please their feeble eyes, and stayed a long time with the savage people to gather breath from her many miseries. During that time, she applied her gentle wit to teach them about the true source of worship, and that they worshipped her in vain, by making her an image of idolatries. When she had managed to restrain their ineffective zeal, they went on to worship her donkey instead.

20 IT HAPPENED THAT THE NOBLE SATYRANE, HALF SATYR, HALF KNIGHT, WAS visiting the forest to seek his kindred, from whence he took his name. He had won much fame abroad, filling far lands with the glory of his might: plain, faithful, true, and the enemy of shame. He ever loved to fight for a lady's right, but never sought to delight in vainglorious battles.

XXI A Satyres sonne yborne in forrest wyld,
By straunge aduenture as it did betyde,
And there begotten of a Lady myld,
Faire *Thyamis* the daughter of *Labryde*,
That was in sacred bands of wedlocke tyde
To *Therion*, a loose vnruly swayne;
Who had more ioy to raunge the forrest wyde,
And chase the saluage beast with busie payne,
Then serue his Ladies loue, and wast in pleasures vayne.

XXII The forlorne mayd did with loues longing burne,
And could not lacke her louers company,
But to the wood she goes, to serue her turne,
And seeke her spouse, that from her still does fly,
And followes other game and venery:
A Satyre chaunst her wandring for to find,
And kindling coles of lust in brutish eye,
The loyall links of wedlocke did vnbind,
And made her person thrall vnto his beastly kind.

XXIII So long in secret cabin there he held
Her captiue to his sensuall desire,
Till that with timely fruit her belly sweld,
And bore a boy vnto that saluage sire:
Then home he suffred her for to retire,
For ransome leauing him the late borne childe;
Whom till to ryper yeares he gan aspire,
He noursled vp in life and manners wilde,
Emongst wild beasts and woods, from lawes of men exilde.

XXIV For all he taught the tender ymp, was but
To banish cowardize and bastard feare;
His trembling hand he would him force to put
Vpon the Lyon and the rugged Beare,
And from the she Beares teats her whelps to teare;
And eke wyld roring Buls he would him make
To tame, and ryde their backes not made to beare;
And the Robuckes in flight to ouertake,
That euery beast for feare of him did fly and quake.

XXV Thereby so fearelesse, and so fell he grew,
That his owne sire and maister of his guise
Did often tremble at his horrid vew,
And oft for dread of hurt would him aduise,
The angry beasts not rashly to despise,
Nor too much to prouoke; for he would learne
The Lyon stoup to him in lowly wise,
(A lesson hard) and make the Libbard sterne
Leaue roaring, when in rage he for reuenge did earne.

21 By a certain strange adventure, it happened that a satyr's son was born in the wild forest, begotten of a genteel lady. Fair Thyamis was her name, daughter of Labryde, already married to Therion. He was a loose and unruly boy preferring to range the wide forest, chase wild beasts, and waste in vain pleasures, than to serve his lady's love.

The forlorn maid burned with longing love, and pined for her lover's company. So off she went, into the woods, to join him on the hunt, hoping to earn his attention. Following game and other wild animals, a satyr chanced to find her wandering alone, and kindling coals of lust in his brutish eye, he unbound the links of wedlock and made her captive to his beastly kind.

For a long time, in a secret cabin in the woods, he held her captive to his sensual pleasure, until her belly swelled with timely fruit, and a boy was born unto that wild woodland sire. Finally, he allowed her to return home, but she had to leave her recently born son as ransom. The boy grew strong and healthy amongst wild beasts and woods, nurtured in life and wild manners, and exiled from the laws of men. For all he taught the tender child, was to banish cowardice and base-born fear. He would force the boy to put his trembling hand upon the lion, or the rugged bear. Then he would wrench the cubs from their mother's teats. Next, he would make Satyrane tame wild roaring bulls by riding on their backs, overtaking the stags in flight, so that every beast would quake and fly from him in fear.

25 Thereby he grew so fearless and deadly, that even his own father and instructor trembled at his rough and shaggy sight. Often fearing the angry beasts might hurt the boy, his father would advise him not to provoke too much. But Satyrane went further: he taught the lion to bow in lowly manner, and the leopard to depart in humble respect, even while roaring for revenge.

XXVI And for to make his powre approued more,
Wyld beasts in yron yokes he would compell;
The spotted Panther, and the tusked Bore,
The Pardale swift, and the Tigre cruell;
The Antelope, and Wolfe both fierce and fell;
And them constraine in equall teme to draw.
Such ioy he had, their stubborne harts to quell,
And sturdie courage tame with dreadfull aw,
That his beheast they feared, as tyrans law,

XXVII His louing mother came vpon a day
Vnto the woods, to see her little sonne;
And chaunst vnwares to meet him in the way,
After his sportes, and cruell pastime donne,
When after him a Lyonesse did runne,
That roaring all with rage, did lowd requere
Her children deare, whom he away had wonne:
The Lyon whelpes she saw how he did beare,
And lull in rugged armes, withouten childish feare.

XXVIII The fearefull Dame all quaked at the sight,
And turning backe, gan fast to fly away,
Vntill with loue reuokt from vaine affright,
She hardly yet perswaded was to stay,
And then to him these womanish words gan say;
Ah *Satyrane*, my dearling, and my ioy,
For loue of me leaue off this dreadfull play;
To dally thus with death, is no fit toy,
Go find some other play-fellowes, mine own sweet boy.

XXIX In these and like delights of bloudy game
He trayned was, till ryper yeares he raught,
And there abode, whilst any beast of name
Walkt in that forest, whom he had not taught
To feare his force: and then his courage haught
Desird of forreine foemen to be knowne,
And far abroad for straunge aduentures sought:
In which his might was neuer ouerthrowne,
But through all Faery lond his famous worth was blown.

XXX Yet euermore it was his manner faire,
After long labours and aduentures spent,
Vnto those natiue woods for to repaire,
To see his sire and offspring auncient.
And now he thither came for like intent;
Where he vnwares the fairest *Vna* found,
Straunge Lady, in so straunge habiliment,
Teaching the Satyres, which her sat around,
Trew sacred lore, which from her sweet lips did redound.

26 To further prove his power, he compelled wild beasts to take iron yokes. The spotted panther, the tusked boar, the swift jaguar, the cruel tiger, the antelope, and the fierce and deadly wolf: he would compel them to haul in an equal team. Such joy he had at taming them with sturdy courage, and quelling their stubborn hearts with dreadful awe, as if his command were a tyrant's law.

One day, his loving mother came unto the woods to see her little son, hoping to meet him after his sports and cruel pastimes were over. She found him running from a roaring, raging lioness whose cubs he fearlessly carried away in his hairy arms. His poor mother quaked at the sight, and she began to turn back and run away, until her love for him stopped her in her tracks.

She began to plead with him with motherly love, "Ah Satyrane, my darling, and my joy, for love of me leave off this dreadful play. To dally thus with death is no fit toy. Go find some different play fellows, my sweet boy!"

But he continued training in this, and similar delights of bloody game, until he reached his riper years, when no beast that did not fear his force walked in that forest. By now, his haughty courage desired to know new and foreign foemen. So, he sought strange adventures far abroad, in which his might was never overthrown, and trumpets heralded his famous worth throughout Faerieland.

30 Yet, after long labors and spent adventures, it had always been his custom to retreat unto his native woods to rest, and to see his old father and ancient kindred. And now he thither came for the same purpose where, unexpectedly, he found the fairest Una: a stranger in strange clothing. She was busy teaching the satyrs about true sacred lore, her words redounding from the sweetest lips, while they all sat around her.

XXXI He wondred at her wisedome heauenly rare,
Whose like in womens wit he neuer knew;
And when her curteous deeds he did compare,
Gan her admire, and her sad sorrowes rew,
Blaming of Fortune, which such troubles threw,
And ioyd to make proofe of her crueltie
On gentle Dame, so hurtlesse, and so trew:
Thenceforth he kept her goodly company,
And learnd her discipline of faith and verity.

XXXII But she all vowd vnto the *Redcrosse* knight,
His wandring perill closely did lament,
Ne in this new acquaintaunce could delight,
But her deare heart with anguish did torment,
And all her wit in secret counsels spent,
How to escape. At last in priuie wise
To *Satyrane* she shewed her intent:
Who glad to gain such fauour, gan deuise,
How with that pensiue Maid he best might thence arise.

XXXIII So on a day when Satyres all were gone,
To do their seruice to *Syluanus* old,
The gentle virgin left behind alone
He led away with courage stout and bold.
Too late it was, to Satyres to be told,
Or euer hope recouer her againe:
In vaine he seekes that hauing cannot hold.
So fast he carried her with carefull paine,
That they the woods are past, and come now to the plaine.

XXXIV The better part now of the lingring day,
They traueild had, when as they farre espide
A wearie wight forwandring by the way,
And towards him they gan in hast to ride,
To weet of newes, that did abroad betide,
Or tydings of her knight of the *Redcrosse*.
But he them spying, gan to turne aside,
For feare as seemd, or for some feigned losse;
More greedy they of newes, fast towards him do crosse.

XXXV A silly man, in simple weedes forworne,
And soild with dust of the long dried way;
His sandales were with toilesome trauell torne,
And face all tand with scorching sunny ray,
As he had traueild many a sommers day,
Through boyling sands of *Arabie* and *Ynde*;
And in his hand a *Iacobs* staffe, to stay
His wearie limbes vpon: and eke behind,
His scrip did hang, in which his needments he did bind.

31 He marveled at her rare heavenly wisdom, the likes of which he had never known in a woman before. When he considered her courteous deeds, he began to admire her even more, and to feel sorry for her sad sorrows, blaming Fortune, who threw such troubles and enjoyed cruelty on such a gentle, harmless and true dame. From then on, he kept her worthy company, and learned the discipline of faith and truth.

Loyal to her chosen knight, Redcross, of whom she continued to quietly lament, Una could not delight in this new acquaintance. Her loving heart continued to be tormented and anguished, and all her thoughts were spent in secret plans on how to escape. At last, in a secretive manner, she revealed her intentions to Satyrane and asked for his help. He was glad to gain such favor, and began to devise how best he might escape with that pensive maid.

So on a day when all the satyrs were away, doing service to old Sylvanus, the gentle maiden left behind alone, he bravely led the way out. The satyrs could not hold her forever, and he who believes that holding is having, is in vain. Speedily, but with great care, he carried her out of the woods, and soon they came to a plain.

THEY HAD TRAVELLED FOR THE BETTER PART OF THAT NOW LINGERING DAY, WHEN they noticed a weary creature wandering astray, along the same road. They rode towards him with great haste, hoping to hear of news abroad, or tidings of her knight Redcross. But when the traveler saw Satyrane and Una approaching, he turned aside and began to retreat, seeming to fear them, and mumbling that he had forgotten something. But, eager for news, they persisted and stood in his path.

35He was a simple man in humble worn-out clothing, soiled with long dried dust. His sandals were also badly worn, and his face was tanned with scorching sunny rays, as he had travelled many a summer's day through the boiling sands of Arabia and India. In his hand, he grasped a Jacob's staff to steady his weary limbs, and on his back hung a pilgrim's pack where he kept his supplies.

XXXVI The knight approching nigh, of him inquerd
Tydings of warre, and of aduentures new;
But warres, nor new aduentures none he herd.
Then *Vna* gan to aske, if ought he knew,
Or heard abroad of that her champion trew,
That in his armour bare a croslet red.
Aye me, Deare dame (quoth he) well may I rew
To tell the sad sight, which mine eies haue red:
These eyes did see that knight both liuing and eke ded.

XXXVII That cruell word her tender hart so thrild,
That suddein cold did runne through euery vaine,
And stony horrour all her sences fild
With dying fit, that downe she fell for paine.
The knight her lightly reared vp againe,
And comforted with curteous kind reliefe:
Then wonne from death, she bad him tellen plaine
The further processe of her hidden griefe;
The lesser pangs can beare, who hath endur'd the chiefe.

XXXVIII Then gan the Pilgrim thus, I chaunst this day,
This fatall day, that shall I euer rew,
To see two knights in trauell on my way
(A sory sight) arraung'd in battell new,
Both breathing vengeaunce, both of wrathfull hew:
My fearefull flesh did tremble at their strife,
To see their blades so greedily imbrew,
That drunke with bloud, yet thristed after life:
What more? the *Redcrosse* knight was slaine with Paynim knife.

XXXIX Ah dearest Lord (quoth she) how might that bee,
And he the stoutest knight, that euer wonne?
Ah dearest dame (quoth he) how might I see
The thing, that might not be, and yet was donne?
Where is (said *Satyrane*) that Paynims sonne,
That him of life, and vs of ioy hath reft?
Not far away (quoth he) he hence doth wonne
Foreby a fountaine, where I late him left
Washing his bloudy wounds, that through the steele were cleft.

XL Therewith the knight thence marched forth in hast,
Whiles *Vna* with huge heauinesse opprest,
Could not for sorrow follow him so fast;
And soone he came, as he the place had ghest,
Whereas that *Pagan* proud him selfe did rest,
In secret shadow by a fountaine side:
Euen he it was, that earst would haue supprest
Faire *Vna*: whom when *Satyrane* espide,
With fowle reprochfull words he boldly him defide.

36 Approaching nigh, the knight enquired of him tidings of war and new adventures. But of wars or new adventures he had heard none. Then Una began to ask if he knew anything about her true champion, describing his armor that bore the red cross.

"Aye me, dear dame," the pilgrim said. "I regret to tell you of a sad sight which mine eyes have seen. These eyes did see that knight, both living, and now dead."

The cruel words pierced her tender heart so hard that sudden cold ran through her veins and stunned horror filled all her senses that, overwhelmed with pain, she crumpled to the ground. Catching her mid-swoon, Satyrane held her head up and tried to comfort her with courteous kind relief. Revived somewhat, Una then began to tell him the rest of the story of her hidden grief. These lesser pains she could bear, she said, so she might as well hear the rest of the pilgrim's account.

So the old man continued his story thus, "I chanced this day, this fatal day, that I shall ever regret, to have seen two knights travelling on my way—such a sorry sight!—who engaged in recent battle. Both were breathing vengeance: both of wrathful nature. My fearful flesh trembled at their strife: to see their blades so greedily tarnished and drunk with blood, yet thirsting after life. What more? The Redcross knight was slain with a pagan's knife."

"Ah dearest sir," replied Una, "how might that be if he is the bravest knight that ever lived?"

"Ah dearest dame," said the pilgrim, "how might I see the thing that might be, and yet was done?"

"What *might be*, or what *was*?" implored Una, desperately.

Satyrane interjected at this point, "Where is that pagan's son: he who has robbed his life and our joy?"

"Not far away," replied the pilgrim, "he is staying a little way hence near the fountain, where I lately left him washing the bloody wounds that steel had cleft."

40 Therewith, the knight Satyrane marched forth in haste, while Una, oppressed with her grieving heart, could not keep up with him for sorrow. Soon he came to the place where the proud pagan rested in a secret shadow by the fountain side.

Satyrane realized that it was he who would have before violated fair Una, and he boldly defied him with reproachful words,

XLI And said, Arise thou cursed Miscreaunt,
That hast with knightlesse guile and trecherous train
Faire knighthood fowly shamed, and doest vaunt
That good knight of the *Redcrosse* to haue slain:
Arise, and with like treason now maintain
Thy guilty wrong, or else thee guilty yield.
The Sarazin this hearing, rose amain,
And catching vp in hast his three square shield,
And shining helmet, soone him buckled to the field.

XLII And drawing nigh him said, Ah misborne Elfe,
In euill houre thy foes thee hither sent,
Anothers wrongs to wreake vpon thy selfe:
Yet ill thou blamest me, for hauing blent
My name with guile and traiterous intent;
That *Redcrosse* knight, perdie, I neuer slew,
But had he beene, where earst his armes were lent,
Th'enchaunter vaine his errour should not rew:
But thou his errour shalt, I hope now prouen trew.

XLIII Therewith they gan, both furious and fell,
To thunder blowes, and fiersly to assaile
Each other bent his enimy to quell,
That with their force they perst both plate and maile,
And made wide furrowes in their fleshes fraile,
That it would pitty any liuing eie.
Large floods of bloud adowne their sides did raile;
But floods of bloud could not them satisfie:
Both hungred after death: both chose to win, or die.

XLIV So long they fight, and fell reuenge pursue,
That fainting each, themselues to breathen let,
And oft refreshed, battell oft renue:
As when two Bores with rancling malice met,
Their gory sides fresh bleeding fiercely fret,
Til breathlesse both them selues aside retire,
Where foming wrath, their cruell tuskes they whet,
And trample th'earth, the whiles they may respire;
Then backe to fight againe, new breathed and entire.

XLV So fiersly, when these knights had breathed once,
They gan to fight returne, increasing more
Their puissant force, and cruell rage attonce,
With heaped strokes more hugely, then before,
That with their drerie wounds and bloudy gore
They both deformed, scarsely could be known.
By this sad *Vna* fraught with anguish sore,
Led with their noise, which through the aire was thrown:
Arriu'd, where they in erth their fruitles bloud had sown.

---

41 "Arise cursed heathen who hastens with unknightly guile, who treacherously and foully shames knighthood, and who boasts to have slain the good knight Redcross. Arise, and with like treachery now defend your wrongs, or else admit your guilt!"

The Saracen, hearing this, rose immediately, and hastily grabbing his triangular shield and shining helmet, he followed him to the field.

Drawing nigh, the Saracen then said, "Ah low-born Elf, in evil hour your foes sent you here to wreak another's wrongs upon yourself. Yet you wrongly blame me for having mixed my name with guile and traitorous intent. That Redcross knight, I swear by God, I never slew. But had Redcross been inside the armor, and not that foolish enchanter, I would not have regretted slaying him. And now I expect to prove the truth in combat!"

Forthwith, they began to fiercely assail, both with furious and deadly thunder blows, each determined to crush the other. They pierced both plate and mail with great force, and made wide furrows in their frail flesh, that would move any living eye to pity. Copious blood flowed down their sides, but even floods could not satisfy them. Both hungered after death: both chose to win or die.

So long they fought and pursued their deadly revenge, so vigorously, that they had to retreat to catch their breath.

Like two boars, with festering malice, who clash until breathless, their gory sides bleeding fiercely, they both retire aside. There, with foaming wrath, they sharpen their cruel tusks, panting and trampling the earth. Then they return to fight, newly oxygenated and refreshed.

45 So with these two knights: once refreshed, they returned to fight, increasing their powerful force and vicious rage at once. With multiplied strokes, stronger than before, their cruel wounds and bloody gore disfiguring them both, one could scarcely recognize them. Led by this loud ruckus, which resounded through the air, sad Una was fraught with anguish when she arrived where they had sown their fruitless blood.

XLVI Whom all so soone as that proud Sarazin
Espide, he gan reuiue the memory
Of his lewd lusts, and late attempted sin,
And left the doubtfull battell hastily,
To catch her, newly offred to his eie:
But *Satyrane* with strokes him turning, staid,
And sternely bad him other businesse plie,
Then hunt the steps of pure vnspotted Maid:
Wherewith he all enrag'd, these bitter speaches said.

XLVII O foolish faeries sonne, what furie mad
Hath thee incenst, to hast thy dolefull fate?
Were it not better, I that Lady had,
Then that thou hadst repented it too late?
Most sencelesse man he, that himselfe doth hate,
To loue another. Lo then for thine ayd
Here take thy louers token on thy pate.
So they to fight; the whiles the royall Mayd
Fled farre away, of that proud Paynim sore afrayd.

XLVIII But that false *Pilgrim*, which that leasing told,
Being in deed old *Archimage*, did stay
In secret shadow, all this to behold,
And much reioyced in their bloudy fray:
But when he saw the Damsell passe away
He left his stond, and her pursewd apace,
In hope to bring her to her last decay.
But for to tell her lamentable cace,
And eke this battels end, will need another place.

46 Then, while catching his breath, that proud Saracen spied her approaching from afar, and he began to revive the memory of his lewd lusts, and late attempted sin. Hastily, he left the doubtful battle to catch what was newly offered to his eye. But Satyrane, turned him back with his sword strokes, and sternly bade him apply himself to the battle, than hunt the steps of such a pure maid.

Enraged, the Saracen began to speak, "O foolish Faerie's son, what mad fury has incensed you to hasten your doleful fate? Were it not better that I captured the lady than killed you? Most senseless man is he who hates to love another himself. Lo, then, for your aid, here take your lover's token on your head!"

So they resumed the fight, while the royal maid fled far away, terrified of that proud pagan.

Meanwhile, that false pilgrim who had told such a lie, being indeed Archimago, stayed hidden in a secret shadow to behold and rejoice in the bloody fray. But when he saw the damsel pass by, he left his hiding place and swiftly pursued, hoping to bring her to her final ruin. Now, to tell of her lamentable case, and of this battle's end, we will need another place.[1]

---

1 *Spenser does not tell us who wins the fight, but Satyrane reappears in Book III and IV where he helps others fight against evil, and Sansloy also appears briefly in Book II. So, whatever the outcome, they both survived.*

NOTES ON CANTO VII

Setting Aside his Armor: This is also symbolic: Redcross not only takes off his physical armor, but the armor of God in Ephesians: 6:10-18

Orgoglio: The giant's name means pride.

Arthur: Although Arthur doesn't play the most significant role in the story's action, he is central to it. Arthur is in search of the Faerie Queene, whom he beheld in a vision. He also claims to originate from western Wales, which connects him to the house of Tudor, Elizabeth's family.

John of Glastonbury (1350AD) claimed that King Arthur was descended from Joseph of Arimathea, who was among the first Christians who came to Britain in the first century. Early church fathers referred to Christianity in Britain as early as 208AD,[1] centuries before the Roman church, and Queen Elizabeth I cited Joseph's missionary work in England when she told Catholic bishops that the Church of England pre-dated the Roman Church.

The "real" Arthur was a king of the Britons in the 5th and 6th century, but the little historical information there is about him is overwhelmed by his legend.

The Horn: represents Truth, and the English Bible.

The Squire: represents Purity, and the Anglican Clergy.

Duessa's pet beast: Based on a scene from Revelation: "And I saw a woman sitting upon a scarlet-colored beast...having seven heads and ten horns. And the woman was clothed in purple and scarlet, and covered with gold...having in her hand a golden cup full of abominations." (Rev.17.3-4)

CANTO VII

REDCROSS AND THE OGRE

The Redcrosse knight is captiue made
By Gyaunt proud opprest,
Prince Arthur meets with Vna greatly with those newes distrest.

I What man so wise, what earthly wit so ware,
As to descry the crafty cunning traine,
By which deceipt doth maske in visour faire,
And cast her colours dyed deepe in graine,
To seeme like Truth, whose shape she well can faine,
And fitting gestures to her purpose frame;
The guiltlesse man with guile to entertaine?
Great maistresse of her art was that false Dame,
The false *Duessa*, cloked with *Fidessaes* name.

II Who when returning from the drery *Night*,
She fownd not in that perilous house of *Pryde*,
Where she had left, the noble *Redcrosse* knight,
Her hoped pray, she would no lenger bide,
But forth she went, to seeke him far and wide.
Ere long she fownd, whereas he wearie sate,
To rest him selfe, foreby a fountaine side,
Disarmed all of yron-coted Plate,
And by his side his steed the grassy forage ate.

III He feedes vpon the cooling shade, and bayes
His sweatie forehead in the breathing wind,
Which through the trembling leaues full gently playes
Wherein the cherefull birds of sundry kind
Do chaunt sweet musick, to delight his mind:
The Witch approching gan him fairely greet,
And with reproch of carelesnesse vnkind
Vpbrayd, for leauing her in place vnmeet,
With fowle words tempring faire, soure gall with hony sweet.

IV Vnkindnesse past, they gan of solace treat,
And bathe in pleasaunce of the ioyous shade,
Which shielded them against the boyling heat,
And with greene boughes decking a gloomy glade,
About the fountaine like a girlond made;
Whose bubbling waue did euer freshly well,
Ne euer would through feruent sommer fade:
The sacred Nymph, which therein wont to dwell,
Was out of *Dianes* fauour, as it then befell.

V The cause was this: one day when *Phoebe* fayre
With all her band was following the chace,
This Nymph, quite tyr'd with heat of scorching ayre,
Sat downe to rest in middest of the race:
The goddesse wroth gan fowly her disgrace,
And bad the waters, which from her did flow,   Thenceforth her waters waxed dull and slow,
Be such as she her selfe was then in place.   And all that drunke thereof, did faint and feeble g

The Redcross knight is taken and made captive by the proud giant.
Greatly distressed with those news, Una meets with Prince Arthur.

WHAT MAN SO WISE, WHAT EARTHLY CREATURE SO WARY, WHAT MORTAL SO worthy can discover the crafty cunning plot of deceit, masked in a beautiful veil? Who can cast her dyed colors so deeply, that the falsehood appears like truth in both warp and weft? Whose shape can she fake so well, framing fitting gestures to her purpose, to entertain the guiltless man with guile? Great mistress of her art was that false dame; the false Duessa, cloaked in the name of Fidessa.

WHEN DUESSA HAD RETURNED FROM THAT DREARY NIGHT, SHE DISCOVERED that her hoped prey, the noble knight Redcross, had left that perilous house of pride. Dismayed, she set off at once to seek him far and wide. Before long, she found weary Redcross sitting by the side of a fountain resting, while his steed grazed on the grassy forage nearby, and his dwarf servant dozed. His iron-coated armor had become too heavy to bear, so he had disarmed himself of it to rest. He was enjoying the cool shade and bathing his sweaty forehead in the tender breeze, while the leaves gently rustled in the trees above, and where cheerful sundry birds chanted sweet music to delight his mind. Then the witch approached and began to greet him with sugar-coated charm, and to reproach him with honey-tempered sourness for his unkind carelessness in deserting her in that awful palace.

Having expressed her dismay, they began to enjoy the solace of the lovely setting together, bathing in the pleasance and joyous shade, which shielded them against the boiling heat. Like a garland, the green boughs decked the fountain, which continued to bubble freshly all through summer.

5 However, it happened that the sacred nymph who usually inhabited this enchanted fountain, was out of favor with the goddess Diana. The nymph had been hunting with Diana and had grown tired from the heat in the scorching air. So she rested by this very fountain in the middle of an important chase. Finding her there, the enraged goddess began to foully disgrace the nymph, and she cursed the waters of the fountain as a punishment, making them dull and slow, like her, so that anyone who drank from them would also faint and grow weak.

VI Hereof this gentle knight vnweeting was,
And lying downe vpon the sandie graile,
Drunke of the streame, as cleare as cristall glas;
Eftsoones his manly forces gan to faile,
And mightie strong was turnd to feeble fraile.
His chaunged powres at first them selues not felt,
Till crudled cold his corage gan assaile,
And chearefull bloud in faintnesse chill did melt,
Which like a feuer fit through all his body swelt.

VII Yet goodly court he made still to his Dame,
Pourd out in loosnesse on the grassy grownd,
Both carelesse of his health, and of his fame:
Till at the last he heard a dreadfull sownd,
Which through the wood loud bellowing, did rebownd,
That all the earth for terrour seemd to shake,
And trees did tremble. Th'Elfe therewith astownd,
Vpstarted lightly from his looser make,
And his vnready weapons gan in hand to take.

VIII But ere he could his armour on him dight,
Or get his shield, his monstrous enimy
With sturdie steps came stalking in his sight,
An hideous Geant horrible and hye,
That with his talnesse seemd to threat the skye,
The ground eke groned vnder him for dreed;
His liuing like saw neuer liuing eye,
Ne durst behold: his stature did exceed
The hight of three the tallest sonnes of mortall seed.

IX The greatest Earth his vncouth mother was,
And blustring *AEolus* his boasted sire,
Who with his breath, which through the world doth pas,
Her hollow womb did secretly inspire,
And fild her hidden caues with stormie yre,
That she conceiu'd; and trebling the dew time,
In which the wombes of women do expire,
Brought forth this monstrous masse of earthly slime,
Puft vp with emptie wind, and fild with sinfull crime.

X So growen great through arrogant delight
Of th'high descent, whereof he was yborne,
And through presumption of his matchlesse might,
All other powres and knighthood he did scorne.
Such now he marcheth to this man forlorne,
And left to losse: his stalking steps are stayde
Vpon a snaggy Oke, which he had torne
Out of his mothers bowelles, and it made
His mortall mace, wherewith his foemen he dismayde.

6 Here the unsuspecting knight, lying down by the fountain side, drank from the crystal-clear liquid. Soon after, his manly forces began to fail, and his mighty strength became feeble and frail. At first, Redcross was not aware of any change in his power, but soon his courage seemed to grow cold and faint, and took over his whole body like a fever.

Yet he continued to court and flirt with his lady friend on the grassy ground, careless of both his health and his honor.

Then, suddenly, he heard a dreadful loud bellowing that echoed all through the woods, so that all the earth seemed to shake with terror, and the trees trembled ominously. The astonished Elf rose deftly to his feet, leaving his lewd mate still on the grass, and grabbed his unready armor and weapons.

But before he could put on his armor, his monstrous enemy came lumbering into view with sturdy, crashing strides. It was a hideous, high and horrible giant: so tall, he seemed to threaten the sky above, while the earth below seemed to groan under him for dread. His stature exceeded three times the size of the tallest of grown men. No one ever saw, or dared behold, such a fearful sight.

The great giant, Orgoglio, was conceived by the uncouth goddess, Earth, and the blustering wind-god, Aeolus. With his breath, which passes throughout all the world, Aeolus impregnated the hidden caves of Earth with stormy ire. Her pregnancy took three times the usual length, then she gave birth to this monstrous mass of earthly slime, puffed up with wind and pride, and filled with sinful crime.

10 Grown great through arrogant delight of his tall stature, and presumption of his matchless might, he scorned all other powers and knighthood. And now he marched towards this forlorn and defenseless man, steadying himself with a crude staff made from a snaggy, knotty oak tree that he had ripped from his mother's bowels, and which doubled as his mace to club his foes.

XI That when the knight he spide, he gan aduance
With huge force and insupportable mayne,
And towardes him with dreadfull fury praunce;
Who haplesse, and eke hopelesse, all in vaine
Did to him pace, sad battaile to darrayne,
Disarmd, disgrast, and inwardly dismayde,
And eke so faint in euery ioynt and vaine,
Through that fraile fountaine, which him feeble made,
That scarsely could he weeld his bootlesse single blade.

XII The Geaunt strooke so maynly mercilesse,
That could haue ouerthrowne a stony towre,
And were not heauenly grace, that him did blesse,
He had beene pouldred all, as thin as flowre:
But he was wary of that deadly stowre,
And lightly lept from vnderneath the blow:
Yet so exceeding was the villeins powre,
That with the wind it did him ouerthrow,
And all his sences stound, that still he lay full low.

XIII As when that diuelish yron Engin wrought
In deepest Hell, and framd by *Furies* skill,
With windy Nitre and quick Sulphur fraught,
And ramd with bullet round, ordaind to kill,
Conceiueth fire, the heauens it doth fill
With thundring noyse, and all the ayre doth choke,
That none can breath, nor see, nor heare at will,
Through smouldry cloud of duskish stincking smoke,
That th'onely breath him daunts, who hath escapt the stroke.

XIV So daunted when the Geaunt saw the knight,
His heauie hand he heaued vp on hye,
And him to dust thought to haue battred quight,
Vntill *Duessa* loud to him gan crye;
O great *Orgoglio*, greatest vnder skye,
O hold thy mortall hand for Ladies sake,
Hold for my sake, and do him not to dye,
But vanquisht thine eternall bondslaue make,
And me thy worthy meed vnto thy Leman take.

XV He hearkned, and did stay from further harmes,
To gayne so goodly guerdon, as she spake:
So willingly she came into his armes,
Who her as willingly to grace did take,
And was possessed of his new found make.
Then vp he tooke the slombred sencelesse corse,
And ere he could out of his swowne awake,
Him to his castle brought with hastie forse,
And in a Dongeon deepe him threw without remorse.

11 When the giant spied the knight, he raised the club into the air with huge and irresistible force, and strutted towards him with dreadful fury. Hapless and hopeless, and all in vain, Redcross paced towards him ready to take on this senseless battle. But, disarmed and disgraced, and inwardly dismayed, Redcross had been weakened in every joint and vein through that fountain of frailty, and could scarcely wield his bootless single blade. The giant struck so powerfully and mercilessly that he could have flattened a stone tower, and if heavenly grace did not bless Redcross, he would have been pulverized as thin as flour. But the knight dodged this deadly assault, leaping lightly from underneath the thundering blow. Yet so exceeding was that villain's power that the wind from the blow overpowered Redcross, and he crashed to the ground, his senses stunned.

Just like that devilish iron canon, wrought in deepest hell, and formed by Furies' skill, stuffed with gunpowder's blast-producing Nitrate and Sulphur, rammed with bullets and designed to kill, it fires and fills the heavens with a thundering noise, so that the air is choked and none can breathe, or see, or hear at will. So ravaged the Ogre's club.

Thinking he had just battered the knight to dust, the giant was daunted and then enraged when he saw him alive, though lying in a faint. But Duessa calmed him, crying out loudly, "O great Orgoglio, greatest under sky, O hold your deadly hand for this lady's sake, and do not let him die! Instead, make me your eternal slave and lover as your worthy prize!"

15He hearkened and refrained from further harms, and ogling Duessa, cheered to gain such an attractive reward. Eagerly, she came running into his arms, and the giant just as eagerly took possession of her. Next, he took the slumbering body of Redcross and brought him to the castle with hasty force, where he flung him into the deepest dungeon, without a shred of remorse.

XVI From that day forth *Duessa* was his deare,
And highly honourd in his haughtie eye,
He gaue her gold and purple pall to weare,
And triple crowne set on her head full hye,
And her endowd with royall maiestye:
Then for to make her dreaded more of men,
And peoples harts with awfull terrour tye,
A monstrous beast ybred in filthy fen
He chose, which he had kept long time in darksome den.

XVII Such one it was, as that renowmed Snake
Which great *Alcides* in *Stremona* slew,
Long fostred in the filth of *Lerna* lake,
Whose many heads out budding euer new,
Did breed him endlesse labour to subdew:
But this same Monster much more vgly was;
For seuen great heads out of his body grew,
An yron brest, and backe of scaly bras,
And all embrewd in bloud, his eyes did shine as glas.

XVIII His tayle was stretched out in wondrous length,
That to the house of heauenly gods it raught,
And with extorted powre, and borrow'd strength,
The euer-burning lamps from thence it braught,
And prowdly threw to ground, as things of naught;
And vnderneath his filthy feet did tread
The sacred things, and holy heasts foretaught.
Vpon this dreadfull Beast with seuenfold head
He set the false *Duessa*, for more aw and dread.

XIX The wofull Dwarfe, which saw his maisters fall,
Whiles he had keeping of his grasing steed,
And valiant knight become a caytiue thrall,
When all was past, tooke vp his forlorne weed,
His mightie armour, missing most at need;
His siluer shield, now idle maisterlesse;
His poynant speare, that many made to bleed,
The ruefull moniments of heauinesse,
And with them all departes, to tell his great distresse.

XX He had not trauaild long, when on the way
He wofull Ladie, wofull *Vna* met,
Fast flying from the Paynims greedy pray,
Whilest *Satyrane* him from pursuit did let:
Who when her eyes she on the Dwarf had set,
And saw the signes, that deadly tydings spake,
She fell to ground for sorrowfull regret,
And liuely breath her sad brest did forsake,
Yet might her pitteous hart be seene to pant and quake.

11 From that day forth, Duessa was the giant's dear, highly honored in his prideful eye. He gave her royal purple and scarlet robes to wear, and set a triple crown upon her head, endowing her with royal majesty. Then, to make her all the more dreaded, and to strike terror into the hearts of people, he found her a pet: a monstrous beast bred in a filthy swamp, which he had long kept in a dark den. What a beast it was! Worse than that well-known Hydra that Hercules slew, long fostered in the filth of Lerna lake, its many heads budding ever new, and breeding endless labor to anyone who tried to slay it. But this monster was even more hideous, for seven great heads grew out of one body. It had a breast of iron, a back of bloodstained scaly brass, and eyes that shone like glass. Its tail was stretched out in such wondrous length that it reached to the heavenly gods, and with extorted power and borrowed strength, it proudly threw anything it deemed unworthy to the ground. Underneath its filthy feet it trod on sacred objects and holy laws. Upon this beast, with its sevenfold head, the giant set the false Duessa, to add more shock and horror.

MEANWHILE, THE WOEFUL DWARF WHO HAD BEEN TAKING CARE OF THE KNIGHT'S grazing steed, had seen his valiant master's fall, and witnessed his capture. When all was past, he took up the knight's forsaken equipment: his mighty armor, cast aside when most needed, his silver shield, now idle and master-less, and his sharpened lance, that had made many a foe bleed. With these tokens of grief, the dwarf departed to tell of his great distress.

20 He hadn't travelled long before he came across the woeful lady Una, fleeing like prey from the greedy pagan, while Satyrane hindered him with the battle pursuit. As soon as she had set eyes on the dwarf, and saw the signs that spoke of deadly tidings, she fell to the ground in sorrow, hardly able to breathe: her piteous heart panting and quaking.

XXI The messenger of so vnhappie newes
Would faine haue dyde: dead was his hart within,
Yet outwardly some little comfort shewes:
At last recouering hart, he does begin
To rub her temples, and to chaufe her chin,
And euery tender part does tosse and turne:
So hardly he the flitted life does win,
Vnto her natiue prison to retourne:
Then gins her grieued ghost thus to lament and mourne.

XXII Ye dreary instruments of dolefull sight,
That doe this deadly spectacle behold,
Why do ye lenger feed on loathed light,
Or liking find to gaze on earthly mould,
Sith cruell fates the carefull threeds vnfould,
The which my life and loue together tyde?
Now let the stony dart of senselesse cold
Perce to my hart, and pas through euery side,
And let eternall night so sad sight fro me hide.

XXIII O lightsome day, the lampe of highest *Ioue*,
First made by him, mens wandring wayes to guyde,
When darknesse he in deepest dongeon droue,
Henceforth thy hated face for euer hyde,
And shut vp heauens windowes shyning wyde:
For earthly sight can nought but sorow breed,
And late repentance, which shall long abyde.
Mine eyes no more on vanitie shall feed,
But seeled vp with death, shall haue their deadly meed.

XXIV Then downe againe she fell vnto the ground;
But he her quickly reared vp againe:
Thrise did she sinke adowne in deadly swownd,
And thrise he her reviu'd with busie paine:
At last when life recouer'd had the raine,
And ouer-wrestled his strong enemie,
With foltring tong, and trembling euery vaine,
Tell on (quoth she) the wofull Tragedie,
The which these reliques sad present vnto mine eie.

XXV Tempestuous fortune hath spent all her spight,
And thrilling sorrow throwne his vtmost dart;
Thy sad tongue cannot tell more heauy plight,
Then that I feele, and harbour in mine hart:
Who hath endur'd the whole, can beare each part.
If death it be, it is not the first wound,
That launched hath my brest with bleeding smart.
Begin, and end the bitter balefull stound;
If lesse, then that I feare, more fauour I haue found.

21 The messenger of such unhappy news would rather have died, and his heart already felt dead within, but he tried to show some comfort to poor Una. Recovering his own courage, he rubbed her temples and chafed her cheeks, he tossed and turned every tender part, until she finally regained consciousness. Then her grieving spirit began to lament and mourn.

"You, eyes, dreary instruments of doleful sight that behold this deadly spectacle, why do you continue to feed on this hated light? Why do you still want to gaze upon earthly forms, since cruel fates have tied my life and love together? Now let the stony dart of senseless cold pierce my heart and pass through every side, and let eternal night hide me from so sad a sight. O lightsome day, the lamp of highest Jove, first made by him to guide men's wandering ways, when darkness drove them into deepest dungeons. Henceforth, forever hide your hated face, and shut heaven's windows shining wide! For earthly sight can only breed sorrow and too late repentance, which shall long abide. Mine eyes shall feed on vanity no more, but sealed up with death shall have their deadly reward."

Then down she fell; onto the ground again. But the dwarf acted quickly and helped her up. Three more times she swooned, and three more times the dwarf revived her with care.

At last, when she regained control of herself, with faltering tongue and trembling vein, she said, "Tell me, then, dwarf, the woeful tragedy that these sad relics present unto mine eye. **25** Tempestuous fortune has spent all her spite, and piercing sorrow has thrown his utmost dart. So, your sad tongue cannot tell a heavier plight than that which I already feel and harbor in mine heart. He who has endured the whole can bear each part. If death it be, it is not the first wound that has pierced my breast with bleeding pain. Tell me, dwarf, and end the bitter baleful ordeal. Begin! And if it be less than I fear, more favor have I found!"

XXVI Then gan the Dwarfe the whole discourse declare,
The subtill traines of *Archimago* old;
The wanton loues of false *Fidessa* faire,
Bought with the bloud of vanquisht Paynim bold:
The wretched payre transform'd to treen mould;
The house of Pride, and perils round about;
The combat, which he with *Sansioy* did hould;
The lucklesse conflict with the Gyant stout,
Wherein captiu'd, of life or death he stood in doubt.

XXVII She heard with patience all vnto the end,
And stroue to maister sorrowfull assay,
Which greater grew, the more she did contend,
And almost rent her tender hart in tway;
And loue fresh coles vnto her fire did lay:
For greater loue, the greater is the losse.
Was neuer Ladie loued dearer day,
Then she did loue the knight of the *Redcrosse*;
For whose deare sake so many troubles her did tosse.

XXVIII At last when feruent sorrow slaked was,
She vp arose, resoluing him to find
A liue or dead: and forward forth doth pas,
All as the Dwarfe the way to her assynd:
And euermore in constant carefull mind
She fed her wound with fresh renewed bale;
Long tost with stormes, and bet with bitter wind,
High ouer hils, and low adowne the dale,
She wandred many a wood, and measurd many a vale.

XXIX At last she chaunced by good hap to meet
A goodly knight, faire marching by the way
Together with his Squire, arayed meet:
His glitterand armour shined farre away,
Like glauncing light of *Phoebus* brightest ray;
From top to toe no place appeared bare,
That deadly dint of steele endanger may:
Athwart his brest a bauldrick braue he ware,
That shynd, like twinkling stars, with stons most pretious rare.

XXX And in the midst thereof one pretious stone
Of wondrous worth, and eke of wondrous mights,
Shapt like a Ladies head, exceeding shone,
Like *Hesperus* emongst the lesser lights,
And stroue for to amaze the weaker sights;
Thereby his mortall blade full comely hong
In yuory sheath, ycaru'd with curious slights;
Whose hilts were burnisht gold, and handle strong
Of mother pearle, and buckled with a golden tong.

26 So, the dwarf began to tell the whole story; about the crafty tricks of old Archimago, the battle with the bold defeated pagan, the wanton loves of fair false Fidessa, of the wretched pair transformed into trees, the castle of pride, and the perils in and around it. He told of the combat between Sansjoy and Redcross, the luckless conflict with the prideful giant, and finally how he was taken captive. But whether he was alive or dead, he still stood in doubt.

She listened patiently right until the end, striving hard to master her sorrowful trial, which grew greater with the more she heard. It almost rent her heart in two, laying fresh coals of love. The greater the love: the greater the loss. For there was never a lady who loved life dearer than she loved her knight of the Redcross, for whose dear sake so many troubles had been tossed her way.

Finally, when her fervent sorrow was quenched, she rose, resolved to find him dead or alive. The dwarf indicated the way and Una followed, still in constant grief but also constant in caring.

They wandered in many a wood and passed through many a vale. Tossed by storms and beaten by bitter wind, they rambled high over hills and low in down dale.

At last, and by good luck, they came across a noble knight who was riding the same way with his squire. The knight was arrayed from top to toe in sparkling armor that shone like the glancing light of Phoebus's brightest rays. Across his breast, he wore a sword belt, studded with rare precious stones that shone like twinkling stars. **30** And, in the midst of these gemstones of wondrous worth and powers, one was shaped like the head of a Faerie Queene, outshining the others like Venus, the Evening Star, and dazzling and bewildering to weaker eyes. Next to his side, in an ivory sheath, that was wrought with curious inscriptions, hung his deadly blade. Its hilt was burnished in gold, the handle of pearl shell, and its buckles of golden tongue.

XXXI His haughtie helmet, horrid all with gold,
Both glorious brightnesse, and great terrour bred;
For all the crest a Dragon did enfold
With greedie pawes, and ouer all did spred
His golden wings: his dreadfull hideous hed
Close couched on the beuer, seem'd to throw
From flaming mouth bright sparkles fierie red,
That suddeine horror to faint harts did show;
And scaly tayle was stretcht adowne his backe full low.

XXXII Vpon the top of all his loftie crest,
A bunch of haires discolourd diuersly,
With sprincled pearle, and gold full richly drest,
Did shake, and seem'd to daunce for iollity,
Like to an Almond tree ymounted hye
On top of greene *Selinis* all alone,
With blossomes braue bedecked daintily;
Whose tender locks do tremble euery one
At euery little breath, that vnder heauen is blowne.

XXXIII His warlike shield all closely couer'd was,
Ne might of mortall eye be euer seene;
Not made of steele, nor of enduring bras,
Such earthly mettals soone consumed bene:
But all of Diamond perfect pure and cleene
It framed was, one massie entire mould,
Hewen out of Adamant rocke with engines keene,
That point of speare it neuer percen could,
Ne dint of direfull sword diuide the substance would.

XXXIV The same to wight he neuer wont disclose,
But when as monsters huge he would dismay,
Or daunt vnequall armies of his foes,
Or when the flying heauens he would affray;
For so exceeding shone his glistring ray,
That *Phoebus* golden face it did attaint,
As when a cloud his beames doth ouer-lay;
And siluer *Cynthia* wexed pale and faint,
As when her face is staynd with magicke arts constraint.

XXXV No magicke arts hereof had any might,
Nor bloudie wordes of bold Enchaunters call,
But all that was not such, as seemd in sight,
Before that shield did fade, and suddeine fall:
And when him list the raskall routes appall,
Men into stones therewith he could transmew,
And stones to dust, and dust to nought at all;
And when him list the prouder lookes subdew,
He would them gazing blind, or turne to other hew.

31 His magnificent helmet was bristled with gold, breeding both glorious brightness and great terror. On the crest was a dragon emblem, with greedy paws, outspread golden wings, and a scaly tail that stretched full low. Lying across the visor, the dragon's hideous head seemed to throw bright-red fiery sparkles that might inflict sudden horror to faint hearts. Then, on top of this lofty crest was an array of richly colored feathers, sprinkled with pearl and gold. The plumes seemed to shake and dance for joy, like an almond tree high on top of Mount Selinis, daintily bedecked with blossoms, whose tender leaves tremble at every breeze.

His warlike shield was like no other beheld by mortal eye. Made neither of steel, nor even enduring brass—such earthly metals soon corroded—this shield was made of pure and clean diamond. Hewn out of Adamantine rock with the sharpest tools, no lance point could pierce, or direful sword could split its solid substance.

This same shield was never revealed to ordinary folk, except when huge monsters needed defeating, when unequal armies of his foes needed daunting, or when the flying Milky Way needed a kickstart to prompt it to keep moving. For its glistering rays shone so exceedingly that they eclipsed Phoebus's golden face, clouding his sunbeams, and as for the already pale and faint silver moon, they would strain it further, like a magic spell.

35 But neither magic spell, nor bloody words of any enchanter's call, had the slightest power over this shield. Before this shield of truth, all that was not as it seemed would fade and fall. When he wished to inspire awe in the commoners, he would turn men into stone, and stones to dust, and dust to nothing. And when he felt the need to subdue the proud, he would dazzle them blind, or turn them into other forms.

XXXVI Ne let it seeme, that credence this exceedes,
For he that made the same, was knowne right well
To haue done much more admirable deedes.
It *Merlin* was, which whylome did excell
All liuing wightes in might of magicke spell:
Both shield, and sword, and armour all he wrought
For this young Prince, when first to armes he fell;
But when he dyde, the Faerie Queene it brought
To Faerie lond, where yet it may be seene, if sought.

XXXVII A gentle youth, his dearely loued Squire
His speare of heben wood behind him bare,
Whose harmefull head, thrice heated in the fire,
Had riuen many a brest with pikehead square;
A goodly person, and could menage faire
His stubborne steed with curbed canon bit,
Who vnder him did trample as the aire,
And chauft, that any on his backe should sit;
The yron rowels into frothy fome he bit.

XXXVIII When as this knight nigh to the Ladie drew,
With louely court he gan her entertaine;
But when he heard her answeres loth, he knew
Some secret sorrow did her heart distraine:
Which to allay, and calme her storming paine,
Faire feeling words he wisely gan display,
And for her humour fitting purpose faine,
To tempt the cause it selfe for to bewray;
Wherewith emmou'd, these bleeding words she gan to say.

XXXIX What worlds delight, or ioy of liuing speach
Can heart, so plung'd in sea of sorrowes deepe,
And heaped with so huge misfortunes, reach?
The carefull cold beginneth for to creepe,
And in my heart his yron arrow steepe,
Soone as I thinke vpon my bitter bale:
Such helplesse harmes yts better hidden keepe,
Then rip vp griefe, where it may not auaile,
My last left comfort is, my woes to weepe and waile.

XL Ah Ladie deare, quoth then the gentle knight,
Well may I weene, your griefe is wondrous great;
For wondrous great griefe groneth in my spright,
Whiles thus I heare you of your sorrowes treat.
But wofull Ladie let me you intrete,
For to vnfold the anguish of your hart:
Mishaps are maistred by aduice discrete,
And counsell mittigates the greatest smart;
Found neuer helpe, who neuer would his hurts impart.

36 Even though it seems to surpass belief, he who made the shield was known to have done much more marvelous deeds. It was Merlin, who had formerly excelled beyond all living creatures in the power of magic spells. It was he who wrought the shield, the sword, and the armor, when the young prince first came to arms. And when he died, the Faerie Queene carried his sword and shield to Faerieland, where it may still be seen to this day.

Behind the great knight, stood the dearly beloved squire: a gentle youth named Timias. He bore an ebony lance, the head of which had been thrice heated in the fire, and had already pierced many an enemy breast. He was a robust young man who could manage his stubborn steed well, deftly pulling on the reins that controlled the animal's bit, when it reared up and trampled the air.

WHEN THE PRINCELY KNIGHT FINALLY DREW CLOSE TO THE LADY, HE BEGAN to entertain her with chivalrous and kindly courtesies. But when he heard her reluctant answers, he knew her heart was distressed by some secret sorrow. To calm her storming pain, he sought the problem with compassion and fair feeling words. Inwardly moved by the knight's efforts to sympathize, Una began to tell her painful story.

"What world's delights or joy of living speech can a heart such as mine, so plunged in a sea of sorrows, and heaped with misfortunes, reach? Death begins to creep into this heart of mine like an arrow, whenever I think of my bitter misfortune. Such hopeless sorrow is better kept hidden, than to stir up grief where it may not help. My only comfort left is to weep and wail my woes."

40 "Ah dear lady," said the gentle knight, "I know very well your grief is great, for wondrous great grief groans in my spirit too. But allow me to entreat you to unfold the anguish of your heart. Mishaps are mastered by discerning advice, and counsel mitigates the greatest pain. He who never imparted his hurts, never found help."

XLI O but (quoth she) great griefe will not be tould,
And can more easily be thought, then said.
Right so; (quoth he) but he, that neuer would,
Could neuer: will to might giues greatest aid.
But griefe (quoth she) does greater grow displaid,
If then it find not helpe, and breedes despaire.
Despaire breedes not (quoth he) where faith is staid.
No faith so fast (quoth she) but flesh does paire.
Flesh may empaire (quoth he) but reason can repaire.

XLII His goodly reason, and well guided speach
So deepe did settle in her gratious thought,
That her perswaded to disclose the breach,
Which loue and fortune in her heart had wrought,
And said; faire Sir, I hope good hap hath brought
You to inquere the secrets of my griefe,
Or that your wisedome will direct my thought,
Or that your prowesse can me yield reliefe:
Then heare the storie sad, which I shall tell you briefe.

XLIII The forlorne Maiden, whom your eyes haue seene
The laughing stocke of fortunes mockeries,
Am th'only daughter of a King and Queene,
Whose parents deare, whilest equall destinies
Did runne about, and their felicities
The fauourable heauens did not enuy,
Did spread their rule through all the territories,
Which *Phison* and *Euphrates* floweth by,
And *Gehons* golden waues doe wash continually.

XLIV Till that their cruell cursed enemy,
An huge great Dragon horrible in sight,
Bred in the loathly lakes of *Tartary*,
With murdrous rauine, and deuouring might
Their kingdome spoild, and countrey wasted quight:
Themselues, for feare into his iawes to fall,
He forst to castle strong to take their flight,
Where fast embard in mightie brasen wall,
He has them now foure yeres besiegd to make them thrall.

XLV Full many knights aduenturous and stout
Haue enterprizd that Monster to subdew;
From euery coast that heauen walks about,
Haue thither come the noble Martiall crew,
That famous hard atchieuements still pursew,
Yet neuer any could that girlond win,
But all still shronke, and still he greater grew:
All they for want of faith, or guilt of sin,
The pitteous pray of his fierce crueltie haue bin.

41 "Oh, but, great grief is less painful to endure when thought rather than spoken," replied Una.

"Right so, but he who never would, never could. Will gives greatest aid to might," countered the knight.

"But grief grows greater when displayed, and if it does not find help, only breeds despair," she said.

"Despair breeds not where faith is solid," he replied.

"But no faith is so firm, that the flesh does not impair," she said.

"Flesh may impair, but reason can repair," he replied.

His wise reasoning and well guided speech settled deeply in her gracious thought, and persuaded her to disclose that which love and misfortune had created in her heart.

"Fair sir," she began, "I hope good fortune has brought you to inquire the secrets of my grief, and either that your wisdom will direct my thought, or your skill can bring me relief. So then, you will hear the sad story, which I will tell in brief.

"This forlorn maiden, whom you see here, is the laughing-stock of fortune's mockeries. I am the only daughter of a king and queen, whom the heavens favored and helped spread their rule through all the territories where the Phison, and the Euphrates rivers flow, and Gehon's[2] golden waves wash the shores. All was peaceful throughout the lands until, one day, a cruel cursed enemy, a great dragon, horrible in sight, bred in the loathsome lakes of Tartarus, with murderous devastation and devouring might, spoiled their kingdom and laid waste to their country. Fearing they would fall into its jaws, they shut themselves up in a strong castle where, for four years now, like slaves, they have been imprisoned and besieged behind a mighty brazen wall. **45** Many brave and adventurous knights, coming from every coast under the sun, have tried to subdue that monster. Yet, for lack of faith or guilt of sin, none could win that garland, and each knight became its piteous prey, while the fierce and cruel monster grew bigger and stronger.

XLVI At last yledd with farre reported praise,
Which flying fame throughout the world had spred,
Of doughtie knights, whom Faery land did raise,
That noble order hight of Maidenhed,
Forthwith to court of *Gloriane* I sped,
Of *Gloriane* great Queene of glory bright,
Whose kingdomes seat *Cleopolis* is red,
There to obtaine some such redoubted knight,
That Parents deare from tyrants powre deliuer might.

XLVI It was my chance (my chance was faire and good)
There for to find a fresh vnproued knight,
Whose manly hands imbrew'd in guiltie blood
Had neuer bene, ne euer by his might
Had throwne to ground the vnregarded right:
Yet of his prowesse proofe he since hath made
(I witnesse am) in many a cruell fight;
The groning ghosts of many one dismaide
Haue felt the bitter dint of his auenging blade.

XLVIII And ye the forlorne reliques of his powre,
His byting sword, and his deuouring speare,
Which haue endured many a dreadfull stowre,
Can speake his prowesse, that did earst you beare,
And well could rule: now he hath left you heare,
To be the record of his ruefull losse,
And of my dolefull disauenturous deare:
O heauie record of the good *Redcrosse*,
Where haue you left your Lord, that could so well you tosse?

XLIX Well hoped I, and faire beginnings had,
That he my captiue langour should redeeme,
Till all vnweeting, an Enchaunter bad
His sence abusd, and made him to misdeeme
My loyalty, not such as it did seeme;
That rather death desire, then such despight.
Be iudge ye heauens, that all things right esteeme,
How I him lou'd, and loue with all my might,
So thought I eke of him, and thinke I thought aright.

L Thenceforth me desolate he quite forsooke,
To wander, where wilde fortune would me lead,
And other bywaies he himselfe betooke,
Where neuer foot of liuing wight did tread,
That brought not backe the balefull body dead;
In which him chaunced false *Duessa* meete,
Mine onely foe, mine onely deadly dread,
Who with her witchcraft and misseeming sweete,
Inueigled him to follow her desires vnmeete.

---

46 "At last, I heard of the sturdy knights from Faerieland who were raised in the Order of the Maidenhead.[3] whose fame and far-reported praise spread throughout the world. So I hurried to the great queen Gloriana's court, whose bright kingdom is referred to as Cleopolis[4]. There I sought a formidable knight who might deliver my dear parents from that tyrant's power. It was my good and fair chance to find a fresh unproven knight, whose manly hands had never been stained in guilty blood, and who had neither disrespected laws nor misused his power. This knight in question has since proven his prowess, as I am witness to many a cruel fight of his. The groaning ghosts of many defeated foes have felt the bitter blow of his avenging blade."

Una stopped to catch her breath, then pointed at the armor the Dwarf was carrying, before continuing her story.

"And yet these forsaken relics of his power, his biting sword, and his devouring lance, which have endured many a dreadful fight, and that he bore so skillfully and can speak of his prowess. Now he has left them here as evidence of his rueful loss, and of my doleful unfortunate beloved: a sad document of the good Redcross. Where did they leave their lord, these arms, that he could so well brandish?

"I had been full of hope that he might redeem my captive suffering and we started out with fair beginnings, until we were tricked unknowingly by an evil enchanter. With deceit and disguises, the enchanter fooled him to question my loyalty, to think it was not as it seemed. But I would rather die than be disloyal! Let the heavens that weigh all things, judge how I loved him with all my might, and how I maintain my loyalty to him.

50 "Thenceforth, I was left desolate to wander where wild fortune might lead, while he took himself off on other byways where no weak-willed creature ventured who expected to return alive. There he met the false Duessa, my only foe, my only dreadful dread, who, with her witchcraft and false sweetness, seduced him to follow her improper desires.

LI At last by subtill sleights she him betraid
Vnto his foe, a Gyant huge and tall,
Who him disarmed, dissolute, dismaid,
Vnwares surprised, and with mightie mall
The monster mercilesse him made to fall,
Whose fall did neuer foe before behold;
And now in darkesome dungeon, wretched thrall,
Remedilesse, for aie he doth him hold;
This is my cause of griefe, more great, then may be told.

LII Ere she had ended all, she gan to faint:
But he her comforted and faire bespake,
Certes, Madame, ye haue great cause of plaint,
That stoutest heart, I weene, could cause to quake.
But be of cheare, and comfort to you take:
For till I haue acquit your captiue knight,
Assure your selfe, I will you not forsake.
His chearefull words reuiu'd her chearelesse spright,
So forth they went, the Dwarfe them guiding euer right.

51 "Finally, by subtle tricks, she betrayed him unto a huge and horrible giant who, brandishing a mighty club, sprang upon him unawares while he was disarmed, dissolute and dismayed. The merciless giant made him fall, then carried him away, and now he is a wretched prisoner in some darksome dungeon. It seems there is no remedy, for he holds him there forever, and this is the cause of my grief, greater than may be told."

When she had finished her story, she began to faint, but he comforted her and addressed her courteously.

"It is certain, madam," the knight began, "that you have cause for great complaint, and a story that would quake even the stoutest heart. But be of good cheer and take comfort. For, until I have rescued your captive knight, be assured that I will not forsake you."

His cheerful words revived her cheerless spirit, and so forth they departed together, with the dwarf as guide.

1   http://sourcebooks.fordham.edu/halsall/mod/elizabeth1.asp

2   *Phison, Euphrates rivers flow, and Gehon's* Three of the four rivers that flow
    from Eden, along with the Tigris (see Genesis 2:10-14)

3   *Maidenhead the Order of the Garter,* of which the Queen Elizabeth I was head
    that is still active today. The figure of St. George slaying the dragon is the
    emblem of this Order.

4   *Cleopolis* London

NOTES ON CANTO VIII

While knights usually rescue damsels in distress, this damsel rescues her knight on two occasions in this story. As you read the next few chapters, can you determine what this might symbolize?

Ignaro: means ignorance: specifically, spiritual ignorance of the Roman Church. He has his head turned backwards, and holds the key to the 'kingdom.' What do you think Spenser might mean by this imagery?

Canto VIII: Arthur intervenes in the eighth canto of each book (except Book III), since eight is the number of regeneration.[1]

CANTO VIII

UNA'S SEARCH AND RESCUE OF REDCROSS

Faire virgin to redeeme her deare
brings Arthur to the fight,
Who slayes the Gyant, wounds the beast,
and strips Duessa quight.

I AY me, how many perils doe enfold
The righteous man, to make him daily fall?
Were not, that heauenly grace doth him vphold,
And stedfast truth acquite him out of all.
Her loue is firme, her care continuall,
So oft as he through his owne foolish pride,
Or weaknesse is to sinfull bands made thrall:
Else should this *Redcrosse* knight in bands haue dyde,
For whose deliuerance she this Prince doth thither guide.

II They sadly traueild thus, vntill they came
Nigh to a castle builded strong and hie:
Then cryde the Dwarfe, lo yonder is the same,
In which my Lord my liege doth lucklesse lie,
Thrall to that Gyants hatefull tyrannie:
Therefore, deare Sir, your mightie powres assay.
The noble knight alighted by and by
From loftie steede, and bad the Ladie stay,
To see what end of fight should him befall that day.

III So with the Squire, th'admirer of his might,
He marched forth towards that castle wall;
Whose gates he found fast shut, ne liuing wight
To ward the same, nor answere commers call.
Then tooke that Squire an horne of bugle small,
Which hong adowne his side in twisted gold,
And tassels gay. Wyde wonders ouer all
Of that same hornes great vertues weren told,
Which had approued bene in vses manifold.

IV Was neuer wight, that heard that shrilling sound,
But trembling feare did feele in euery vaine;
Three miles it might be easie heard around,
And Ecchoes three answerd it selfe againe:
No false enchauntment, nor deceiptfull traine
Might once abide the terror of that blast,
But presently was voide and wholly vaine:
No gate so strong, no locke so firme and fast,
But with that percing noise flew open quite, or brast.

V The same before the Geants gate he blew,
That all the castle quaked from the ground,
And euery dore of freewill open flew.
The Gyant selfe dismaied with that sownd,
Where he with his *Duessa* dalliance fownd,
In hast came rushing forth from inner bowre, with staring countenance sterne, as one astownd,
And staggering steps, to weet, what suddein stow
Had wrought that horror strange, and dar'd
his dreaded powre.

Fair maiden brings Arthur to the fight to redeem
her love. He slays the giant, wounds the beast,
and quite strips Duessa.

AYE ME, HOW MANY PERILS SURROUND THE RIGHTEOUS MAN THAT WOULD DAILY make him fall, were it not for heavenly grace that upholds him, and steadfast truth that rescues him? Her[2] love is firm and her care continual, while he, through his own foolish pride or weakness, is in bondage to sin. Without her, this Redcross knight, for whose deliverance she thither guides this prince, would have died in such bindings.

THE BAND TRAVELLED TOGETHER THUS, UNTIL THEY CAME UNTO A CASTLE THAT was built strong and high.

The dwarf then cried, "Lo, yonder is the same castle in which my lord and liege lies luckless, prisoner to that giant's hateful tyranny. Therefore, dear Sir, your mighty powers will be put to the test."

Immediately, the noble knight alighted from his lofty steed, and bade the lady stay to see what end of fight should befall them that day. Then, with his squire, the admirer of his might, he marched forth towards the castle wall. But the gates were shut fast, and neither guard nor living creature would answer his call. So, his squire took up the small bugle horn that hung by his side. Fashioned with twisted gold, and decorated with gay tassels, the horn's great powers were told all over the land, having proven itself in many ways. No living creature had heard that shrill sound that did not tremble with fear in every vein. Three miles it might easily have been heard, and three times its echoes answered back. No false enchantment or deceitful trick could withstand the terror of that blast: its powers being immediately subdued. No gate so strong, no lock so firm and fast, would not open at its piercing blast.

5 When the squire blew the horn before the giant's gate, the whole castle trembled from the ground, and every door flew open freely. The giant himself, dismayed by that sound, came rushing out of his room where he had been busy courting Duessa. Glaring in fury, and with staggering steps, the giant leapt to see what the sudden and strange ruckus was about, and who dared challenge his dreaded power.

VI And after him the proud *Duessa* came,
High mounted on her manyheaded beast,
And euery head with fyrie tongue did flame,
And euery head was crowned on his creast,
And bloudie mouthed with late cruell feast.
That when the knight beheld, his mightie shild
Vpon his manly arme he soone addrest,
And at him fiercely flew, with courage fild,
And eger greedinesse through euery member thrild.

VII Therewith the Gyant buckled him to fight,
Inflam'd with scornefull wrath and high disdaine,
And lifting vp his dreadfull club on hight,
All arm'd with ragged snubbes and knottie graine,
Him thought at first encounter to haue slaine,
But wise and warie was that noble Pere,
And lightly leaping from so monstrous maine,
Did faire auoide the violence him nere;
It booted nought, to thinke, such thunderbolts to beare.

VIII Ne shame he thought to shunne so hideous might:
The idle stroke, enforcing furious way,
Missing the marke of his misaymed sight
Did fall to ground, and with his heauie sway
So deepely dinted in the driuen clay,
That three yardes deepe a furrow vp did throw:
The sad earth wounded with so sore assay,
Did grone full grieuous vnderneath the blow,
And trembling with strange feare, did like an earthquake show.

IX As when almightie *Ioue* in wrathfull mood,
To wreake the guilt of mortall sins is bent,
Hurles forth his thundring dart with deadly food,
Enrold in flames, and smouldring dreriment,
Through riuen cloudes and molten firmament;
The fierce threeforked engin making way,
Both loftie towres and highest trees hath rent,
And all that might his angrie passage stay,
And shooting in the earth, casts vp a mount of clay.

X His boystrous club, so buried in the ground,
He could not rearen vp againe so light,
But that the knight him at auantage found,
And whiles he stroue his combred clubbe to quight
Out of the earth, with blade all burning bright
He smote off his left arme, which like a blocke
Did fall to ground, depriu'd of natiue might;
Large streames of bloud out of the truncked stocke
Forth gushed, like fresh water streame from riuen rocke.

6 After him, rushed proud Duessa, riding on the back of her many-headed beast. Every head was topped with a crown, every mouth flamed with fiery tongues, and every jaw dribbled with bloody gobbets from its latest cruel feast. When the great knight beheld this sight, his mighty shield ready upon his arm, he flew at the giant fiercely, filled with courage and eager to do battle.

Therewith the great ogre readied himself for the fight, inflamed with scornful wrath and proud disdain. Lifting his dreadful club, all armed with ragged snags and knotted roots, he expected an easy win. He slammed it down upon the knight, and thought he had slain him on the first encounter. But that noble champion was wise and wary, and leapt lightly from so monstrous a power. He then continued to dodge the hideous strokes and idle strikes that kept missing their mark. It proved useless to think such boulders to bear, and there was no knightly shame in dodging such immense might. So the giant's club missed its mark and fell to the ground with such heavy sway, that he deeply dented the driven clay and left a furrow, three yards deep. The sad wounded earth groaned grievously underneath the blow, and trembled with strange fear like an earthquake.

When mighty Jove is in a wrathful mood, and determined to punish mortal sins, he hurls forth his thundering dart with deadly strife. Enrolled in flames and smoldering gloom, the forces of nature make their way through riven clouds and molten earth, the battering ram of thunder, fire and darkness rips up lofty towers, highest trees, and everything else that might prevent his angry passage. Then, while shooting at the earth, Jove casts up a mountain eruption of molten clay.

10 The giant struggled hard to retrieve the colossal club that was now stuck fast in the ground. Meanwhile, the knight took advantage of this opportunity, and with his bright, burning blade, he smote off the giant's left arm, which fell like a lump of stone to the ground, depriving him of his natural might. Large streams of blood gushed out of the truncated stump, like a fresh stream of water from a riven rock.

XI Dismaied with so desperate deadly wound,
And eke impatient of vnwonted paine,
He loudly brayd with beastly yelling sound,
That all the fields rebellowed againe;
As great a noyse, as when in Cymbrian plaine
An heard of Bulles, whom kindly rage doth sting,
Do for the milkie mothers want complaine,
And fill the fields with troublous bellowing,
The neighbour woods around with hollow murmur ring.

XII That when his deare *Duessa* heard, and saw
The euill stownd, that daungerd her estate,
Vnto his aide she hastily did draw
Her dreadfull beast, who swolne with bloud of late
Came ramping forth with proud presumpteous gate,
And threatned all his heads like flaming brands.
But him the Squire made quickly to retrate,
Encountring fierce with single sword in hand,
And twixt him and his Lord did like a bulwarke stand.

XIII The proud *Duessa* full of wrathfull spight,
And fierce disdaine, to be affronted so,
Enforst her purple beast with all her might
That stop out of the way to ouerthroe,
Scorning the let of so vnequall foe:
But nathemore would that courageous swayne
To her yeeld passage, gainst his Lord to goe,
But with outrageous strokes did him restraine,
And with his body bard the way atwixt them twaine.

XIV Then tooke the angrie witch her golden cup,
Which still she bore, replete with magick artes;
Death and despeyre did many thereof sup,
And secret poyson through their inner parts,
Th'eternall bale of heauie wounded harts;
Which after charmes and some enchauntments said,
She lightly sprinkled on his weaker parts;
Therewith his sturdie courage soone was quayd,
And all his senses were with suddeine dread dismayd.

XV So downe he fell before the cruell beast,
Who on his necke his bloudie clawes did seize,
That life nigh crusht out of his panting brest:
No powre he had to stirre, nor will to rize.
That when the carefull knight gan well auise,
He lightly left the foe, with whom he fought,
And to the beast gan turne his enterprise;
For wondrous anguish in his hart it wrought,
To see his loued Squire into such thraldome brought.

11 Dismayed with so desperate and deadly a wound, as well as frantic with unwanted pain, he brayed loudly with beastly yelling, until the fields themselves echoed. The noise was so great that it sounded like a herd of bulls on a Cymbrian plain, whose natural urges for their mothers' milk made them fill the fields with troublous bellowing, reverberating in neighboring woods.

Then when the giant's dear Duessa heard and saw the evil plight that endangered her state, she hastily drew unto his aid. On her dreadful beast's back, swollen with blood from its latest feast, its bobbing heads threatening like flaming brands, she came bounding forth with proud presumptuous pace. But the squire countered fiercely with his single sword in hand, forcing her to retreat quickly while he stood like a barricade for his knight lord. Proud Duessa, full of wrathful spite and fierce disdain to have been confronted like this, compelled her purple beast to overthrow this hindrance to her unequal foe. But that courageous youth would not give passage to his lord, and barred the way between the two.

Then the angry witch took her golden cup, filled with magic arts. Many drank of its death and despair, and secret poison seeped through their inner parts, eternally tormenting their hearts. After uttering some charms and enchantments, Duessa sprinkled the magic potion on the squire's weaker parts, and his strength and senses began to dwindle.

15 Down he fell before the cruel beast who seized him by the neck with his bloody claws, trying to crush the life out of his panting breast. No more power had that brave squire to stir, or will to rise. But when the caring knight noticed this, he left fighting the giant foe and turned his enterprise to the beast, for such anguish it wrought in his heart to see his beloved squire in such a lowly state.

XVI And high aduauncing his bloud-thirstie blade,
Stroke one of those deformed heads so sore,
That of his puissance proud ensample made;
His monstrous scalpe downe to his teeth it tore,
And that misformed shape mis-shaped more:
A sea of bloud gusht from the gaping wound,
That her gay garments staynd with filthy gore,
And ouerflowed all the field around;
That ouer shoes in bloud he waded on the ground.

XVII Thereat he roared for exceeding paine,
That to haue heard, great horror would haue bred,
And scourging th'emptie ayre with his long traine,
Through great impatience of his grieued hed
His gorgeous ryder from her loftie sted
Would haue cast downe, and trod in durtie myre,
Had not the Gyant soone her succoured;
Who all enrag'd with smart and franticke yre,
Came hurtling in full fierce, and forst the knight retyre.

XVIII The force, which wont in two to be disperst,
In one alone left hand he now vnites,
Which is through rage more strong then both were erst;
With which his hideous club aloft he dites,
And at his foe with furious rigour smites,
That strongest Oake might seeme to ouerthrow.
The stroke vpon his shield so heauie lites,
That to the ground it doubleth him full low
What mortall wight could euer beare so monstrous blow?

XIX And in his fall his shield, that couered was,
Did loose his vele by chaunce, and open flew:
The light whereof, that heauens light did pas,
Such blazing brightnesse through the aier threw,
That eye mote not the same endure to vew.
Which when the Gyaunt spyde with staring eye,
He downe let fall his arme, and soft withdrew
His weapon huge, that heaued was on hye
For to haue slaine the man, that on the ground did lye.

XX And eke the fruitfull-headed beast, amaz'd
At flashing beames of that sunshiny shield,
Became starke blind, and all his senses daz'd,
That downe he tumbled on the durtie field,
And seem'd himselfe as conquered to yield.
Whom when his maistresse proud perceiu'd to fall,
Whiles yet his feeble feet for faintnesse reeld,
Vnto the Gyant loudly she gan call,
O helpe *Orgoglio*, helpe, or else we perish all.

16 Lifting his sword up high, the knight slammed his blade down upon one of those deformed heads so strongly, that its skull was torn down to its teeth. That malformed twisted shape, now even more misshapen, gushed blood from its gaping wound, while Duessa's gay garments were soon stained with filthy gore. The gaping wound overflowed into the field around them, and they were now wading in blood.

The monster roared with intense pain: a noise that, to have heard, would have bred great horror. Scourging the empty air with its long tail over its riven head in a frenzy, it would have thrown its gorgeous rider from her lofty seat and trod on her in dirty mud, had not the giant come to her aid. Enraged with pain and frantic ire, he came hurtling in full fierce, and forced the great knight to retreat.

The giant's strength, which was usually dispersed between two arms, was now united in the one remaining hand. With even fiercer rage than when he had both arms, the giant raised his grotesque club and aimed it at his foe. With furious ferocity, he smote that strongest oak upon the knight's shield so heavily, that he doubled over and fell on the ground. What mortal creature could ever bear so monstrous a blow?

But as it struck his enchanted shield, its veil flew open, beaming blazing brightness through the air. Surpassing the light of the heavens, its brilliance was unendurable to the eye.

When the giant beheld this light with staring eyes, he let his arm fall softly, dropping his huge weapon that had been hefted on high, ready to slay the knight lying on ground.

20 The many-headed beast, stunned by the flashing beams of that sunshiny shield, became stark blind. With all its senses so dazed, it tumbled down on a dirty field: a jumbled mass of twisted features and wobbling flesh.

When proud Duessa saw the giant reeling on his feeble feet, about to fall, she called loudly unto him, "Oh help, Orgoglio, help, or else we all perish!"

XXI At her so pitteous cry was much amoou'd
Her champion stout, and for to ayde his frend,
Againe his wonted angry weapon proou'd:
But all in vaine: for he has read his end
In that bright shield, and all their forces spend
Themselues in vaine: for since that glauncing sight,
He hath no powre to hurt, nor to defend;
As where th'Almighties lightning brond does light,
It dimmes the dazed eyen, and daunts the senses quight.

XXII Whom when the Prince, to battell new addrest,
And threatning high his dreadfull stroke did see,
His sparkling blade about his head he blest,
And smote off quite his right leg by the knee,
That downe he tombled; as an aged tree,
High growing on the top of rocky clift,
Whose hartstrings with keene steele nigh hewen be,
The mightie trunck halfe rent, with ragged rift
Doth roll adowne the rocks, and fall with fearefull drift.

XXIII Or as a Castle reared high and round,
By subtile engins and malitious slight
Is vndermined from the lowest ground
And her foundation forst, and feebled quight,
At last downe falles, and with her heaped hight
Her hastie ruine does more heauie make,
And yields it selfe vnto the victours might;
Such was this Gyaunts fall, that seemd to shake
The stedfast globe of earth, as it for feare did quake.

XXIV The knight then lightly leaping to the pray,
With mortall steele him smot againe so sore,
That headlesse his vnweldy bodie lay,
All wallowd in his owne fowle bloudy gore,
Which flowed from his wounds in wondrous store,
But soone as breath out of his breast did pas,
That huge great body, which the Gyaunt bore,
Was vanisht quite, and of that monstrous mas
Was nothing left, but like an emptie bladder was.

XXV Whose grieuous fall, when false *Duessa* spyde,
Her golden cup she cast vnto the ground,
And crowned mitre rudely threw aside;
Such percing griefe her stubborne hart did wound,
That she could not endure that dolefull stound,
But leauing all behind her, fled away:
The light-foot Squire her quickly turnd around,
And by hard meanes enforcing her to stay,
So brought vnto his Lord, as his deserued pray.

21 At her so piteous cry, her brave champion again tried to raise his angry weapon, but it was all in vain, for he had read his end in the reflection of that bright shield, and knew his forces were now in vain. For in that dazzling light, he had neither power to harm, nor means to defend. As where the Almighty's lightening torch alights, it dims the dazzled eyes, and daunts the senses.

The princely knight then renewed his battle, threatening a high dreadful stroke, and brandishing his sparkling blade above his head. Briefly blessing the air between them, he then swung his sword downwards and chopped off the giant's right leg at the knee.

Down tumbled the giant, just like an old tree, long growing on a rocky cliff top, its hardy remaining roots still clinging to the earth. The mighty trunk splits in half as it crashes on the ragged rocks, and falls with a fearful shudder. Or as a castle, built high and mighty, but is undermined from the ground by canons, battering rams, and clever battle strategies. Since her foundations are broken down and weakened, down she falls, and is reduced to rubble. Her hasty ruin then makes her heavier, easily yielding herself to her victor's might. Such was this giant's fall that seemed to shake the steadfast globe of the entire earth, as it quaked in fear.

Leaping lightly upon his prey, the knight smote him a deadly blow, leaving his headless unwieldy body to wallow in its own foul and bloody gore, which flowed out of a store of wounds. Like a deflated balloon, the huge body that the giant had borne quite vanished so that, of his monstrous mass, there was nothing more.

25 But when false Duessa saw this grievous fall, she cast her golden cup onto the ground, and threw her crown aside in a violent tantrum. Such piercing grief now wounded her stubborn heart that she could not endure that doleful sight, and began to flee. But the light-footed squire quickly seized her and brought her to his lord as his deserved prey.

XXVI The royall Virgin, which beheld from farre,
In pensiue plight, and sad perplexitie,
The whole atchieuement of this doubtfull warre,
Came running fast to greet his victorie,
With sober gladnesse, and myld modestie,
And with sweet ioyous cheare him thus bespake;
Faire braunch of noblesse, flowre of cheualrie,
That with your worth the world amazed make,
How shall I quite the paines, ye suffer for my sake?

XXVII And you fresh bud of vertue springing fast,
Whom these sad eyes saw nigh vnto deaths dore,
What hath poore Virgin for such perill past,
Wherewith you to reward? Accept therefore
My simple selfe, and seruice euermore;
And he that high does sit, and all things see
With equall eyes, their merites to restore,
Behold what ye this day haue done for mee,
And what I cannot quite, requite with vsuree.

XXVIII But sith the heauens, and your faire handeling
Haue made you maister of the field this day,
Your fortune maister eke with gouerning,
And well begun end all so well, I pray,
Ne let that wicked woman scape away;
For she it is, that did my Lord bethrall,
My dearest Lord, and deepe in dongeon lay,
Where he his better dayes hath wasted all.
O heare, how piteous he to you for ayd does call.

XXIX Forthwith he gaue in charge vnto his Squire,
That scarlot whore to keepen carefully;
Whiles he himselfe with greedie great desire
Into the Castle entred forcibly,
Where liuing creature none he did espye;
Then gan he lowdly through the house to call:
But no man car'd to answere to his crye.
There raignd a solemne silence ouer all,
Nor voice was heard, nor wight was seene in bowre or hall.

XXX At last with creeping crooked pace forth came
An old old man, with beard as white as snow,
That on a staffe his feeble steps did frame,
And guide his wearie gate both too and fro:
For his eye sight him failed long ygo,
And on his arme a bounch of keyes he bore,
The which vnused rust did ouergrow:
Those were the keyes of euery inner dore,
But he could not them vse, but kept them still in store.

---

26 The royal maiden, who beheld the whole achievement of this doubtful and dreaded war in fearful plight and sad anguish, came running fast to greet his victory with gracious gladness.

Addressing the knight with sweet joyous cheer, she said, "Fair child of nobility, flower of chivalry, that with your worth the world stands amazed, how shall I repay you for the pains you have suffered for my sake? And you, O squire, fresh bud of virtue blossoming fast, whom these sad eyes saw so close to death's door, how can a poor maiden reward you for such peril now past? Accept, then, my simple self at your service evermore. And may He who sits high, who sees all things with the eyes of justice, and rewards our merits, behold what you did this day for me. And that which I cannot quite repay, God will, plus interest.

"But since the heavens and your fair handling have made you master of the field this day, I pray for that which began well, will end just as well. Let not the wicked woman escape, for it is she who enslaved my dearest lord knight Redcross, where he still lies deep in the dungeon, wasting his better days. O hear how piteously he calls to you for aid!"

Forthwith, the princely knight ordered his squire to keep careful charge of that scarlet whore. Then, with keen determination, he forcibly entered the castle and found it deserted.

"Anyone there?" he shouted, and paused to listen. But no answer came, and there seemed to reign a solemn silence over all. No voice was heard, no living creature was seen, in bower or in hall.

30 At length, Arthur heard sluggish footsteps creeping towards him with a crooked pace, and an old, old man appeared. His beard was as white as snow, and he held a tall staff to support his feeble footsteps and weary gait, for his eyesight had failed him long ago. On his arm he bore a bunch of keys that looked unused, from the amount of overgrown rust. They were the keys to every inner door, but he would not use them, and kept the kingdom locked up.

XXXI But very vncouth sight was to behold,
How he did fashion his vntoward pace,
For as he forward moou'd his footing old,
So backward still was turnd his wrincled face,
Vnlike to men, who euer as they trace,
Both feet and face one way are wont to lead.
This was the auncient keeper of that place,
And foster father of the Gyant dead;
His name *Ignaro* did his nature right aread.

XXXII His reuerend haires and holy grauitie
The knight much honord, as beseemed well,
And gently askt, where all the people bee,
Which in that stately building wont to dwell.
Who answerd him full soft, he could not tell.
Againe he askt, where that same knight was layd,
Whom great *Orgoglio* with his puissaunce fell
Had made his caytiue thrall; againe he sayde,
He could not tell: ne euer other answere made.

XXXIII Then asked he, which way he in might pas:
He could not tell, againe he answered.
Thereat the curteous knight displeased was,
And said, Old sire, it seemes thou hast not red
How ill it sits with that same siluer hed
In vaine to mocke, or mockt in vaine to bee:
But if thou be, as thou art pourtrahed
With natures pen, in ages graue degree,
Aread in grauer wise, what I demaund of thee.

XXXIV His answere likewise was, he could not tell.
Whose senceless speach, and doted ignorance
When as the noble Prince had marked well,
He ghest his nature by his countenance,
And calmd his wrath with goodly temperance.
Then to him stepping, from his arme did reach
Those keyes, and made himselfe free enterance.
Each dore he opened without any breach;
There was no barre to stop, nor foe him to empeach.

XXXV There all within full rich arayd he found,
With royall arras and resplendent gold.
And did with store of euery thing abound,
That greatest Princes presence might behold.
But all the floore (too filthy to be told)
With bloud of guiltlesse babes, and innocents trew,
Which there were slaine, as sheepe out of the fold,
Defiled was, that dreadfull was to vew,
And sacred ashes ouer it was strowed new.

31 He was not a very pleasant sight to behold either because, as he moved his old feet forward, his wrinkled face was turned backwards, unlike the usual, where men's feet and face lead the same way. But this was the ancient keeper of the place, foster father of the dead giant. His name was Ignaro, his nature being aligned with ignorance.

The noble knight bowed low in respect, honoring his age and holy gravity. Then he politely asked the old man where, in a stately building such as this, all the people might be.

"I cannot tell," came the soft reply.

Puzzled by this enigmatic reply, but not deterred, the knight then asked where that young knight, whom the great Orgoglio felled with his deadly power and made captive, might be kept.

"I cannot tell," came the answer once again.

Then the knight asked which way he might pass.

"I cannot tell," again he answered.

At that, the courteous knight was displeased, and he said, "Old sire, it seems you have not understood how ill it sits with that same silver head, to mock in vain, or to be mocked in vain. But if you be, as you are portrayed with nature's pen, old enough to be in the grave, be equally wise in proportion to your age, and grant what I ask of you."

"I cannot tell," came his answer yet again.

The princely knight calmed his own wrath with goodly temperance, marking well that the ignorant old man was probably feeble-minded and incapable of sensible speech. Stepping towards him, he reached forward and simply took the keys unopposed.

35 With them, he was able to open every door in the castle without any force. There was no bar to stop him, and no foe to oppose him. Therein, he found every room richly arrayed with royal tapestries and resplendent gold. Everything abounded with such abundance, befitting the presence of even the greatest prince. But the floor—too filthy to be told—was defiled with the blood of guiltless babes and true innocents, slain like sheep out of the fold. This dreadful sight was then strewn with fresh and recent sacred ashes.

XXXVI And there beside of marble stone was built
An Altare, caru'd with cunning imagery,
On which true Christians bloud was often spilt,
And holy Martyrs often doen to dye,
With cruell malice and strong tyranny:
Whose blessed sprites from vnderneath the stone
To God for vengeance cryde continually,
And with great griefe were often heard to grone,
That hardest heart would bleede, to heare their piteous mone.

XXXVII Through euery rowme he sought, and euery bowr,
But no where could he find that wofull thrall:
At last he came vnto an yron doore,
That fast was lockt, but key found not at all
Emongst that bounch, to open it withall;
But in the same a little grate was pight,
Through which he sent his voyce, and lowd did call
With all his powre, to weet, if liuing wight
Were housed therewithin, whom he enlargen might.

XXXVIII Therewith an hollow, dreary, murmuring voyce
These piteous plaints and dolours did resound;
O who is that, which brings me happy choyce
Of death, that here lye dying euery stound,
Yet liue perforce in balefull darkenesse bound?
For now three Moones haue changed thrice their hew,
And haue beene thrice hid vnderneath the ground,
Since I the heauens chearefull face did vew,
O welcome thou, that doest of death bring tydings trew.

XXXIX Which when that Champion heard, with percing point
Of pitty deare his hart was thrilled sore,
And trembling horrour ran through euery ioynt,
For ruth of gentle knight so fowle forlore:
Which shaking off, he rent that yron dore,
With furious force, and indignation fell;
Where entred in, his foot could find no flore,
But all a deepe descent, as darke as hell,
That breathed euer forth a filthie banefull smell.

XL But neither darkenesse fowle, nor filthy bands,
Nor noyous smell his purpose could withhold,
(Entire affection hateth nicer hands)
But that with constant zeale, and courage bold,
After long paines and labours manifold,
He found the meanes that Prisoner vp to reare;
Whose feeble thighes, vnhable to vphold
His pined corse, him scarse to light could beare,
A ruefull spectacle of death and ghastly drere.

36 In the midst of it all, was a marble altar, carved with cunning imagery, on which true Christian blood was often spilt, and holy martyrs left to die. [3] From underneath the altar, those blessed spirits were often heard to groan, crying continually for God's vengeance. Even the hardest heart would bleed to hear their piteous moans.

The noble knight sought through every room and bower, but nowhere could he find that woeful captive. At last he came upon an iron door that was locked fast, but that no key in the bunch would open. In the same door was a little window grate, and through it he called loudly with all his power, asking if there were any living creature within whom he might free.

Therewith, a hollow, dreary murmuring voice echoed with these piteous plaints and laments, "O who is he who brings me happy choice of death, to him who here dies every moment, forced in baleful darkness bound? For three months now I have been hidden underneath the ground, and it is three months since I viewed the cheerful heavens. O welcome, you who brings me true tidings of death!"

When that champion heard this, his heart was full of pity to piercing point, and trembling horror ran in every vein with sympathy for the gentle knight who was now so foul forlorn. With furious force, and fierce indignation, he ripped that iron door off its hinges with his bare hands. But when his foot tried to find the floor, he realized that there was none: only a deep descent, dark as hell, from which rose a filthy baneful smell.

40 But neither foul darkness nor filthy bonds, nor noxious smell could withhold his purpose, for true love does not hesitate to get its hands dirty in service of another. With constant zeal and bold courage, after long pains and many labors, he finally found a means to get the prisoner out.

The youth's now feeble body and wasted thigh muscles were barely able to hold him up. He could scarcely tolerate the light, and was a rueful sight to behold.

XLI His sad dull eyes deepe sunck in hollow pits,
Could not endure th'vnwonted sunne to view;
His bare thin cheekes for want of better bits,
And empty sides deceiued of their dew,
Could make a stony hart his hap to rew;
His rawbone armes, whose mighty brawned bowrs
Were wont to riue steele plates, and helmets hew,
Were cleane consum'd, and all his vitall powres
Decayd, and all his flesh shronk vp like withered flowres.

XLII Whom when his Lady saw, to him she ran
With hasty ioy: to see him made her glad,
And sad to view his visage pale and wan,
Who earst in flowres of freshest youth was clad.
Tho when her well of teares she wasted had,
She said, Ah dearest Lord, what euill starre
On you hath fround, and pourd his influence bad,
That of your selfe ye thus berobbed arre,
And this misseeming hew your manly looks doth marre?

XLIII But welcome now my Lord, in wele or woe,
Whose presence I haue lackt too long a day;
And fie on Fortune mine auowed foe,
Whose wrathfull wreakes them selues do now alay.
And for these wrongs shall treble penaunce pay
Of treble good: good growes of euils priefe.
The chearelesse man, whom sorrow did dismay,
Had no delight to treaten of his griefe;
His long endured famine needed more reliefe.

XLIV Faire Lady, then said that victorious knight,
The things, that grieuous were to do, or beare,
Them to renew, I wote, breeds no delight:
Best musicke breeds delight in loathing eare:
But th'onely good, that growes of passed feare,
Is to be wise, and ware of like agein.
This dayes ensample hath this lesson deare
Deepe written in my heart with yron pen,
That blisse may not abide in state of mortall men.

XLV Henceforth sir knight, take to you wonted strength,
And maister these mishaps with patient might;
Loe where your foe lyes stretcht in monstrous length,
And loe that wicked woman in your sight,
The roote of all your care, and wretched plight,
Now in your powre, to let her liue, or dye.
To do her dye (quoth *Vna*) were despight,
And shame t'auenge so weake an enimy;
But spoile her of her scarlot robe, and let her fly.

41 With his sad dull eyes, sunk deep in hollow pits, he squinted at the unaccustomed view of sunlight. His bare cheeks were sunken for want of proper food, and his waist was thin, having almost starved to death. His lanky arms, whose mighty brawny muscles could at one time shatter steel plates and split helmets in half, were just skin and bone. All his vital powers were decayed, and all his flesh shriveled like withered flowers.

When his lady saw him, she ran to him with hasty joy. To see her Redcross made her glad, but also sad to see his visage so pale and wasted who, before, was the freshest flower of youth.

When her well of tears had been used up, she said, "Oh dearest lord knight, what evil star on you has frowned and poured his bad fortunes, so that you are so pale and robbed of your manly looks? But welcome now my lord knight, in sickness and in health, whose company I have missed for too long a day. Fie on Fortune, my avowed foe, whose wrathful troubles themselves do now allay. For these wrongs, she shall pay triple penance of triple good, because good grows out of man's evil lessons."

The cheerless man, dismayed by sorrow, had no delight to talk of his distress. He had too long endured a famine and now needed some relief.

"Fair lady," then said the victorious noble knight. "To recall the things that were grievous to do, or bear, breeds no delight. Only the best music, not a recital, may breed delight in loathing ear. But the only good that grows out of passed fear, is to grow wise from the experience, and to be wary not to repeat the errors. This day's example, and this dire lesson, has been written deep in my heart with iron pen: that earthly pleasures are fleeting in the state of mortal men. **45** Henceforth, Sir knight of the Redcross, take back your strength and learn from these mishaps with patient might. Lo, there lies your foe, stretched in monstrous length, and lo, that wicked woman in your sight, the root of all your trouble and wretched plight, is now in your power to let live or die."

"To kill her would just be vindictive," cautioned Una, "and shameful to avenge so weak an enemy. But strip her of her scarlet robe, and then let her flee."

XLVI So as she bad, that witch they disaraid,
And robd of royall robes, and purple pall,
And ornaments that richly were displaid;
Ne spared they to strip her naked all.
Then when they had despoild her tire and call,
Such as she was, their eyes might her behold,
That her misshaped parts did them appall,
A loathly, wrinckled hag, ill fauoured, old,
Whose secret filth good manners biddeth not be told.

XLVII Her craftie head was altogether bald,
And as in hate of honorable eld,
Was ouergrowne with scurfe and filthy scald;
Her teeth out of her rotten gummes were feld,
And her sowre breath abhominably smeld;
Her dried dugs, like bladders lacking wind,
Hong downe, and filthy matter from them weld;
Her wrizled skin as rough, as maple rind,
So scabby was, that would haue loathd all womankind.

XLVIII Her neather parts, the shame of all her kind,
My chaster Muse for shame doth blush to write;
But at her rompe she growing had behind
A foxes taile, with dong all fowly dight;
And eke her feete most monstrous were in sight;
For one of them was like an Eagles claw,
With griping talaunts armd to greedy fight,
The other like a Beares vneuen paw:
More vgly shape yet neuer liuing creature saw.

XLIX Which when the knights beheld, amazd they were,
And wondred at so fowle deformed wight.
Such then (said *Vna*) as she seemeth here,
Such is the face of falshood, such the sight
Of fowle *Duessa*, when her borrowed light
Is laid away, and counterfesaunce knowne.
Thus when they had the witch disrobed quight,
And all her filthy feature open showne,
They let her goe at will, and wander wayes vnknowne.

L She flying fast from heauens hated face,
And from the world that her discouered wide,
Fled to the wastfull wildernesse apace,
From liuing eyes her open shame to hide,
And lurkt in rocks and caues long vnespide.
But that faire crew of knights, and *Vna* faire
Did in that castle afterwards abide,
To rest them selues, and weary powres repaire,
Where store they found of all, that dainty was and rare.

---

46 So, as Una suggested, they stripped the witch of her robbed royal robes and purple gown, and of her richly displayed ornaments. Then off came the tiara and headdress: they spared nothing in stripping her naked. Finally, she stood in front of them as she really was: a loathsome, ill favored, wrinkled old hag, whose secret filth had been hidden behind fake good manners. They stood appalled at the misshapen parts their eyes beheld. Her deceitful head was altogether bald, having preferred that to honorable grey hair. Her scalp was overgrown with sores and filthy scabs. Her teeth were falling out of their rotten gums, and her sour breath smelled abominably. Her shriveled breasts hung down like deflated balloons, oozing filthy matter. Her frizzled skin was as rough as maple bark, and so scabby, that it was an insult to womankind.

My modest Muse blushes to write about her nether parts: the shame of all her kindred. But, behind her rump, she grew a crafty fox's tail all covered in dung. And her feet were a monstrous sight, for one of them was like a predatory eagle's claw, with gripping talons armed to greedy fight. The other foot was like a cruel bear's rugged paw, and no living creature saw such an ugly shape.

When the knights beheld this sight they were amazed, and they wondered at how so foul a deformed creature could exist.

"Such then," said Una, "as she seems here, such is the face of falsehood, such is the sight of the foul Duessa, when her borrowed virtue is laid away, and her deceit uncovered."

Thus, when they had disrobed the witch, and all her filthy features were brought to light, they let her go at will to wander unknown ways.

50 Fast she fled from heaven's hated face, and from the world that had discovered her. Swiftly, she fled to the desolate wilderness to hide her shame away from living eyes. There she lurked in long forgotten rocks and caves.

BUT THAT FAIR COMPANY OF KNIGHTS, SQUIRE, DWARF AND FAIR UNA, STAYED IN that castle to rest themselves and repair their strength. In the well stocked pantry there, they found all the fare they needed, including precious and rare treats.

1 Hamilton, AC. Spenser The Faerie Queene. New York: Routledge, 2007. Print

2 Her: both Truth and Una

3 holy martyrs left to die: referring to persecutions of Protestants

CANTO IX

ESCAPE FROM THE CAVE OF DESPAIR

His loues and lignage Arthur tells
The knights knit friendly bands:
Sir Treuisan flies from Despayre,
Whom Redcrosse knight withstands.

I O Goodly golden chaine, wherewith yfere
The vertues linked are in louely wize:
And noble minds of yore allyed were,
In braue poursuit of cheualrous emprize,
That none did others safety despize,
Nor aid enuy to him, in need that stands,
But friendly each did others prayse deuize
How to aduaunce with fauourable hands,
As this good Prince redeemd the *Redcrosse* knight from bands.

II Who when their powres, empaird through labour long,
With dew repast they had recured well,
And that weake captiue wight now wexed strong,
Them list no lenger there at leasure dwell,
But forward fare, as their aduentures fell,
But ere they parted, *Vna* faire besought
That straunger knight his name and nation tell;
Least so great good, as he for her had wrought,
Should die vnknown, and buried be in thanklesse thought.

III Faire virgin (said the Prince) ye me require
A thing without the compas of my wit:
For both the lignage and the certain Sire,
From which I sprong, from me are hidden yit.
For all so soone as life did me admit
Into this world, and shewed heauens light,
From mothers pap I taken was vnfit:
And streight deliuered to a Faery knight,
To be vpbrought in gentle thewes and martiall might.

IV Vnto old *Timon* he me brought byliue,
Old *Timon*, who in youthly yeares hath beene
In warlike feates th'expertest man aliue,
And is the wisest now on earth I weene;
His dwelling is low in a valley greene,
Vnder the foot of *Rauran* mossy hore,
From whence the riuer *Dee* as siluer cleene
His tombling billowes rolls with gentle rore:
There all my dayes he traind me vp in vertuous lore.

V Thither the great Magicien *Merlin* came,
As was his vse, ofttimes to visit me:
For he had charge my discipline to frame,
And Tutours nouriture to ouersee.
Him oft and oft I askt in priuitie,
Of what loines and what lignage I did spring:
Whose aunswere bad me still assured bee,
That I was sonne and heire vnto a king,
As time in her iust terme the truth to light should bring.

Arthur tells of his loves and linage, and the knights knit friendly bands.
Sir Trevisan flies from Despair, whom the Redcross knight withstands.

O GOODLY GOLDEN CHAIN WHEREWITH THE VIRTUES ARE LINKED TOGETHER IN lovely ways, and noble minds of yore were allied in brave pursuit of chivalrous enterprise. None did others' safety disregard, nor begrudge him aid in need. But each composed friendly praises to the other. Advancing as such, in favorable hands, this good prince knight redeemed the Redcross knight from bonds.

WHEN THEIR POWERS, IMPAIRED THROUGH LONG LABOR, WERE WELL RECOVERED from due rest, and that weak captive creature had now grown strong, they resolved to dwell no longer at leisure. It was time to forward fare, and discover where their adventures fell. But before they parted, fair Una asked that stranger knight to tell them his name and nation, so that his great good should not be forgotten.

"Fair maiden," began the prince, "I am Arthur. But, beyond my name, you request a thing outside the scope of my knowledge. Both the lineage, and the certain father from which I sprang, are still hidden from me. For as so soon as I entered this world and saw heaven's light, I was taken, unripe, from my mother's breast, and delivered to a Faerie knight to be brought up in gentlemanly disciplines of martial might.

"I was hastily brought unto old Timon who, in his youth, had been the most expert man alive in warlike feats, and I believe he is now the wisest man on earth. His dwelling lies low in a green valley, under the foot of moss-covered Mount Rauran[1]. From there flows the river Dee, silver clean: its tumbling billows rolling with gentle roar. There, all my days, he trained me up in virtuous lore.

5 "Thither, the great Magician Merlin came oftentimes to visit me, as was his habit. For he had charge of my education, formation, and tutor's nurturance to oversee. So many times, I asked him in secret, "Of what lineage did I spring?" His answer was always the same: that I was the son and heir unto a king, and when the time was right, he would bring the truth to light."

VI Well worthy impe, said then the Lady gent,
And Pupill fit for such a Tutours hand.
But what aduenture, or what high intent
Hath brought you hither into Faery land,
Aread Prince *Arthur*, crowne of Martiall band?
Full hard it is (quoth he) to read aright
The course of heauenly cause, or vnderstand
The secret meaning of th'eternall might,
That rules mens wayes, and rules the thoughts of liuing wight.

VII For whether he through fatall deepe foresight
Me hither sent, for cause to me vnghest,
Or that fresh bleeding wound, which day and night
Whilome doth rancle in my riuen brest,
With forced fury following his behest,
Me hither brought by wayes yet neuer found,
You to haue helpt I hold my selfe yet blest.
Ah curteous knight (quoth she) what secret wound
Could euer find, to grieue the gentlest hart on ground?

VIII Deare Dame (quoth he) you sleeping sparkes awake,
Which troubled once, into huge flames will grow,
Ne euer will their feruent fury slake,
Till liuing moysture into smoke do flow,
And wasted life do lye in ashes low.
Yet sithens silence lesseneth not my fire,
But told it flames, and hidden it does glow,
I will reuele, what ye so much desire:
Ah Loue, lay downe thy bow, the whiles I may respire.

IX It was in freshest flowre of youthly yeares,
When courage first does creepe in manly chest,
Then first the coale of kindly heat appeares
To kindle loue in euery liuing brest;
But me had warnd old *Timons* wise behest,
Those creeping flames by reason to subdew,
Before their rage grew to so great vnrest,
As miserable louers vse to rew,
Which still wex old in woe, whiles woe still wexeth new.

X That idle name of loue, and louers life,
As losse of time, and vertues enimy
I euer scornd, and ioyd to stirre vp strife,
In middest of their mournfull Tragedy,
Ay wont to laugh, when them I heard to cry,
And blow the fire, which them to ashes brent:
Their God himselfe, grieu'd at my libertie,
Shot many a dart at me with fiers intent,
But I them warded all with wary gouernment.

6 "Well worthy child," said the lady gently, "And pupil fit for such a tutor's hand. But what adventure, or what high intent has brought you hither into Faerieland? Tell us, Prince Arthur; crown of martial band."

"It is hard to correctly discern the course of heavenly cause," replied the noble knight, "Or understand the secret meaning of the eternal might that rules men's ways and thoughts. For whether He, through fated deep foresight, sent me hither for a cause unguessed by me, or for that fresh bleeding wound, which day and night does constantly rankle in my riven breast, or by ways yet never found? Yet I hold myself blessed to have helped you."

"Oh courteous knight," she said, "what secret wound could ever find to grieve the gentlest heart on earth?"

"Dear Dame," he replied, "you are awakening sleeping sparks which, once troubled, will grow into huge flames. Their ever-burning fury will not subside till living moisture flows into smoke, and wasted life lies in low ashes. Yet since silence does not lessen my fire, but enflames it, and hidden it glows, I will reveal what you so much desire to know. Oh Cupid, lay down your bow a while, so that I may take some respite.

"It was during the freshest flower of my youthly years, when courage first creeps into a manly chest, and first appears the coal of natural heat to kindle love in every living heart. But old Timon had warned me with wise instructions to use reason to subdue those creeping flames before their rage grew to great unrest. He advised me that miserable lovers rue and grow old in woe, while their woe still grows new. **10** That idle name of love, that loss of time in a lover's life, that enemy of virtue, I ever scorned. I even enjoyed stirring up strife at the theatre during a play about a mournful tragedy. I would want to laugh when I heard them cry, and blow the fire which burnt them to ashes. Their god, Cupid, grieved at my liberty to do this, shot many a dart at me with fierce intent. But I avoided them all with wary self control.

XI But all in vaine: no fort can be so strong,
Ne fleshly brest can armed be so sound,
But will at last be wonne with battrie long,
Or vnawares at disauantage found;
Nothing is sure, that growes on earthly ground:
And who most trustes in arme of fleshly might,
And boasts, in beauties chaine not to be bound,
Doth soonest fall in disauentrous fight,
And yeeldes his caytiue neck to victours most despight.

XII Ensample make of him your haplesse ioy,
And of my selfe now mated, as ye see;
Whose prouder vaunt that proud auenging boy
Did soone pluck downe, and curbd my libertie.
For on a day prickt forth with iollitie
Of looser life, and heat of hardiment,
Raunging the forest wide on courser free,
The fields, the floods, the heauens with one consent
Did seeme to laugh on me, and fauour mine intent.

XIII For wearied with my sports, I did alight
From loftie steed, and downe to sleepe me layd;
The verdant gras my couch did goodly dight,
And pillow was my helmet faire displayd:
Whiles euery sence the humour sweet embayd,
And slombring soft my hart did steale away,
Me seemed, by my side a royall Mayd
Her daintie limbes full softly down did lay:
So faire a creature yet saw neuer sunny day.

XIV Most goodly glee and louely blandishment
She to me made, and bad me loue her deare,
For dearely sure her loue was to me bent,
As when iust time expired should appeare.
But whether dreames delude, or true it were,
Was neuer hart so rauisht with delight,
Ne liuing man like words did euer heare,
As she to me deliuered all that night;
And at her parting said, She Queene of Faeries hight.

XV When I awoke, and found her place deuoyd,
And nought but pressed gras, where she had lyen,
I sorrowed all so much, as earst I ioyd,
And washed all her place with watry eyen.
From that day forth I lou'd that face diuine;
From that day forth I cast in carefull mind,
To seeke her out with labour, and long tyne,
And neuer vow to rest, till her I find,
Nine monethes I seeke in vaine yet ni'll that vow vnbind.

11 Yet all was in vain. No fort can be so strong, no armored fleshy breast can be so sound, that will not at last be won by long term battering, or found unawares at a disadvantage. Nothing that grows on earthly ground is certain. He who most trusts in arms of fleshy might, and boasts not to be bound by beauty's chain, falls the soonest into unlucky flight, and yields his captive neck to Cupid's revenge.

To make an example of this unlucky joy, you see here checkmated, whose prouder boasting that proud avenging Cupid plucked down and curbed my liberty. For, one day, I was out riding with great jollity and freedom, looking for dares, freely ranging the wide forest, fields, and floods on a swift horse, while the heavens seemed to laugh on me and favor my intent. Once wearied with my sports, I dismounted from my lofty steed, and laid me down to sleep in the verdant grass, whose softness made a delightful bed, and my fair helmet, a pillow. While every sense was bathed in the sweet humor of sleep, and slumbering soft my heart did steal away, I sensed a royal maid by my side, her dainty limbs softly lying down. Never a sunny day yet saw such a fair creature. Most goodly glee and lovely flatteries she made to me, and bade me love her dear. For dearly sure her love was directed towards me, and would appear in full, when the proper time had expired. But whether dreams delude, or true it were, was never a heart so ravished with delight, nor living man like words did ever hear as she delivered to me all that night. And at her parting, she said she was called the Queene of Faeries.

15 "When I awoke and found the place deserted, and nothing but the flattened grass beside me where she had lain, I sorrowed as much as I had before rejoiced, and washed the empty place with watery tears. From that day forth I loved that divine face, and from that day forth I resolved, in careful mind, to seek her out with labor and long toil, and vowed never to rest until I find her. Nine months I have now been seeking in vain, yet never will that vow be unbound."

XVI Thus as he spake, his visage wexed pale,
And chaunge of hew great passion did bewray;
Yet still he stroue to cloke his inward bale,
And hide the smoke, that did his fire display,
Till gentle *Vna* thus to him gan say;
O happy Queene of Faeries, that hast found
Mongst many, one that with his prowesse may
Defend thine honour, and thy foes confound:
True Loues are often sown, but seldom grow on ground.

XVII Thine, O then, said the gentle *Redcrosse* knight,
Next to that Ladies loue, shalbe the place,
O fairest virgin, full of heauenly light,
Whose wondrous faith, exceeding earthly race,
Was firmest fixt in mine extremest case,
And you, my Lord, the Patrone of my life,
Of that great Queene may well gaine worthy grace:
For onely worthy you through prowes priefe
Yf liuing man mote worthy be, to be her liefe.

XVIII So diuersly discoursing of their loues,
The golden Sunne his glistring head gan shew,
And sad remembraunce now the Prince amoues,
With fresh desire his voyage to pursew:
Als *Vna* earnd her traueill to renew.
Then those two knights, fast friendship for to bynd,
And loue establish each to other trew,
Gaue goodly gifts, the signes of gratefull mynd,
And eke as pledges firme, right hands together ioynd.

XIX Prince *Arthur* gaue a boxe of Diamond sure,
Embowd with gold and gorgeous ornament,
Wherein were closd few drops of liquor pure,
Of wondrous worth, and vertue excellent,
That any wound could heale incontinent:
Which to requite, the *Redcrosse* knight him gaue
A booke, wherein his Saueours testament
Was writ with golden letters rich and braue;
A worke of wondrous grace, and able soules to saue.

XX Thus beene they parted, *Arthur* on his way
To seeke his loue, and th'other for to fight
With *Vnaes* foe, that all her realme did pray.
But she now weighing the decayed plight,
And shrunken synewes of her chosen knight,
Would not a while her forward course pursew,
Ne bring him forth in face of dreadfull fight,
Till he recouered had his former hew:
For him to be yet weake and wearie well she knew.

16 As Arthur spoke, his face became pale, and the change of hue revealed a great passion. Yet he still strove to cloak his inward pain and hide the smoke his inner fire displayed.

Then gentle Una began to speak, "O happy Queene of the Faeries who has found, amongst so many, one who with his prowess may defend her honor and confound her foes. True loves are often sown, but seldom grown on ground."

Then the gentle Redcross knight addressed Una, "Yours, O then, next to that of the Faerie Queene's love, shall be your place, O fairest maiden, full of heavenly light, whose wondrous loyalty exceeds our earthly race. These thoughts were strongest in my extreme plight. And you, my lord, Prince Arthur, shall be the patron of my life, and of that Great Queen, may you gain worthy grace. For your prowess will prove you worthy of her love."

And thus they sat together all night, discussing diverse ideas about love, until the golden sun's glistering head began to show, along with the sad realization that the princely knight will be moving on, with fresh desire to pursue his voyage. Loving friendship between the two knights had grown strong during their stay in the castle, and as a sign of loyalty and gratitude, they exchanged gifts, shook hands, and made pledges of loyalty. Prince Arthur gave them a box of pure diamond encircled with gold, and a gorgeous chalice containing a few drops of pure liquor of wondrous worth and excellent virtue, that could instantly heal any bleeding wound. In return, Redcross gave him a book wherein his Savior's testament was written in rich and splendid golden letters: a work of wondrous grace and salvation.

20 Thus, they parted: Arthur on his way to seek his love, and the other to fight the foe that plundered and preyed upon Una's realm. Meanwhile, Una weighed in on the situation with her chosen knight, who remained weak and weary. Until he had recovered his former self, she knew that Redcross would be incapable of pursuing the quest where he would certainly face a dreadful fight.

~

XXI So as they traueild, lo they gan espy
An armed knight towards them gallop fast,
That seemed from some feared foe to fly,
Or other griesly thing, that him agast.
Still as he fled, his eye was backward cast,
As if his feare still followed him behind;
Als flew his steed, as he his bands had brast,
And with his winged heeles did tread the wind,
As he had beene a fole of *Pegasus* his kind.

XXII Nigh as he drew, they might perceiue his head
To be vnarmd, and curld vncombed heares
Vpstaring stiffe, dismayd with vncouth dread;
Nor drop of bloud in all his face appeares
Nor life in limbe: and to increase his feares,
In fowle reproch of knighthoods faire degree,
About his neck an hempen rope he weares,
That with his glistring armes does ill agree;
But he of rope or armes has now no memoree.

XXIII The *Redcrosse* knight toward him crossed fast,
To weet, what mister wight was so dismayd:
There him he finds all sencelesse and aghast,
That of him selfe he seemd to be afrayd;
Whom hardly he from flying forward stayd,
Till he these wordes to him deliuer might;
Sir knight, aread who hath ye thus arayd,
And eke from whom make ye this hasty flight:
For neuer knight I saw in such misseeming plight.

XXIV He answerd nought at all, but adding new
Feare to his first amazment, staring wide
With stony eyes, and hartlesse hollow hew,
Astonisht stood, as one that had aspide
Infernall furies, with their chaines vntide.
Him yet againe, and yet againe bespake
The gentle knight; who nought to him replide,
But trembling euery ioynt did inly quake,
And foltring tongue at last these words seemd forth to shake.

XXV For Gods deare loue, Sir knight, do me not stay;
For loe he comes, he comes fast after mee.
Eft looking backe would faine haue runne away;
But he him forst to stay, and tellen free
The secret cause of his perplexitie:
Yet nathemore by his bold hartie speach,
Could his bloud-frosen hart emboldned bee,
But through his boldnesse rather feare did reach,
Yet forst, at last he made through silence suddein breach.

21 SO ON THEY JOURNEYED TOGETHER AS BEFORE: THE LOYAL DWARF, FAIR UNA, and still weary Redcross. But they had not been travelling long, before they noticed a knight in armor, galloping towards them at a speedy pace, as though he were fleeing some fearful foe or other grisly thing that horrified him. As he fled, he kept looking back as if he feared something ghastly were following on behind. His steed flew as though his bonds had burst, treading the wind as if he had winged heels, like a foal of Pegasus.

As he drew near, they noticed that the knight's helmet was missing, and his uncombed curly hair standing on end with strange dread. Not a drop of blood appeared on his face, nor was there loss of life or limb to increase his fears, seeming to discredit knighthood to a fair degree. About his neck he wore a noose of hemp rope, that didn't quite match his glistening armor.

But of the rope, or arms, he had no memory.

The Redcross knight quickly rode to meet him, to find out what manner of creature he was, and what concern so dismayed him. There he found him senseless and aghast, as though he were afraid of his very own self.

Redcross had trouble catching up, and called out, "Sir knight! Declare who has arrayed you with that rope around your neck, and from whom you flee in such a hasty manner? For never did I see a knight in such an unfitting plight."

The unseemly knight came to a halt, but did not answer. Instead, he looked even more afraid, staring in amazement with wide stony eyes that were set in hollow sockets. His visage was of a bloodless hue, astonished, as though he had seen the very Furies of hell out of their chains. Once again, the gentle knight spoke to him, attempting to gain an understanding of his predicament, but again he did not answer, and instead, trembled in every joint. At last, with faltering tongue, his words seeming to shake, he spoke these words:

25 "For God's dear love, sir knight, do not hold me up, for lo, he comes, he comes fast after me."

Looking over his shoulder again, the quaking knight would rather have kept riding, but Redcross urged him to stay and explain the full story, and the cause of his distress. Even his encouraging and heart-felt speech could not embolden this knight's blood-frozen heart, only seeming to arouse more fear instead. Yet his boldness at last forced the knight to breach his sudden silence.

XXVI And am I now in safetie sure (quoth he)
From him, that would haue forced me to dye?
And is the point of death now turnd fro mee,
That I may tell this haplesse history?
Feare nought: (quoth he) no daunger now is nye?
Then shall I you recount a ruefull cace,
(Said he) the which with this vnlucky eye
I late beheld, and had not greater grace
Me reft from it, had bene partaker of the place.

XXVII I lately chaunst (Would I had neuer chaunst)
With a faire knight to keepen companee,
Sir *Terwin* hight, that well himselfe aduaunst
In all affaires, and was both bold and free,
But not so happie as mote happie bee:
He lou'd, as was his lot, a Ladie gent,
That him againe lou'd in the least degree:
For she was proud, and of too high intent,
And ioyd to see her louer languish and lament.

XXVIII From whom returning sad and comfortlesse,
As on the way together we did fare,
We met that villen (God from him me blesse)
That cursed wight, from whom I scapt whyleare,
A man of hell, that cals himselfe *Despaire*:
Who first vs greets, and after faire areedes
Of tydings strange, and of aduentures rare:
So creeping close, as Snake in hidden weedes,
Inquireth of our states, and of our knightly deedes.

XXIX Which when he knew, and felt ourfeeble harts
Embost with bale, and bitter byting griefe,
Which loue had launched with his deadly darts,
With wounding words and termes of foule repriefe
He pluckt from vs all hope of due reliefe,
That earst vs held in loue of lingring life;
Then hopelesse hartlesse, gan the cunning thiefe
Perswade vs die, to stint all further strife:
To me he lent this rope, to him a rusty knife.

XXX With which sad instrument of hastie death,
That wofull louer, loathing lenger light,
A wide way made to let forth liuing breath.
But I more fearefull, or more luckie wight,
Dismayd with that deformed dismall sight,
Fled fast away, halfe dead with dying feare:
Ne yet assur'd of life by you, Sir knight,
Whose like infirmitie like chaunce may beare:
But God you neuer let his charmed speeches heare.

26 "Am I now in sure safety," he asked, still quivering, "from him who would have forced me to die? And is the point of death now turned from me, so that I may tell this luckless history?"

Redcross answered, "Fear not! No danger now is nigh."

"Then," replied the mysterious knight, "I shall recount to you a rueful event which this unlucky eye recently beheld, and from which, if greater grace had not wrenched me, I would have been its victim. Lately, I chanced—would I had never chanced!—to keep company of a fair knight. His name was Sir Terwin, and he was well advanced in all affairs, as well as bold and free, but not so happy as happy might be. He loved, as was his lot, a noble lady to the highest degree, who in return, loved him back to the least degree. She was proud and ambitious, and enjoyed seeing her lover languish and lament.

"He had been returning from this sad and comfortless affair, and we had decided to accompany each other along the way, when we met that villain:"

He paused to cross himself and ask God's blessing, before continuing, "that cursed creature from whom I recently escaped. He is a man from hell, and he calls himself Despair. He greeted us first and told us of strange tidings and rare adventures. Creeping close to us, like a snake hidden in weeds, he enquired of our rank and knightly deeds. Once he knew our feeble hearts were exhausted with sorrow and bitter biting grief, which love has lanced with his enticing arrows, he plucked all hope or relief, that before held us in love of lingering life, with wounding words and terms of foul reproof. Heartlessly, that cunning thief began to persuade us to kill ourselves to avoid further strife. He lent me this rope, and to my friend: a bloody knife. **30** And with that sad instrument of hasty death, that woeful lover, loathing to see the light any longer, stabbed himself in the chest. Dismayed and disgusted by that dismal sight, I fled away fast, half dead with the fear of dying."

The shaken knight paused and stared at Redcross for a few moments, then said, "You, sir knight, in the infirmity I now see you in, could suffer the same fate. May God never let you hear his charmed speeches!"

XXXI How may a man (said he) with idle speach
Be wonne, to spoyle the Castle of his health?
I wote (quoth he) whom triall late did teach,
That like would not for all this worldes wealth:
His subtill tongue, like dropping honny, mealt'th
Into the hart, and searcheth euery vaine,
That ere one be aware, by secret stealth
His powre is reft, and weaknesse doth remaine.
O neuer Sir desire to try his guilefull traine.

XXXII Certes (said he) hence shall I neuer rest,
Till I that treachours art haue heard and tride;
And you Sir knight, whose name mote I request,
Of grace do me vnto his cabin guide.
I that hight *Treuisan* (quoth he) will ride
Against my liking backe, to doe you grace:
But nor for gold nor glee will I abide
By you, when ye arriue in that same place;
For leuer had I die, then see his deadly face.

XXXIII Ere long they come, where that same wicked wight
His dwelling has, low in an hollow caue,
Farre vnderneath a craggie clift ypight,
Darke, dolefull, drearie, like a greedie graue,
That still for carrion carcases doth craue:
On top whereof aye dwelt the ghastly Owle,
Shrieking his balefull note, which euer draue
Farre from that haunt all other chearefull fowle;
And all about it wandring ghostes did waile and howle.

XXXIV And all about old stockes and stubs of trees,
Whereon nor fruit, nor leafe was euer seene,
Did hang vpon the ragged rocky knees;
On which had many wretches hanged beene,
Whose carcases were scattered on the greene,
And throwne about the cliffs. Arriued there,
That bare-head knight for dread and dolefull teene,
Would faine haue fled, ne durst approchen neare,
But th'other forst him stay, and comforted in feare.

XXXV That darkesome caue they enter, where they find
That cursed man, low sitting on the ground,
Musing full sadly in his sullein mind;
His griesie lockes, long growen, and vnbound,
Disordred hong about his shoulders round,
And hid his face; through which his hollow eyne
Lookt deadly dull, and stared as astound;
His raw-bone cheekes through penurie and pine,
Were shronke into his iawes, as he did neuer dine.

31 "How on earth may a man," asked Redcross, "be convinced to spoil the castle of his health, by idle and foolish speech?"

"I would not undergo this trail again for all this world's wealth, nor wish it on anyone else. But his subtle tongue, like dripping honey, melts into the heart, and sneaks though your every vein, so that before you know it, he has you in his power by secret stealth. O Sir, never desire to test his cunning deceit!"

"For certain," declared Redcross, on hearing this, "I shall never rest until I have heard and tried that treacherous fiend's heart. And you, sir knight, whose name I now request, please do me a favor and guide me to his cavern."

"My name is Trevisan," he said, "and, against my liking, I will ride back with you out of graciousness. But not for gold or glitter will I abide there, for I would rather die than see that face again!

BEFORE LONG, REDCROSS, UNA, THE DWARF, AND THE FRIGHTENED KNIGHT, arrived at that wicked creature's dwelling, which was a low hollow cave. Far underneath a craggy cliff, it gaped like a dark, doleful, dreary grave that still craved for carrion carcasses. On top on the cliff, dwelt a ghastly owl, shrieking his baleful note, driving away sunnier fowl, and draining any residual cheer of those who ventured near. Around the entrance, many ghosts wailed and howled.

Worse still, on every stalk or stump of tree, whereon neither fruit nor leaf were seen, and on every ragged crag, hung many wretches, whose carcasses were scattered on the green, and thrown about the cliffs. Arriving at this ghastly scene, the bare-headed knight would have fled immediately, if it were not for the others who urged him to stay, comforting his fear.

35Together, they crept into the darksome cave, where they found that cursed man, sitting low on the ground. He was musing sadly with his sullen mind, his greasy dreadlocks, long grown and unkempt, hung raggedly about his shoulders and hid most of his face. His deadly dull and hollow eyes stared as if astounded. His raw-bone cheeks were shrunk to his jaws from poverty and starvation, as he never ate a thing.

XXXVI His garment nought but many ragged clouts,
With thornes together pind and patched was,
The which his naked sides he wrapt abouts;
And him beside there lay vpon the gras
A drearie corse, whose life away did pas,
All wallowd in his owne yet luke-warme blood,
That from his wound yet welled fresh alas;
In which a rustie knife fast fixed stood,
And made an open passage for the gushing flood.

XXXVII Which piteous spectacle, approuing trew
The wofull tale that *Treuisan* had told,
When as the gentle *Redcrosse* knight did vew,
With firie zeale he burnt in courage bold,
Him to auenge, before his bloud were cold,
And to the villein said, Thou damned wight,
The author of this fact, we here behold,
What iustice can but iudge against thee right,
With thine owne bloud to price his bloud, here shed in sight.

XXXVIII What franticke fit (quoth he) hath thus distraught
Thee, foolish man, so rash a doome to giue?
What iustice euer other iudgement taught,
But he should die, who merites not to liue?
None else to death this man despayring driue,
But his owne guiltie mind deseruing death.
Is then vniust to each his due to giue?
Or let him die, that loatheth liuing breath?
Or let him die at ease, that liueth here vneath?

XXXIX Who trauels by the wearie wandring way,
To come vnto his wished home in haste,
And meetes a flood, that doth his passage stay,
Is not great grace to helpe him ouer past,
Or free his feet, that in the myre sticke fast?
Most enuious man, that grieues at neighbours good,
And fond, that ioyest in the woe thou hast,
Why wilt not let him passe, that long hath stood
Vpon the banke, yet wilt thy selfe not passe the flood?

XL He there does now enioy eternall rest
And happie ease, which thou doest want and craue,
And further from it daily wanderest:
What if some litle paine the passage haue,
That makes fraile flesh to feare the bitter waue?
Is not short paine well borne, that brings long ease,
And layes the soule to sleepe in quiet graue?
Sleepe after toyle, port after stormie seas,
Ease after warre, death after life does greatly please.

36 He was wearing a garment made of many rags that were patched and pinned together with thorns. Upon the grass beside him, lay a dreary corpse, still wallowing in lukewarm blood that still welled fresh from its wound, and in which a bloody knife was fixed: an open passage for the gushing blood.

This piteous spectacle proved that Trevisan's woeful tale was true.

When gentle Redcross glanced around, his fiery zeal burned in bold courage, and he challenged the villain, wanting to avenge him, before Sir Terwin's blood was cold, "You damned creature! The author of this crime we here behold. What justice can but judge against you right? Therefore, with your own blood you will pay for this sight!"

"What frantic fit," replied the villain, "has thus distraught you, foolish man: so rash to give such a judgement? What justice taught you, that he who deserves to die should live? This man's own guilty mind made him deserve nothing other than death. Is it then unjust to give each his due? Or let him die on that loathed living breath? Or let him die at ease: he who lives so uneasy? Who travels by the weary wandering way to come unto his wished home in haste, only to meet a river that prevents his passage? Is not great grace to help him pass over, or free his feet that are stuck fast in the mud? You are just an envious man who grieves at a man's *good*! You are foolish not to let him pass who has stood upon the bank. Why not pass the bank yourself?

40"Look at him," shrugged the dark villain, pointing to the man with the knife in his chest. "Doesn't he now enjoy eternal rest and happy ease, that you also want and crave, and from which you keep further wandering? So what if the passage entails a little pain that makes frail flesh fear? Isn't short-lived pain well borne if it brings long ease, and lays the soul to sleep in a quiet grave? Sleep after toil, rest in port after stormy seas, ease after war … and death after life does greatly please."

XLI The knight much wondred at his suddeine wit,
And said, The terme of life is limited,
Ne may a man prolong, nor shorten it;
The souldier may not moue from watchfull sted,
Nor leaue his stand, vntill his Captaine bed.
Who life did limit by almightie doome,
(Quoth he) knowes best the termes established;
And he, that points the Centonell his roome,
Doth license him depart at sound of morning droome.

XLII Is not his deed, what euer thing is donne,
In heauen and earth? did not he all create
To die againe? all ends that was begonne.
Their times in his eternall booke of fate
Are written sure, and haue their certaine date.
Who then can striue with strong necessitie,
That holds the world in his still chaunging state,
Or shunne the death ordaynd by destinie?
When hour of death is come, let none aske whence, nor why.

XLIII The lenger life, I wote the greater sin,
The greater sin, the greater punishment:
All those great battels, which thou boasts to win,
Through strife, and bloud-shed, and auengement,
Now praysd, hereafter deare thou shalt repent:
For life must life, and bloud must bloud repay.
Is not enough thy euill life forespent?
For he, that once hath missed the right way,
The further he doth goe, the further he doth stray.

XLIV Then do no further goe, no further stray,
But here lie downe, and to thy rest betake,
Th'ill to preuent, that life ensewen may.
For what hath life, that may it loued make,
And giues not rather cause it to forsake?
Feare, sicknesse, age, losse, labour, sorrow, strife,
Paine, hunger, cold, that makes the hart to quake;
And euer fickle fortune rageth rife,
All which, and thousands mo do make a loathsome life.

XLV Thou wretched man, of death hast greatest need,
If in true ballance thou wilt weigh thy state:
For neuer knight, that dared warlike deede,
More lucklesse disauentures did amate:
Witnesse the dongeon deepe, wherein of late
Thy life shut vp, for death so oft did call;
And though good lucke prolonged hath thy date,
Yet death then, would the like mishaps forestall,
Into the which hereafter thou maiest happen fall.

41 The knight wondered much at his quick mind, but replied, boldly, "The term of life is limited. A man may neither prolong it, nor shorten it. The solider may not move from watchful station, nor leave his post until the captain bids him!"

"He who limited life by almighty doom," came the villain's hissing reply, "knows best the terms established. And he who assigned the sentinel his station also allows him to depart at the sound of the morning drum. Is not God's deed, what ever thing is done in heaven and earth? Did he not create all to die again? All ends that was begun. Their times are written in his eternal book of fate, and have a certain date. Who then can strive with strong necessity by shunning the death ordained by destiny? When the hour of death is come, let no one ask whence or why. I know for certain: the longer life, the greater the sin. The greater the sin, the greater the punishment. All those great battles that you boast to win, through strife and bloodshed and vengeance, now praised, but hereafter you shall greatly repent. For life for a life, and blood must repay blood. Is not a misspent evil life enough? For he who once missed the right way, the further he goes in life, the further he strays.

"So do not go any further, so that you will not stray any further. But lie down here and go to you rest, so that you can prevent any possible ill life may bring. Think about it! What has life ever done for you, young knight? Fear, sickness, age, loss, labor, sorrow, strife, pain, hunger, cold, and all that makes the heart quake, and always that fickle wheel of fortune rages rife. All which, and thousands more reasons do make life loathsome.

45 "You wretched man, if you really think about it, and if you weigh your state with true assessment, death is your greatest need, not life. For never a knight who dared warlike deeds met with such misfortunes. Witness the dungeon deep, wherein of late your life was shut inside. Did you not call for death so often down there? And only through good luck have you prolonged your death date. You see? Death will forestall further mishaps like this, and you could fall into many more in the future.

XLVI Why then doest thou, O man of sin, desire
To draw thy dayes forth to their last degree?
Is not the measure of thy sinfull hire
High heaped vp with huge iniquitie,
Against the day of wrath, to burden thee?
Is not enough, that to this Ladie milde
Thou falsed hast thy faith with periurie,
And sold thy selfe to serue *Duessa* vilde,
With whom in all abuse thou hast thy selfe defilde?

XLVII Is not he iust, that all this doth behold
From highest heauen, and beares an equall eye?
Shall he thy sins vp in his knowledge fold,
And guiltie be of thine impietie?
Is not his law, Let euery sinner die:
Die shall all flesh? what then must needs be donne,
Is it not better to doe willinglie,
Then linger, till the glasse be all out ronne?
Death is the end of woes: die soone, O faeries sonne.

XLVIII The knight was much enmoued with his speach,
That as a swords point through his hart did perse,
And in his conscience made a secret breach,
Well knowing true all, that he did reherse,
And to his fresh remembrance did reuerse
The vgly vew of his deformed crimes,
That all his manly powres it did disperse,
As he were charmed with inchaunted rimes,
That oftentimes he quakt, and fainted oftentimes.

XLIX In which amazement, when the Miscreant
Perceiued him to wauer weake and fraile,
Whiles trembling horror did his conscience dant,
And hellish anguish did his soule assaile,
To driue him to despaire, and quite to quaile,
He shew'd him painted in a table plaine,
The damned ghosts, that doe in torments waile,
And thousand feends that doe them endlesse paine
With fire and brimstone, which for euer shall remaine.

L The sight whereof so throughly him dismaid,
That nought but death before his eyes he saw,
And euer burning wrath before him laid,
By righteous sentence of th'Almighties law:
Then gan the villein him to ouercraw,
And brought vnto him swords, ropes, poison, fire,
And all that might him to perdition draw;
And bad him choose, what death he would desire:
For death was due to him, that had prouokt Gods ire.

46 "Why then do you, O man of sin, desire to draw your days forth to their last degree? Is not the measure of your sinful wages heaped with vices that so burden you? Is it not enough that you betrayed this mild lady here, as well as your faith, with lies, and sold yourself to serve vile Duessa, defiling your soul? Is He not just, that He sees all this from highest heaven with unbiased eye? Should God take your sins up into his fold, and be guilty of *your* impiety? Is it not his law to let every sinner die? Doesn't all flesh die? What then must needs be done? Is it not better to kill yourself willingly, than linger till the hourglass runs out? Death would be the end of your woes. Die right now, O Faerie's son!"

The knight was so moved by this speech that it pierced his heart like a sword's point, and his mind began to weaken. The villain's arguments seemed logical and irrefutable, and in despair, Redcross turned his thoughts onto his ugly misdemeanors. The more he pondered on his regrets, the more his manly powers dispersed, and he began to quake and faint, as if he were charmed with enchanted rhymes. When the villain noticed Redcross waver and weaken, trembling horror daunting his mind, and hellish anguish assailing his soul, he set about driving him to full despair. He showed Redcross a lurid painting of eternally damned wailing ghosts, eternally tormented by a thousand fiends that do them endless pain with fire and brimstone. **50** The sight whereof upset Redcross so thoroughly, that he could see no future but death, and ever burning wrath. Misusing the righteous judgment of the Almighty's Law, the villain worked even harder to win him over to the side of death, bringing him a sword, ropes, poison, and fire, and asking him to choose which death he would desire. For, he suggested, death was due to him who had provoked God's ire.

LI But when as none of them he saw him take,
He to him raught a dagger sharpe and keene,
And gaue it him in hand: his hand did quake,
And tremble like a leafe of Aspin greene,
And troubled bloud through his pale face was seene
To come, and goe with tydings from the hart,
As it a running messenger had beene.
At last resolu'd to worke his finall smart,
He lifted vp his hand, that backe againe did start.

LII Which when as *Vna* saw, through euery vaine
The crudled cold ran to her well of life,
As in a swowne: but soone reliu'd againe,
Out of his hand she snatcht the cursed knife,
And threw it to the ground, enraged rife,
And to him said, Fie, fie, faint harted knight,
What meanest thou by this reprochfull strife?
Is this the battell, which thou vauntst to fight
With that fire-mouthed Dragon, horrible and bright?

LIII Come, come away, fraile, seely, fleshly wight,
Ne let vaine words bewitch thy manly hart,
Ne diuelish thoughts dismay thy constant spright.
In heauenly mercies hast thou not a part?
Why shouldst thou then despeire, that chosen art?
Where iustice growes, there grows eke greater grace,
The which doth quench the brond of hellish smart,
And that accurst hand-writing doth deface,
Arise, Sir knight arise, and leaue this cursed place.

LIV So vp he rose, and thence amounted streight.
Which when the carle beheld, and saw his guest
Would safe depart, for all his subtill sleight,
He chose an halter from among the rest,
And with it hung himselfe, vnbid vnblest.
But death he could not worke himselfe thereby;
For thousand times he so himselfe had drest,
Yet nathelesse it could not doe him die,
Till he should die his last, that is eternally.

51 But when he saw Redcross waiver at the deathly choices, the villain swiftly reached for a sharp and keen dagger instead, and placed it in his hand. Redcross's hand quaked and trembled like a leaf of Aspen green, and he grew pale from his troubled heart. At last, resolved to do the deed, he lifted the dagger above his chest.

When Una saw this, curdled cold ran through every vein to her heart, as in a swoon. But she quickly revived.

"No!" she cried, snatching the cursed knife out of his hand, and hurling it on the ground.

Filled with enraged rife, she rebuked him, "Fie fie, faint-hearted knight, what do you mean by this reproachful strife? Is this the battle which you boasted to fight with that fire mouthed dragon, horrible and bright? Come, come away, frail and feeble fleshy creature! Do not let vain words bewitch your manly heart, or devilish thoughts dismay your faithful spirit. Have you not a part in heavenly mercies? Why should you despair if you are already chosen by God: not unto wrath, but *salvation*? Then do not be deceived anymore. Where error increases, grace grows even greater, quenching the blades of evil. Remember that our condemnations were nailed to the cross. Arise, sir knight, arise, and leave this cursed place!"

So up he rose and thence mounted his steed, and they continued on their way.

BUT THE VILE VILLAIN, BEHOLDING HIS FAILED TEMPTATION, AND DESPAIRING that his cunning tricks were of no avail, chose a noose and tried to hang himself, unbidden and unblessed. But death did not work on him, for he had already tried a thousand times before. He was fated to stay alive until he should die his last: that is eternally.

---

1   *Mount Rauran: a mountain in Wales. Spenser places Arthur's origins in the same region as the Tudor royal family, connecting him to Queen Elizabeth I.*

NOTES ON CANTO X

Una doesn't prepare Redcross to battle the great dragon by taking him to the gym. Instead, she takes him to the House of Holiness, implying that this will be a spiritual battle rather than a physical one. Here, Redcross undergoes a regime of contemplation and mortification: fasting, sackcloth, self-flagellation and salt baths, and in this Canto, Spenser seems to contradict his earlier critiques of similar practices and rituals of the Roman Church. Mortification of the flesh was, and still is, understood to be a noble discipline in the Catholic Church, citing Romans 8:13 (*For if you live according to the flesh you will die, but if by the Spirit you put to death the deeds of the body, you will live*). Protestants, especially Reformed traditions, understand Romans 8:13 to mean inner sanctification as a gift of grace, rather than an action. However, Martin Luther still engaged in these practices alongside his preaching of Sola Gratia and Sola Fide[1] and it could be that these early Protestants took a while to change their beliefs and traditions. Spenser scholar, Carol Kaske, argues that the regime Redcross undergoes in this chapter is correctional of the Roman Catholic teachings. Where contemplation and mortification are understood as central and necessary for salvation in Catholicism, Spenser's Protestantism corrects this view and presents them as solely an *aid* to good deeds. In the House of Holiness, good deeds are more important, and Caelia's beads are not meritorious in themselves, but an aid to concentration.[2]

Una Rescuing The Knight: Redcross—Man—cannot save himself without the help of 'Truth.' Una's rescues symbolize God's grace. Redcross must rely on a power greater than himself, not on his own strength. While Dante, from The *Divine Comedy*, and Christian, from *Pilgrim's Progress*, both work their own salvation, Redcross is 'rescued.'
Caelia: "Heavenly"
The three daughters Fidelia, Sperenza and Charissa are Faith, Hope, and Charity: the three greatest virtues, according to St. Paul in 1Cor 13:13, and each one instructs Redcross in her own specialty. Charity is translated from the Greek 'agape:' the highest of the four loves, and the selfless love demonstrated by Christ. Charissa has just given birth to a new baby son, which is symbolic for Redcross being "born again" (John 3).
The physicians: who tend to his body are the counterparts to the seven bodily vices of the House of Pride.
City: symbolizes the New Jerusalem from the book of Revelation.

CANTO X

THE HOUSE OF HOLINESS

I Her faithfull knight faire Vna brings
to house of Holinesse,
Where he is taught repentance, and
the way to heauenly blesse.

I What man is he, that boasts of fleshly might,
And vaine assurance of mortality,
Which all so soone, as it doth come to fight,
Against spirituall foes, yeelds by and by,
Or from the field most cowardly doth fly?
Ne let the man ascribe it to his skill,
That thorough grace hath gained victory.
If any strength we haue, it is to ill,
But all the good is Gods, both power and eke will.

II By that, which lately hapned, *Vna* saw,
That this her knight was feeble, and too faint;
And all his sinews woxen weake and raw,
Through long enprisonment, and hard constraint,
Which he endured in his late restraint,
That yet he was vnfit for bloudie fight:
Therefore to cherish him with diets daint,
She cast to bring him, where he chearen might,
Till he recouered had his late decayed plight.

III There was an auntient house not farre away,
Renowmd throughout the world for sacred lore,
And pure vnspotted life: so well they say
It gouernd was, and guided euermore,
Through wisedome of a matrone graue and hore;
Whose onely ioy was to relieue the needes
Of wretched soules, and helpe the helpelesse pore:
All night she spent in bidding of her bedes,
And all the day in doing good and godly deedes.

IV Dame *Cælia* men did her call, as thought
From heauen to come, or thither to arise,
The mother of three daughters, well vpbrought
In goodly thewes, and godly exercise:
The eldest two most sober, chast, and wise,
Fidelia and *Speranza* virgins were,
Though spousd, yet wanting wedlocks solemnize;
But faire *Charissa* to a louely fere
Was lincked, and by him had many pledges dere.

V Arriued there, the dore they find fast lockt;
For it was warely watched night and day,
For feare of many foes: but when they knockt,
The Porter opened vnto them streight way:
He was an aged syre, all hory gray,
With lookes full lowly cast, and gate full slow,
Wont on a staffe his feeble steps to stay,
Hight *Humiltá*. They passe in stouping low;
For streightand narrow was the way,
which he did show.

Fair Una brings her faithful knight to the house of Holiness,
where he is taught repentance and the way to heavenly bliss.

WHAT KIND OF MAN IS HE WHO BOASTS OF FLESHY MIGHT AND VAIN ASSURANCE of mortality, but who cowers when it comes to fighting against spiritual foes, yielding to them, or fleeing the field like a coward? Neither should the man ascribe his victory to his own skill, for it is gained by grace, and if we have any strength at all, it is inclined to ill. For all good belongs to God, as well as power and will.

AFTER THESE RECENT TRIALS, UNA REALIZED THAT HER KNIGHT WAS FEEBLE, AND lacking in strength and courage. His muscles had grown weak and raw through long imprisonment and arduous constraint, and she knew he was yet unfit for the great fight. Therefore, to nourish him with a wholesome diet, she resolved to bring him to where he might be cheered until he had recovered his former state.

There was an ancient house not far away, renowned throughout the world for sacred lore and pure spotted life. It was well governed and guided by a wise and venerable old matron. Her only joy was to relieve the needs of wretched souls and help the helpless poor. All night she spent with her beads in prayer, and all day in doing good and godly deeds. She was Dame Caelia, named after the heavens above from whence she came, and to where she will ascend. She was mother to three daughters who were well brought up in good manners and godly deeds. The older sisters, Fidelia and Speranza, were sober, virtuous and wise, and were engaged to be married. While the younger sister, fair Charissa, was already wed to a loving husband, and by him had many dear children.

5 When Una and Redcross arrived at the door, they found it locked fast, for it was carefully watched, night and day, for fear of many foes. But when they knocked, the door was immediately opened to them. The porter was an old grey man with humble looks and slow pace, leaning on a staff to steady his feeble steps. His name was Humilta, and he showed them through. The trio passed inside, stooping low, for straight and narrow was the passage that led forward.

VI Each goodly thing is hardest to begin,
But entred in a spacious court they see,
Both plaine, and pleasant to be walked in,
Where them does meete a francklin faire and free,
And entertaines with comely courteous glee,
His name was *Zele*, that him right well became,
For in his speeches and behauiour hee
Did labour liuely to expresse the same,
And gladly did them guide, till to the Hall they came.

VII There fairely them receiues a gentle Squire,
Of milde demeanure, and rare courtesie,
Right cleanly clad in comely sad attire;
In word and deede that shew'd great modestie,
And knew his good to all of each degree,
Hight *Reuerence*. He them with speeches meet
Does faire entreat; no courting nicetie,
But simple true, and eke vnfained sweet,
As might become a Squire so great persons to greet.

VIII And afterwards them to his Dame he leades,
That aged Dame, the Ladie of the place:
Who all this while was busie at her beades:
Which doen, she vp arose with seemely grace,
And toward them full matronely did pace.
Where when that fairest *Vna* she beheld,
Whom well she knew to spring from heauenly race,
Her hart with ioy vnwonted inly sweld,
As feeling wondrous comfort in her weaker eld.

IX And her embracing said, O happie earth,
Whereon thy innocent feet doe euer tread,
Most vertuous virgin borne of heauenly berth,
That to redeeme thy woefull parents head,
From tyrans rage, and euer-dying dread,
Hast wandred through the world now long a day;
Yet ceasest not thy wearie soles to lead,
What grace hath thee now hither brought this way?
Or doen thy feeble feet vnweeting hither stray?

X Strange thing it is an errant knight to see
Here in this place, or any other wight,
That hither turnes his steps. So few there bee,
That chose the narrow path, or seeke the right:
All keepe the broad high way, and take delight
With many rather for to go astray,
And be partakers of their euill plight,
Then with a few to walke the rightest way;
O foolish men, why haste ye to your owne decay?

6 The hardest part of every good thing is the beginning. But once they entered, they saw a spacious courtyard, quite ordinary, but pleasant to walk in. There they met a fair and free franklin, who entertained them with pleasant and courteous glee. His name is Zeal, and that name suited him because his speech and actions were lively, and he joyfully guided them to the hall.

There, a gentle squire of mild demeanor and rare courtesy received them. He was completely clad in pleasant and humble attire, showing great modesty in word and deed, and respect to social setting and rank. His name was Reverence, and he met them with fitting speeches and genuine words, while avoiding false courtesies, as might become a squire. Afterwards, he led lady Una to meet the aged dame, the lady of the place, who was busy in prayer. When done, she arose with seemly grace and strolled warmly towards them. When she beheld the fairest Una, whom she knew must have sprung from a heavenly race, her heart swelled with uncommon joy, bringing her comfort in her old age.

Embracing her, the old lady said, "O happy earth whereon your innocent feet do ever tread! Most virtuous maiden, born of heavenly birth who, to redeem your woeful parents' sad state, has long wandered through the world with that ever-threatening dread of the tyrant's rage, and eternal death. Yet you cease not to weary your soles to lead. What grace has brought you hither? Or do your feeble feet unknowingly wander astray?**10** Strange thing it is to see an errant knight here in this place, or any other creature, who hither turns his steps. So few choose the narrow path or seek the right way. Most prefer to keep the broad highway and take delight with the many, to go astray and be partakers of their evil plight, than with a few to walk the rightest way. *O foolish men, why do you hasten your own destruction?*"

XI Thy selfe to see, and tyred limbs to rest,
O matrone sage (quoth she) I hither came,
And this good knight his way with me addrest,
Led with thy prayses and broad-blazed fame,
That vp to heauen is blowne. The auncient Dame
Him goodly greeted in her modest guise,
And entertaynd them both, as best became,
With all the court'sies, that she could deuise.
Ne wanted ought, to shew her bounteous or wise.

XII Thus as they gan of sundry things deuise,
Loe two most goodly virgins came in place,
Ylinked arme in arme in louely wise,
With countenance demure, and modest grace,
They numberd euen steps and equall pace:
Of which the eldest, that *Fidelia* hight,
Like sunny beames threw from her Christall face,
That could haue dazd the rash beholders sight,
And round about her head did shine like heauens light.

XIII She was araied all in lilly white,
And in her right hand bore a cup of gold,
With wine and water fild vp to the hight,
In which a Serpent did himselfe enfold,
That horrour made to all, that did behold;
But she no whit did chaunge her constant mood:
And in her other hand she fast did hold
A booke, that was both signd and seald with blood,
Wherein darke things were writ, hard to be vnderstood.

XIV Her younger sister, that *Speranza* hight,
Was clad in blew, that her beseemed well;
Not all so chearefull seemed she of sight,
As was her sister; whether dread did dwell,
Or anguish in her hart, is hard to tell:
Vpon her arme a siluer anchor lay,
Whereon she leaned euer, as befell:
And euer vp to heauen, as she did pray,
Her stedfast eyes were bent, ne swarued other way.

XV They seeing *Vna*, towards her gan wend,
Who them encounters with like courtesie;
Many kind speeches they betwene them spend,
And greatly ioy each other well to see:
Then to the knight with shamefast modestie
They turne themselues, at *Vnaes* meeke request,
And him salute with well beseeming glee:
Who faire them quites, as him beseemed best,
And goodly gan discourse of many a noble gest.

11 "We came to see you and rest our tired limbs, O wise matron," replied Una. "We came hither because of this good knight, led by rumors of your praises and widely proclaimed fame, and whose renown reaches to heaven."

The old lady greeted Redcross warmly in her modest way, and entertained them both the best she could, with all the courtesies and generosities she could devise.

As they began to discuss all manner of things, the two fair maidens, Fidelia and Speranza, entered the room, linked arm in arm in a loving manner. With demure countenances and modest grace, they walked at an equal pace. The eldest was called Fidelia, and her luminous face glowed like sunbeams, and could have dazzled an unprepared onlooker. Around her head, heaven's light shone brightly, and she was dressed in lily white. In her right hand, she bore a golden goblet filled to the brim with wine and water, and in which the Serpent of Healing was coiled. It was frightening to behold, but Fidelia did not change her constant mood. In her other hand she held a book that was signed and sealed in blood, wherein profound things were written, though not easy to understand.[3]

Her younger sister, Speranza, was smartly dressed in blue. She wasn't quite as cheerful as her sister, and whether dread or anguish dwelled in her heart, it was difficult to tell. On her arm, she carried a silver anchor, which she appeared to be leaning on, while she cast her eyes to heaven and seemed to be praying in an unswerving manner.

15 Seeing Una, they began to approach her and exchange courtesies. Many kind exchanges were spent between them, and they greatly enjoyed each other's company. Next, at Una's meek request, they moved towards the knight with humble modesty and greeted him warmly. Redcross returned their greetings in a similar manner, and they began a discussion about many a noble deed.

XVI Then *Vna* thus; But she your sister deare;
The deare *Charissa* where is she become?
Or wants she health, or busie is elsewhere?
Ah no, said they, but forth she may not come:
For she of late is lightned of her wombe,
And hath encreast the world with one sonne more,
That her to see should be but troublesome.
Indeede (quoth she) that should her trouble sore,
But thankt be God, and her encrease so euermore.

XVII Then said the aged *Caelia*, Deare dame,
And you good Sir, I wote that of your toyle,
And labours long, through which ye hither came,
Ye both forwearied be: therefore a whyle
I read you rest, and to your bowres recoyle.
Then called she a Groome, that forth him led
Into a goodly lodge, and gan despoile
Of puissant armes, and laid in easie bed;
His name was meeke *Obedience* rightfully ared.

XVIII Now when their wearie limbes with kindly rest,
And bodies were refresht with due repast,
Faire *Vna* gan *Fidelia* faire request,
To haue her knight into her schoolehouse plaste,
That of her heauenly learning he might taste,
And heare the wisedome of her words diuine.
She graunted, and that knight so much agraste,
That she him taught celestiall discipline,
And opened his dull eyes, that light mote in them shine.

XIX And that her sacred Booke, with bloud ywrit,
That none could read, except she did them teach,
She vnto him disclosed euery whit,
And heauenly documents thereout did preach,
That weaker wit of man could neuer reach,
Of God, of grace, of iustice, of free will,
That wonder was to heare her goodly speach:
For she was able, with her words to kill,
And raise againe to life the hart, that she did thrill.

XX And when she list poure out her larger spright,
She would commaund the hastie Sunne to stay,
Or backward turne his course from heauens hight;
Sometimes great hostes of men she could dismay,
Dry-shod to passe, she parts the flouds in tway;
And eke huge mountaines from their natiue seat
She would commaund, themselues to beare away,
And throw in raging sea with roaring threat.
Almightie God her gaue such powre, and puissance great.

16 Then Una said, "But where is your dear sister, Charissa? Is she ill, or busy elsewhere?"

"No, she is neither ill nor away," replied Fidelia and Speranza, "but has recently given birth to a baby son, and it is best she is not disturbed."

"Indeed," said Una, "she needs her rest right now. But thanks to God and may she may increase her fold evermore."

Then Caelia said, "Dear lady Una, and you good sir, I know that your toil and labors are long, and that you must be utterly wearied. Therefore I bid you rest, and will show you to your rooms."

Then she called to a meek servant, whose name was Obedience. He led Redcross to a restful lodging, where he began to help him off with his armor. Then the knight lay down on the soft bed and slept soundly.

The next morning, with their weary limbs well rested, and refreshed with nourishing victuals, fair Una approached Fidelia with her request. She explained that the purpose of their visit was for her knight to be placed under her tutelage, so that he would taste heavenly learning and hear the wisdom of her divine words. Fidelia agreed to Una's request, since he was so favored with grace.

Then she took Redcross under her wing and taught him celestial discipline to open his dull eyes to the light that would shine into them. With her sacred book, written in the life-blood of Christ, she guided his reading, revealing its meanings and heavenly teachings: of God, of grace, of justice, of free will. What a wonder it was to hear her guidance. For she was able, with her words, to pierce and raise the heart back to life again.

20 And when she intended on a longer and more powerful teaching, she would command the hasty sun to stay or turn backward on its course from heaven's height. With her words, she could conquer great hosts of men, part floods and allow others to pass without even wetting their feet. She could even move mountains, rip them up, and throw them into a raging sea with thundering commands. Almighty God gave her such power over the word.

XXI The faithfull knight now grew in litle space,
By hearing her, and by her sisters lore,
To such perfection of all heauenly grace,
That wretched world he gan for to abhore,
And mortall life gan loath, as thing forlore,
Greeu'd with remembrance of his wicked wayes,
And prickt with anguish of his sinnes so sore,
That he desirde to end his wretched dayes:
So much the dart of sinfull guilt the soule dismayes.

XXII But wise *Speranza* gaue him comfort sweet,
And taught him how to take assured hold
Vpon her siluer anchor, as was meet;
Else had his sinnes so great, and manifold
Made him forget all that *Fidelia* told.
In this distressed doubtfull agonie,
When him his dearest *Vna* did behold,
Disdeining life, desiring leaue to die,
She found her selfe assayld with great perplexity.

XXIII And came to *Caelia* to declare her smart,
Who well acquainted with that commune plight,
Which sinfull horror workes in wounded hart,
Her wisely comforted all that she might,
With goodly counsell and aduisement right;
And streightway sent with carefull diligence,
To fetch a Leach, the which had great insight
In that disease of grieued conscience,
And well could cure the same; His name was *Patience*.

XXIV Who comming to that soule-diseased knight,
Could hardly him intreat, to tell his griefe:
Which knowne, and all that noyd his heauie spright
Well searcht, eftsoones he gan apply reliefe
Of salues and med'cines, which had passing priefe,
And thereto added words of wondrous might:
By which to ease he him recured briefe,
And much asswag'd the passion of his plight,
That he his paine endur'd, as seeming now more light.

XXV But yet the cause and root of all his ill,
Inward corruption, and infected sin,
Not purg'd nor heald, behind remained still,
And festring sore did rankle yet within,
Close creeping twixt the marrow and the skin.
Which to extirpe, he laid him priuily
Downe in a darkesome lowly place farre in,
Whereas he meant his corrosiues to apply,
And with streight diet tame his stubborne malady.

21 By hearing Fidelia and Speranza's lore, Redcross grew quickly in mind and spirit, and attained such perfection of heavenly grace, that he began to loathe the wretched world and mortal life, that is doomed to destruction. He grieved and repented of his wicked ways, and was so pierced with anguish from his previous transgressions, that he desired to end his wretched days: such does the dart of sinful guilt dismay the soul. But wise Speranza gave him sweet comfort, teaching him how to take an assured hold of her silver anchor of hope, telling him not to let his sins, while great and manifold, cloud all that Fidelia had shown him.

When Una saw him in this distressed doubtful agony, disdaining life and desiring death, she became afraid, remembering the recent incident in the Cave of Despair. So she came to Caelia to express her concerns, and Caelia assured her that she was well acquainted with that common plight, where sinful horror worked in a wounded heart, and she comforted Una with her wisdom and good counsel. Next, Caelia sent for a doctor, named Patience. He had great insight into the disease of the grieved conscience, and could cure it.

Dr Patience visited the soul-diseased Redcross and persuaded him to tell of his grief. Once he had confessed all that troubled his well-searched heavy spirit, Patience began to apply his relief. First came the salves and medicines, which had passing effects, then he added words of wondrous might. Soon Redcross was absolved of his plight and pain, and his burden greatly lightened. **25** But the cause and root of all his ill, inward corruption and infected sin, not purged or healed, remained behind and festered within, creeping close between the marrow and skin. To extricate this stubborn malady, Dr Patience laid him in a separate room in some darksome lowly place where he could prescribe his remedies and order a strict regime.

XXVI In ashes and sackcloth he did array
His daintie corse, proud humors to abate,
And dieted with fasting euery day,
The swelling of his wounds to mitigate,
And made him pray both earely and eke late:
And euer as superfluous flesh did rot
Amendment readie still at hand did wayt,
To pluck it out with pincers firie whot,
That soone in him was left no one corrupted iot.

XXVII And bitter *Penance* with an yron whip,
Was wont him once to disple euery day:
And sharpe *Remorse* his hart did pricke and nip,
That drops of bloud thence like a well did play;
And sad *Repentance* vsed to embay
His bodie in salt water smarting sore,
The filthy blots of sinne to wash away.
So in short space they did to health restore
The man that would not liue, but earst lay at deathes dore.

XXVIII In which his torment often was so great,
That like a Lyon he would cry and rore,
And rend his flesh, and his owne synewes eat.
His owne deare *Vna* hearing euermore
His ruefull shriekes and gronings, often tore
Her guiltlesse garments, and her golden heare,
For pitty of his paine and anguish sore;
Yet all with patience wisely she did beare;
For well she wist, his crime could else be neuer cleare.

XXIX Whom thus recouer'd by wise Patience,
And trew *Repentance* they to *Vna* brought:
Who ioyous of his cured conscience,
Him dearely kist, and fairely eke besought
Himselfe to chearish, and consuming thought
To put away out of his carefull brest.
By this *Charissa*, late in child-bed brought,
Was woxen strong, and left her fruitfull nest;
To her faire *Vna* brought this vnacquainted guest.

XXX She was a woman in her freshest age,
Of wondrous beauty, and of bountie rare,
With goodly grace and comely personage,
That was on earth not easie to compare;
Full of great loue, but *Cupids* wanton snare
As hell she hated, chast in worke and will;
Her necke and breasts were euer open bare,
That ay thereof her babes might sucke their fill;
The rest was all in yellow robes arayed still.

26 He then dressed Redcross's handsome body in sackcloth and ashes to abate his proud passions, and increase his self control. He fasted every day to ease his swelling wounds, and was made to pray both early and late. Just as puffed-up flesh will rot, correction was always ready at hand to pluck it out with hot fiery pincers, and soon he was left with not one corrupted jot.

Every day he was wont to discipline his weaker flesh with the iron lash of penance.[6] The sharp remorse pricked the conscience of his heart and welled drops of blood. He then bathed his stinging body in salt water, and the filthy blots of sin were washed away. So, in a short space, they restored the man who would not live, but before lay at death's door.

Sometimes his torment was so great, he would roar and cry like a lion, rend his flesh and torment his own sinews. His own dear Una, hearing his rueful shrieks and groaning, often tore her guiltless garments and her golden hair. She pitied his pain and severe anguish, yet she bore it all with wise patience, for she knew there was no other way for his crime to be cleared.

When he had finally recovered, Dr Patience and Dr Repentance brought Redcross to Una. Joyous at his cured conscience, she kissed him dearly and gently urged him to cherish his own life, and to put away the consuming thoughts of death. By this time, Charissa had now grown strong after the birth of her son, and Una brought Redcross to introduce him to her.

30 Charissa was a woman in her freshest age, of wondrous beauty and rare goodness, with goodly grace and a charming nature that was not easy to match on earth. Being full of true and pure love, and chaste in work and will, she disdained Cupid's wanton snare like hell. While arrayed in a yellow robe of marriage,

XXXI A multitude of babes about her hong,
Playing their sports, that ioyd her to behold,
Whom still she fed, whiles they were weakeand young,
But thrust them forth still, as they wexed old:
And on her head she wore a tyre of gold,
Adornd with gemmes and owches wondrous faire,
Whose passing price vneath was to be told;
And by her side there sate a gentle paire
Of turtle doues, she sitting in an yuorie chaire.

XXXII The knight and *Vna* entring, faire her greet,
And bid her ioy of that her happie brood;
Who them requites with court'sies seeming meet,
And entertaines with friendly chearefull mood.
Then *Vna* her besought, to be so good,
As in her vertuous rules to schoole her knight,
Now after all his torment well withstood,
In that sad house of *Penaunce*, where his spright
Had past the paines of hell, and long enduring night.

XXXIII She was right ioyous of her iust request,
And taking by the hand that Faeries sonne,
Gan him instruct in euery good behest,
Of loue, and righteousnesse, and well to donne,
And wrath, and hatred warely to shonne,
That drew on men Gods hatred, and his wrath,
And many soules in dolours had fordonne:
In which when him she well instructed hath,
From thence to heauen she teacheth him the ready path.

XXXIV Wherein his weaker wandring steps to guide,
An auncient matrone she to her does call,
Whose sober lookes her wisedome well descride:
Her name was *Mercie*, well knowne ouer all,
To be both gratious, and eke liberall:
To whom the carefull charge of him she gaue,
To lead aright, that he should neuer fall
In all his wayes through this wide worldes waue,
That Mercy in the end his righteous soule might saue.

XXXV The godly Matrone by the hand him beares
Forth from her presence, by a narrow way,
Scattred with bushy thornes, and ragged breares,
Which still before him she remou'd away,
That nothing might his ready passage stay:
And euer when his feet encombred were,
Or gan to shrinke, or from the right to stray,
She held him fast, and firmely did vpbeare,
As carefull Nourse her child from falling oft does reare.

31 she continued to breastfeed a multitude of babes that hung about her neck, or played around her feet, rejoicing to behold. She fed the weak and young, but urged them forth as they grew older. On her head, she wore a golden tiara that was adorned with wondrously fair gems and jewels of inestimable value. Seated upon an ivory chair, a pair of gentle turtle doves perched by her side.

Redcross and Una entered her room and greeted her warmly, bidding her joy with her happy brood of little ones. She returned their courtesies with well fitting words, and received them with a friendly cheerful mood. Then Una asked Charissa if she would be so good as to tutor her knight in her virtuous ways, since his torment, and his stint in the house of penance, where he had passed through the pains of hell and long enduring darkness, were now over.

Charissa's eyes lit up at the request, and taking the Faerie's son by the hand, she began to instruct him in truth. She told him about true love, of righteousness, and of well-doing. She coached him to shun all wrath and hatred that drew God's wrath and hatred on those who indulged in it, and had ruined many souls in misery. Once she had instructed him, from there, she taught him about the direct path to heaven.

To further guide his weaker wandering steps, Charissa called to a wise old woman, whose wisdom was revealed by her sober looks, and whose name was Mercy: well known everywhere to be both gracious and free. She now gave Mercy charge of Redcross, asking her to lead him rightly so that, in all his wanderings in the wide world, he should never fall, and that, in the end, Mercy shall save his soul. **35** The wise old woman took him by the hand and led him by a narrow way, scattered with thornbushes and ragged briars. As they passed, Mercy pushed back the prickly branches so that nothing would obstruct his passage. And when his feet were tempted to flee, she held him firmly and carefully helped him, as a nursemaid raises a child.

XXXVI Eftsoones vnto an holy Hospitall,
That was fore by the way, she did him bring,
In which seuen Bead-men that had vowed all
Their life to seruice of high heauens king
Did spend their dayes in doing godly thing:
Their gates to all were open euermore,
That by the wearie way were traueiling,
And one sate wayting euer them before,
To call in-commers by, that needy were and pore.

XXXVII The first of them that eldest was, and best,
Of all the house had charge and gouernement,
As Guardian and Steward of the rest:
His office was to giue entertainement
And lodging, vnto all that came, and went:
Not vnto such, as could him feast againe,
And double quite, for that he on them spent,
But such, as want of harbour did constraine:
Those for Gods sake his dewty was to entertaine.

XXXVIII The second was as Almner of the place,
His office was, the hungry for to feed,
And thristy giue to drinke, a worke of grace:
He feard not once him selfe to be in need,
Ne car'd to hoord for those, whom he did breede:
The grace of God he layd vp still in store,
Which as a stocke he left vnto his seede;
He had enough, what need him care for more?
And had he lesse, yet some he would giue to the pore.

XXXIX The third had of their wardrobe custodie,
In which were not rich tyres, nor garments gay,
The plumes of pride, and wings of vanitie,
But clothes meet to keepe keene could away,
And naked nature seemely to aray;
With which bare wretched wights he dayly clad,
The images of God in earthly clay;
And if that no spare cloths to giue he had,
His owne coate he would cut, and it distribute glad.

XL The fourth appointed by his office was,
Poore prisoners to relieue with gratious ayd,
And captiues to redeeme with price of bras,
From Turkes and Sarazins, which them had stayd;
And though they faultie were, yet well he wayd,
That God to vs forgiueth euery howre
Much more then that, why they in bands were layd,
And he that harrowd hell with heauie stowre,
The faultie soules from thence brought to his heauenly bowre

36 Soon they came unto a holy hostel nearby, and she brought him inside. There, seven monks who had vowed all their lives to service, spent their days doing good deeds. Their gates were always open to all who were travelling by the weary way, while a porter sat watching to call in passers-by who were needy and poor.

The eldest and foremost had charge of running and governing the house, and acting as guardian and steward of the rest. His duty was to give provisions and lodging to all who came and went. Those who could afford a feast would twice repay him for what was spent, if want of shelter had forced them to come to him. Those, for dear God's sake, his duty was to provide.

The second was Almer, distributer of alms. His job was to feed the hungry and replenish the thirsty: a work of grace. He never feared scarcity, nor cared to hoard for his family. Instead, he stored his treasures in heaven, and this was the fund he left unto his children. He had enough on earth, so why need more? And even though he had too little, he still gave to the poor.

The third oversaw the hostel wardrobe, in which there were no rich tiaras or gay garments, which are the plumes of pride and wings of vanity. Instead, he kept clothing that was suitable in keeping away the cold, and he daily clad naked wretched creatures, since they were also made in the image of God. And if he had no spare clothes to give, he would gladly give his own coat.

40 The fourth monk's job was to help poor prisoners and to relieve their suffering with gracious aid. He would redeem those kidnapped by Turks and Saracens, and pay the ransoms. And although they were sinful, he treated them well, because, every hour, God forgives much more than that. For that which they were laid in bonds, He descended into hell, broke the gates, and thence brought the guilty souls to his heavenly bower.

XLI The fift had charge sicke persons to attend,
And comfort those, in point of death which lay;
For them most needeth comfort in the end,
When sin, and hell, and death do most dismay
The feeble soule departing hence away.
All is but lost, that liuing we bestow,
If not well ended at our dying day.
O man haue mind of that last bitter throw;
For as the tree does fall, so lyes it euer low.

XLII The sixt had charge of them now being dead,
In seemely sort their corses to engraue,
And deck with dainty flowres their bridall bed,
That to their heauenly spouse both sweet and braue
They might appeare, when he their soules shall saue.
The wondrous workemanship of Gods owne mould,
Whose face he made, all beasts to feare, and gaue
All in his hand, euen dead we honour should.
Ah dearest God me graunt, I dead be not defould.

XLIII The seuenth now after death and buriall done,
Had charge the tender Orphans of the dead
And widowes ayd, least they should be vndone:
In face of iudgement he their right would plead,
Ne ought the powre of mighty men did dread
In their defence, nor would for gold or fee
Be wonne their rightfull causes downe to tread:
And when they stood in most necessitee,
He did supply their want, and gaue them euer free.

XLIV There when the Elfin knight arriued was,
The first and chiefest of the seuen, whose care
Was guests to welcome, towardes him did pas:
Where seeing *Mercie*, that his steps vp bare,
And alwayes led, to her with reuerence rare
He humbly louted in meeke lowlinesse,
And seemely welcome for her did prepare:
For of their order she was Patronesse,
Albe *Charissa* were their chiefest founderesse.

XLV There she awhile him stayes, him selfe to rest,
That to the rest more able he might bee:
During which time, in euery good behest
And godly worke of Almes and charitee
She him instructed with great industree;
Shortly therein so perfect he became,
That from the first vnto the last degree,
His mortall life he learned had to frame
In holy righteousnesse, without rebuke or blame.

41 The fifth had charge of sick persons. He would comfort those who lay at the point of death, because that was when they most needed comfort: when sin, and hell, and death most trouble the feeble soul departing hence away. All is but lost of that which we store up when living, if not well ended in our dying day. *O man, have mind of that bitter throe of death, for as the tree falls, so it lies forever more.*

The sixth had charge of burying the dead. He would gracefully deck their funeral bed with dainty flowers, so that in heaven they would appear sweet and brave when it came to the salvation of their souls. The wondrous workmanship of God's own image, whose face he made all beasts to fear, delivering them into his hand, and we should honor even the dead. *Oh dearest God, grant me: may I not be defiled when dead!*

The seventh had charge of orphans and widow's aid, lest they should be undone. He would go to court to plead for their rights, and did not fear the power of mighty men in their defense. Nor would he accept fees or bribes to discredit their rightful causes. And when they were most in need, he would supply their every want for free.

When the Elfin knight arrived there, the chief monk, whose job it was to welcome guests, strode warmly towards him. When he noticed Mercy following him, the monk bowed reverently, and prepared a seemly welcome for her. For of their Order, she was their patroness and protector, even though Charissa was their chief founder.

45 Mercy stayed a while with Redcross so that he could rest before completing his journey. During this time she instructed him in the godly work of alms-giving and charity. Shortly, he became so perfect that, from the first unto the last, he realized he had to frame his whole life in holy righteousness, without rebuke or blame.

XLVI Thence forward by that painfull way they pas,
Forth to an hill, that was both steepe and hy;
On top whereof a sacred chappell was,
And eke a litle Hermitage thereby,
Wherein an aged holy man did lye,
That day and night said his deuotion,
Ne other worldly busines did apply;
His name was heauenly *Contemplation*;
Of God and goodnesse was his meditation.

XLVII Great grace that old man to him giuen had;
For God he often saw from heauens hight,
All were his earthly eyen both blunt and bad,
And through great age had lost their kindly sight,
Yet wondrous quick and persant was his spright,
As Eagles eye, that can behold the Sunne:
That hill they scale with all their powre and might,
That his frayle thighes nigh wearie and fordonne
Gan faile, but by her helpe the top at last he wonne.

XLVIII There they do finde that godly aged Sire,
With snowy lockes adowne his shoulders shed,
As hoarie frost with spangles doth attire
The mossy braunches of an Oke halfe ded.
Each bone might through his body well be red,
And euery sinew seene through his long fast:
For nought he car'd his carcas long vnfed;
His mind was full of spirituall repast,
And pyn'd his flesh, to keepe his body low and chast.

XLIX Who when these two approching he aspide,
At their first presence grew agrieued sore,
That forst him lay his heauenly thoughts aside;
And had he not that Dame respected more,
Whom highly he did reuerence and adore,
He would not once haue moued for the knight.
They him saluted standing far afore;
Who well them greeting, humbly did requight,
And asked, to what end they clomb that tedious height.

L What end (quoth she) should cause vs take such paine,
But that same end, which euery liuing wight
Should make his marke, high heauen to attaine?
Is not from hence the way, that leadeth right
To that most glorious house, that glistreth bright
With burning starres, and euerliuing fire,
Whereof the keyes are to thy hand behight
By wise *Fidelia*? she doth thee require,
To shew it to this knight, according his desire.

46 Thence forward, they travelled again by the thorn path, and came to a hill that was both steep and high. On top thereof, a sacred chapel and hermitage stood, wherein lived an old holy man. Day and night, he said his devotions and did not apply himself to any worldly business. His name was heavenly Contemplation, and his meditation was on God and goodness. That old wise man had been given great grace, for he often saw God from heaven's height. Even though, with great age, he had lost his earthly sight, and was blind in both eyes, his insight was quick and piercing like an eagle's eye, that can behold the sun. Redcross and Mercy began to scale the hill with all their power and might. At times Redcross felt his frail thighs were too weary to go on, and he began to fail. But with Mercy's help and encouragement, they at least reached the summit.

There they found the godly aged hermit, Contemplation, with snowy locks that fell upon his shoulders like icicles. Like the mossy branches of a half-dead oak tree, his bones were easily seen through his skin, and every tendon and ligament was visible, due to frequent fasting. His mind was too full of spiritual food, so he starved his flesh to keep his body humble and chaste.

When he perceived these two approaching, he was aggrieved to be forced to lay his heavenly thoughts aside. And had he not realized it was Mercy, whom he greatly respected, revered and adored, he would not have moved once for the knight. When Redcross and Mercy greeted him from a distance, as a token of respect, the old man returned their greetings and asked them why they had climbed that wearying height.

50 "What end," began Mercy, "should cause us to take such pain, but that same end which every living creature should seek: to attain high heaven? Is not from hence the way that leads to that glorious house, glistering bright, with burning stars and ever living fire of the Kingdom of Heaven, whereof the keys are entrusted in your hand by wise Fidelia? She has requested that you should show it to this knight, granting his desire."

LI Thrise happy man, said then the father graue,
Whose staggering steps thy steady hand doth lead,
And shewes the way, his sinfull soule to saue.
Who better can the way to heauen aread,
Then thou thy selfe, that was both borne and bred
In heauenly throne, where thousand Angels shine?
Thou doest the prayers of the righteous sead
Present before the maiestie diuine,
And his auenging wrath to clemency incline.

LII Yet since thou bidst, thy pleasure shalbe donne.
Then come thou man of earth, and see the way,
That neuer yet was seene of Faeries sonne,
That neuer leads the traueiler astray,
But after labours long, and sad delay,
Brings them to ioyous rest and endlesse blis.
But first thou must a season fast and pray,
Till from her bands the spright assoiled is,
And haue her strength recur'd from fraile infirmitis.

LIII That done, he leads him to the highest Mount;
Such one, as that same mighty man of God,
That bloud-red billowes like a walled front
On either side disparted with his rod,
Till that his army dry-foot through them yod,
Dwelt fortie dayes vpon; where writ in stone
With bloudy letters by the hand of God,
The bitter doome of death and balefull mone
He did receiue, whiles flashing fire about him shone.

LIV Or like that sacred hill, whose head full hie,
Adornd with fruitfull Oliues all arownd,
Is, as it were for endlesse memory
Of that deare Lord, who oft thereon was fownd,
For euer with a flowring girlond crownd:
Or like that pleasaunt Mount, that is for ay
Through famous Poets verse each where renownd,
On which the thrise three learned Ladies play
Their heauenly notes, and make full many a louely lay.

LV From thence, far off he vnto him did shew
A litle path, that was both steepe and long,
Which to a goodly Citie led his vew;
Whose wals and towres were builded high and strong
Of perle and precious stone, that earthly tong
Cannot describe, nor wit of man can tell;
Too high a ditty for my simple song;
The Citie of the great king hight it well,
Wherein eternall peace and happinesse doth dwell.

51 "Thrice happy man," began the old grave hermit, "is he whose staggering steps you have led here showing him the way: his sinful soul to save. Who better can understand the way to heaven than you, Mercy, who was born and bred in a heavenly throne, where a thousand angels shine? You pray for the redeemed souls present before the divine majesty, inclining His avenging wrath to mercy. Yet since you bid, your will shall be done. Then come, you, man of earth, and see what no Faerie's son has ever seen. Glimpse that which never leads the traveler astray, but after long labors and sad delay, brings him to joyous rest and endless bliss. But first you must pray and fast for a season, until the spirit is released from her Adamic bonds, and her strength is restored to health from frail infirmities."

After that, he led them to the highest mount: such a one as Moses stood on—he whom the Red Sea billowed and parted with his rod, like a walled front on either side, until his army had moved through without even wetting their feet. Moses dwelt forty days upon Mt Sinai, writing in stone with the life-blood letters of the Covenant. Meanwhile, he endured the bitter doom of death and sad moaning, while flashes of lighting shone around him.

Or like that sacred hill that was adorned with fruitful olive trees, forever crowned with a flowering garland, as if it were an everlasting memorial of the dear Lord, who was often found thereon.

Or like Mount Parnassus, that inspired famous poets' verse, and on which those thrice-three learned ladies, the Muses, played their heavenly notes and composed many a lovely melody.

55 From the top of the mountain, the old man took Redcross down a little path and showed him a splendid city on the other side[4]. Its strong, high walls and towers were built of pearl and precious stone, so wonderful, that no earthly tongue could describe it, or mind of man convey: a too high refrain for my simple song. A great king dwelt in the city, wherein eternal peace and happiness dwelt for all.

LVI As he thereon stood gazing, he might see
The blessed Angels to and fro descend
From highest heauen, in gladsome companee,
And with great ioy into that Citie wend,
As commonly as friend does with his frend.
Whereat he wondred much, and gan enquere,
What stately building durst so high extend
Her loftie towres vnto the starry sphere,
And what vnknowen nation there empeopled were.

LVII Faire knight (quoth he) *Hierusalem* that is,
The new *Hierusalem*, that God has built
For those to dwell in, that are chosen his,
His chosen people purg'd from sinfull guilt,
With pretious bloud, which cruelly was spilt
On cursed tree, of that vnspotted lam,
That for the sinnes of all the world was kilt:
Now are they Saints all in that Citie sam,
More deare vnto their God, then yoūglings to their dam.

LVIII Till now, said then the knight, I weened well,
That great *Cleopolis*, where I haue beene,
In which that fairest *Faerie Queene* doth dwell,
The fairest Citie was, that might be seene;
And that bright towre all built of christall cleene,
Panthea, seemd the brightest thing, that was:
But now by proofe all otherwise I weene;
For this great Citie that does far surpas,
And this bright Angels towre quite dims that towre of glas.

LIX Most trew, then said the holy aged man;
Yet is *Cleopolis* for earthly frame,
The fairest peece, that eye beholden can:
And well beseemes all knights of noble name,
That couet in th'immortall booke of fame
To be eternized, that same to haunt,
And doen their seruice to that soueraigne Dame,
That glorie does to them for guerdon graunt:
For she is heauenly borne, and heauen may iustly vaunt.

LX And thou faire ymp, sprong out from English race,
How euer now accompted Elfins sonne,
Well worthy doest thy seruice for her grace,
To aide a virgin desolate foredonne.
But when thou famous victorie hast wonne,
And high emongst all knights hast hong thy shield,
Thenceforth the suit of earthly conquest shonne,
And wash thy hands from guilt of bloudy field:
For bloud can nought but sin, and wars but sorrowes yield.

56 As he stood there gazing, Redcross thought he could see a ladder, and angels descending to and fro in gladsome company, coming and going into the city as casually as friend does with his friend's home. Gazing at this incredible sight, Redcross began to wonder how the lofty towers reached the starry sphere, and who lived there, and he turned to ask the old man.

"Fair knight," said the old hermit, "that is the New Jerusalem that God has built for those to dwell in, who are his chosen ones. They, who were purged of sin with the precious blood that was cruelly spilt upon that cursed tree, the innocent lamb, killed for the sins of the world, are now all saints together in that city, dearer to God than are children to their mother."

"Till now," said the knight, "I thought that my own city, Cleopolis, in which the fairest Faerie Queene dwells, was the fairest city of all, and that the great crystal tower, the Panthea[5], seemed the brightest thing. But now I have seen something greater. For this great city far surpasses mine, and this bright angel tower quite dims our tower of glass."

"Most true," replied the holy man. "Yet Cleopolis, as an earthly city, is still the fairest masterpiece the eye can behold. And it well befits all knights of noble name who wish eternity in the immortal Book of Life. For the sovereign queen is heavenly born, and glory will be the reward for those who serve her.

60 "And you, fair youth, sprung out of the English race, hitherto accounted as an Elfin's son, you are doing a worthy service for her grace, aiding a desolate and wearied maiden. But when you have won your famous victory, have been honored amongst all knights, and have hung up your shield, thenceforth, you must shun earthly conquest and wash your hands from the guilt of bloody field. For blood yields to sin, and wars to sorrows.

LXI Then seeke this path, that I to thee presage,
Which after all to heauen shall thee send;
Then peaceably thy painefull pilgrimage
To yonder same *Hierusalem* do bend,
Where is for thee ordaind a blessed end:
For thou emongst those Saints, whom thou doest see,
Shalt be a Saint, and thine owne nations frend
And Patrone: thou Saint *George* shalt called bee,
Saint *George* of mery England, the signe of victoree.

LXII Vnworthy wretch (quoth he) of so great grace,
How dare I thinke such glory to attaine?
These that haue it attaind, were in like cace
(Quoth he) as wretched, and liu'd in like paine.
But deeds of armes must I at last be faine,
And Ladies loue to leaue so dearely bought?
What need of armes, where peace doth ay remaine,
(Said he) and battailes none are to be fought?
As for loose loues they are vaine, and vanish into nought.

LXIII O let me not (quoth he) then turne againe
Backe to the world, whose ioyes so fruitlesse are;
But let me here for aye in peace remaine,
Or streight way on that last long voyage fare,
That nothing may my present hope empare.
That may not be (said he) ne maist thou yit
Forgo that royall maides bequeathed care,
Who did her cause into thy hand commit,
Till from her cursed foe thou haue her freely quit.

LXIV Then shall I soone, (quoth he) so God me grace,
Abet that virgins cause disconsolate,
And shortly backe returne vnto this place,
To walke this way in Pilgrims poore estate.
But now aread, old father, why of late
Didst thou behight me borne of English blood,
Whom all a Faeries sonne doen nominate?
That word shall I (said he) auouchen good,
Sith to thee is vnknowne the cradle of thy brood.

LXV For well I wote, thou springst from ancient race
Of *Saxon* kings, that haue with mightie hand
And many bloudie battailes fought in place
High reard their royall throne in *Britane* land,
And vanquisht them, vnable to withstand:
From thence a Faerie thee vnweeting reft,
There as thou slepst in tender swadling band,
And her base Elfin brood there for thee left.
Such men do Chaungelings call, so chaungd by Faeries theft.

61 "Then seek the path that I reveal to you: the path that will send you to heaven. After your service, you must peacefully turn your path to Jerusalem, where a blessed end is ordained for you. For you will be one of the saints that you see down there, right now. Not only a saint, but your nation's friend and patron saint. You shall be called Saint George: Saint George of merry England: the emblem of victory."

Redcross gazed at the old man, aghast, and said, "But I am just an unworthy wretch. How dare I dream so great a grace to attain such glory?"

The old man replied, "The people you see in that city were once like you: wretched, and living with similar griefs."

Redcross shook his head in disbelief, "But must I now leave my quest and lady love, for whom I have toiled so hard?"

"What need of arms do you have when there is eternal peace, and no more battles fought? As for loves: they are vain and vanish into nothing," said the old man.

"O, then, don't make return to the world, whose joys are fruitless," said Redcross, "but let me remain here forever in peace, or send me on that last voyage now, so that nothing may impair my present hope."

The old man shook his head softly, "That may not be," said he. "Nor may you yet forgo that royal maid's bequeathed care, that she committed into your hand, until you have entirely delivered her from that cursed foe."

"Then I promise—and God give me grace—to aid that maiden's dreadful quest, so that I can shortly return to this place and walk the pilgrim's way," said Redcross.

Then he turned to the old man and asked, "But now, old father, please explain why you just referred to me as one born of English blood, when everyone else calls me a Faerie's son?"

"That I shall, since your family is yet unknown to you," began the old man, **65** "for I know that you spring from an ancient race of Saxon kings who have fought with mighty hand and raised high their royal throne in Britain, vanquishing those unable to withstand them. From thence, unbeknown to you, a Faerie removed you as you slept in infant swaddling clothes, and left her common Elfin baby in your stead. Such babies, stolen and exchanged by Faeries, are called changelings.

LXVI Thence she thee brought into this Faerie lond,
And in an heaped furrow did thee hyde,
Where thee a Ploughman all vnweeting fond,
As he his toylesome teme that way did guyde,
And brought thee vp in ploughmans state to byde,
Whereof *Georgos* he thee gaue to name;
Till prickt with courage, and thy forces pryde,
To Faery court thou cam'st to seeke for fame,
And proue thy puissaunt armes, as seemes thee best became.

LXVII O holy Sire (quoth he) how shall I quight
The many fauours I with thee haue found,
That hast my name and nation red aright,
And taught the way that does to heauen bound?
This said, adowne he looked to the ground,
To haue returnd, but dazed were his eyne,
Through passing brightnesse, which did quite confound
His feeble sence, and too exceeding shyne.
So darke are earthly things compard to things diuine.

LXVIII At last whenas himselfe he gan to find,
To *Vna* back he cast him to retire;
Who him awaited still with pensiue mind.
Great thankes and goodly meed to that good syre,
He thence departing gaue for his paines hyre.
So came to *Vna*, who him ioyd to see,
And after litle rest, gan him desire,
Of her aduenture mindfull for to bee.
So leaue they take of *Caelia*, and her daughters three.

66 Thence she brought you into Faerieland, and hid you in a furrow inside a hill where a surprised farmer, ploughing the fields with his toilsome team, unexpectedly discovered you. He brought you up in ploughman's rank, and gave you the name George. One day, you were pricked with courage and youthful prime, and came to the Faerie court to seek fame and prove your power in arms, as best suited to you.

"O, holy father," replied Redcross, "how shall I repay the many favors I have found with you, who has revealed the truth about my name and nation, and taught the way that leads to heaven?"

There was no answer, but suddenly a great light dazzled Redcross so that he had to look to the ground. The surpassing brightness confounded his feeble senses, for it shone so exceedingly. *So dark are earthly things compared to things divine*!

At last, when he had recovered himself from this bright vision, he resolved to return to Una, who still waited for him with anxious mind. Thence departing, Redcross rewarded that good old sire with great thanks, as was fitting for his pain's reward.

Soon, he returned to Una who was overjoyed to see him, and after a little rest, he began to set his mind on the final quest. So, they took leave of Caelia and her three daughters.

1   Lindberg, Carter (1988). *Martin Luther: Justified by Grace*. Graded Press.

2   Edmund Spenser, Carol V. Kaske, *The Faerie Queene: Book One* Paperback—2006

3   *The New Testament*

4   *splendid city: 1 Rev 21:10-21*

5   *Panthea: Greek for both "all goddess" and "all see" Spenser might have meant an English Pantheon,*

6   *Penance: the Greek 'Metanoia' (repentance, or more literally "with mind"), was translated into Latin as 'paenitentia' by Jerome in 405AD, and later as "do penance" in the early English Bibles (Wycliffe and Douay-Rheims Catholic Bible). No such word exists in the NT, though the word continued to be used in Christian contexts. The mistranslation, that affected theology for 1000 years, was corrected by Tyndale, and he was executed for it.*

NOTES ON CANTO XI

Dragon: symbolizes the enemies of Queen Elizabeth I and her subjects: the Medieval Roman Catholic Church, Philip II of Spain, and Satan.

The battle lasts for 40 stanzas, suggesting a spiritual battle (Jesus' 40 days in the wilderness Matt 4).

The Well of Life symbolizes Living Water (John:4) and baptism. **The Tree of Life** is the Eucharist, the symbol of Christ's body and blood. Both well and tree represent the grace that God bestows on mankind through the sacraments.

CANTO XI

THE BATTLE WITH THE DRAGON

The knight with that old Dragon fights
two dayes incessantly:
The third him ouerthrowes, and gayns
most glorious victory.

I HIgh time now gan it wex for *Vna faire,*
To thinke of those her captiue Parents deare,
And their forwasted kingdome to repaire:
Whereto whenas they now approched neare,
With hartie words her knight she gan to cheare,
And in her modest manner thus bespake;
Deare knight, as deare, as euer knight was deare,
That all these sorrowes suffer for my sake,
High heauen behold the tedious toyle, ye for me take.

II Now are we come vnto my natiue soyle,
And to the place, where all our perils dwell;
Here haunts that feend, and does his dayly spoyle,
Therefore henceforth be at your keeping well,
And euer ready for your foeman fell.
The sparke of noble courage now awake,
And striue your excellent selfe to excell;
That shall ye euermore renowmed make,
Aboue all knights on earth, that batteill vndertake.

III And pointing forth, lo yonder is (said she)
The brasen towre in which my parents deare
For dread of that huge feend emprisond be
Whom I from far see on the walles appeare
Whose sight my feeble soule doth greatly cheare:
And on the top of all I do espye
The watchman wayting tydings glad to heare,
That O my parents might I happily
Vnto you bring, to ease you of your misery.

IV With that they heard a roaring hideous sound,
That all the ayre with terrour filled wide,
And seemd vneath to shake the stedfast ground.
Eftsoones that dreadfull Dragon they espide,
Where stretcht he lay vpon the sunny side
Of a great hill, himselfe like a great hill.
But all so soone, as he from far descride
Those glistring armes, that heauen with light did fill,
He rousd himselfe full blith, and hastned them vntill.

V Then badd the knight his Lady yede aloofe,
And to an hill her selfe with draw aside,
From whence she might behold that battailles proof
And eke be safe from daunger far descryde:
She him obayd, and turnd a little wyde.
Now O thou sacred Muse, most learned Dame,
Faire ympe of *Phoebus,* and his aged bride,
The Nourse of time, and euerlasting fame,
That warlike hands ennoblest with immortall name;

The knight fights with that old dragon for two days incessantly. On the third day, he overthrows him, and gains the most glorious victory.

IT WAS HIGH TIME NOW FOR FAIR UNA TO THINK OF HER DEAR CAPTIVE PARENTS, and to the task of restoring their forsaken kingdom, and once they started to approach her home, she began to cheer her knight with hearty words.

And in her modest manner, she said, "Dear knight, as dear as any knight was dear, who suffers all these sorrows for my sake, high heaven, behold the tedious toil you endure for me. Now we are soon approaching unto my native soil, to the place where all our perils dwell, where that fiend haunts and does his daily spoil. Therefore, henceforth, be at your keeping well, and ever ready for your deadly foeman. Awake now the spark of noble courage, and strive for your most excellent self to excel, so that with the coming battle you are about to undertake, you shall be renowned above all knights on earth."

And, pointing forth, she said, "Lo, you see yonder, that brazen tower in which my dear parents are imprisoned, for dread of that huge fiend? I can see them appearing on the walls, and they shall soon be cheered by my feeble soul. And at the very top, I see the watchman waiting to hear the glad tidings that, *O mother and father*, might I happily bring unto you, to ease you of your misery! '"

Just then, they heard a hideous roaring that filled the air, far and wide, with terror, and seemed to shake the steadfast ground underneath them. And soon they glimpsed that dreadful dragon lying stretched out upon the sunny side of the hill, like a great hill himself. But it wasn't long before, from afar, that dreadful dragon discerned those glittering arms, that heaven had filled with light. He calmly and blithely raised himself, then hastened towards them.

5Redcross quickly bade Una ride apart, and withdraw herself to the hill from whence she might behold the outcome of the battle, as well as remain safe from danger. She obeyed and galloped away to shelter.

NOW, O SACRED MUSE, MOST LEARNED DAME, FAIR CHILD OF PHOEBUS AND HIS aged bride, the nurse of time and everlasting fame, that warlike hands ennobles with immortal name,

VI O gently come into my feeble brest,
Come gently, but not with that mighty rage,
Wherewith the martiall troupes thou doest infest,
And harts of great Heroës doest enrage,
That nought their kindled courage may aswage,
Soone as thy dreadfull trompe begins to sownd;
The God of warre with his fiers equipage
Thou doest awake, sleepe neuer he so sownd,
And scared nations doest with horrour sterne astownd.

VII Faire Goddesse lay that furious fit aside,
Till I of warres and bloudy *Mars* do sing,
And Briton fields with Sarazin bloud bedyde,
Twixt that great faery Queene and Paynim king,
That with their horrour heauen and earth did ring,
A worke of labour long, and endlesse prayse:
But now a while let downe that haughtie string,
And to my tunes thy second tenor rayse,
That I this man of God his godly armes may blaze.

VIII By this the dreadfull Beast drew nigh to hand,
Halfe flying, and halfe footing in his hast,
That with his largenesse measured much land,
And made wide shadow vnder his huge wast;
As mountaine doth the valley ouercast.
Approching nigh, he reared high afore
His body monstrous, horrible, and vast,
Which to increase his wondrous greatnesse more,
Was swolne with wrath, and poyson, and with bloudy gore.

IX And ouer, all with brasen scales was armd,
Like plated coate of steele, so couched neare,
That nought mote perce, ne might his corse be harmd
With dint of sword, nor push of pointed speare;
Which as an Eagle, seeing pray appeare,
His aery plumes doth rouze, full rudely dight,
So shaked he, that horrour was to heare,
For as the clashing of an Armour bright,
Such noyse his rouzed scales did send vnto the knight.

X His flaggy wings when forth he did display,
Were like two sayles, in which the hollow wynd
Is gathered full, and worketh speedy way:
And eke the pennes, that did his pineons bynd,
Were like mayne-yards, with flying canuas lynd,
With which whenas him list the ayre to beat,
And there by force vnwonted passage find,
The cloudes before him fled for terrour great,
And all the heauens stood still amazed with his threat.

6 *O gently come into my feeble breast. Come gently: but not with that mighty rage with which you infest the martial troops and enrage the hearts of great heroes. For, as soon as your dreadful trumpet sounds, nothing will assuage their kindled courage. You awake the god of war who never sleeps soundly, and with his armaments, you astound the sacred nations with stern horror.*

Fair goddess, lay that strain of music aside till I sing of the wars and of bloody Mars, of Briton fields dyed with Saracen blood, of the war between the great Faerie Queene and pagan king,[1] that heaven and earth rang with their horror: a work of long labor and endless praise. But now loosen the high strings of your harp to a lower pitch, and produce deeper notes to my tunes, so that I may glorify this man of godly arms.

BEFORE LONG, THE DREADFUL BEAST DREW CLOSE TO REDCROSS, HALF FLYING and half footing in haste. His size measured much land, and cast a wide, dark shadow under his huge girth: just as a mountain casts shadow on a valley.

Approaching nigh, he reared up before the knight: his body monstrous, horrible and vast, which, to increase his wondrous greatness even more, was swollen with wrath, poison and bloody gore. Tightly meshed brass-like scales covered his entire body like a plated coat of steel, so that no dint of sword or pointed lance might pierce or harm his bulk.

The dragon shook himself, like an eagle that delights in seeing a prey, his airy plumes ruggedly arrayed and ruffled. But what a horror to hear! For the clashing and crashing scales of that bright armor sent such a chilling clamor unto the knight.

10 When the monster displayed his gigantic drooping wings, they gathered wind and billowed outwards like two sails, working a speedy way. The ribs that bound the wings were like the yard-arms of a sailing ship, lined with flying canvas. And when he beat the air, and forced the wind to find passage, the clouds would flee in terror before him, and the heavens would stand amazed at his powerful thrusts.

XI His huge long tayle wound vp in hundred foldes,
Does ouerspred his long bras-scaly backe,
Whose wreathed boughts when euer he vnfoldes,
And thicke entangled knots adown does slacke.
Bespotted all with shields of red and blacke,
It sweepeth all the land behind him farre,
And of three furlongs does but litle lacke;
And at the point two stings in-fixed arre,
Both deadly sharpe, that sharpest steele exceeden farre.

XII But stings and sharpest steele did far exceed
The sharpnesse of his cruell rending clawes;
Dead was it sure, as sure as death in deed,
What euer thing does touch his rauenous pawes,
Or what within his reach he euer drawes.
But his most hideous head my toung to tell
Does tremble: for his deepe deuouring iawes
Wide gaped, like the griesly mouth of hell,
Through which into his darke abisse all rauin fell.

XIII And that more wondrous was, in either iaw
Three ranckes of yron teeth enraunged were,
In which yet trickling bloud and gobbets raw
Of late deuoured bodies did appeare,
That sight thereof bred cold congealed feare:
Which to increase, and as atonce to kill,
A cloud of smoothering smoke and sulphur seare
Out of his stinking gorge forth steemed still,
That all the ayre about with smoke and stench did fill.

XIV His blazing eyes, like two bright shining shields,
Did burne with wrath, and sparkled liuing fyre;
As two broad Beacons, set in open fields,
Send forth their flames farre off to euery shyre,
And warning giue, that enemies conspyre,
With fire and sword the region to inuade;
So flam'd his eyne with rage and rancorous yre:
But farre within, as in a hollow glade,
Those glaring lampes were set, that made a dreadfull shade.

XV So dreadfully he towards him did pas,
Forelifting vp aloft his speckled brest,
And often bounding on the brused gras,
As for great ioyance of his newcome guest.
Eftsoones he gan aduance his haughtie crest,
As chauffed Bore his bristles doth vpreare,
And shoke his scales to battell readie drest;
That made the *Redcrosse* knight nigh quake for feare,
As bidding bold defiance to his foeman neare.

11 His huge, long tail was wound up in hundreds of folds, and when he unfolded the wreathed coils of thick entangled knots, it eclipsed his enormous, brassy, scaly back. Bespotted with armored plates of red and black, the tail swept all the land far behind him, and measured just short of three furlongs. And fixed in the tail's pointy end, lay two deadly-sharp stings of the sharpest steel, exceeding all by far.

But the sharpness of his cruel rending claws was even more lethal than the stings and steel. Whatever creature touched his ravenous paws, or was grasped within his reach, was dead as death indeed. And as for his hideous head, my tongue trembles to describe it. Gaping wide, his deep devouring jaws were like the grisly mouth of hell, and into its dark abyss, all of his prey would fall.

Even more wondrous, was that both his upper and lower jaws were spiked with three rows of iron teeth, that were entangled with trickling blood and raw gobbets of late devoured bodies: a sight that bred cold congealed fear. To increase his power even further, as at once to kill, a cloud of smothering smoke and Sulphur continually seared forth from his stinking gorge, so that all the air about him was filled with smoke and stench.

His blazing eyes, like two bright shining shields, burned with wrath and sparkled with living fire, like two broad beacons, set in open fields, sending forth their flames far off to every shire, and giving warning that enemies loom, ready to invade with fire and sword. So flamed the dragon's eyes, with rage and rancorous ire. But deep within, as in a hollow glade, were set those glaring lamps that made a dreadful shade.

15 So dreadfully did that monster pace towards him, raising high his speckled breast, and often bounding on the bruised grass, as if for great joy at his newcomer guest. Soon, he began to advance with haughty crest, rearing his bristles like an restless boar, and shaking his scales, ready for battle. All of this made Redcross inwardly quake for fear, but outwardly he bid bold defiance to his nearby foeman.

XVI The knight gan fairely couch his steadie speare,
And fiercely ran at him with rigorous might:
The pointed steele arriuing rudely theare,
His harder hide would neither perce, nor bight,
But glauncing by forth passed forward right;
Yet sore amoued with so puissant push,
The wrathfull beast about him turned light,
And him so rudely passing by, did brush
With his long tayle, that horse and man to ground did rush.

XVII Both horse and man vp lightly rose againe,
And fresh encounter towards him addrest:
But th'idle stroke yet backe recoyld in vaine,
And found no place his deadly point to rest.
Exceeding rage enflam'd the furious beast,
To be auenged of so great despight;
For neuer felt his imperceable brest
So wondrous force, from hand of liuing wight;
Yet had he prou'd the powre of many a puissant knight.

XVIII Then with his wauing wings displayed wyde,
Himselfe vp high he lifted from the ground,
And with strong flight did forcibly diuide
The yielding aire, which nigh too feeble found
Her flitting partes, and element vnsound,
To beare so great a weight: he cutting way
With his broad sayles, about him soared round:
At last low stouping with vnweldie sway,
Snatcht vp both horseand man, to beare them quite away.

XIX Long he them bore aboue the subiect plaine,
So farre as Ewghen bow a shaft may send,
Till struggling strong did him at last constraine,
To let them downe before his flightes end:
As hagard hauke presuming to contend
With hardie fowle, aboue his hable might,
His wearie pounces all in vaine doth spend,
To trusse the pray too heauie for his flight;
Which comming downe to ground, does free it selfe by fight.

XX He so disseized of his gryping grosse,
The knight his thrillant speare againe assayd
In his bras-plated body to embosse,
And three mens strength vnto the stroke he layd;
Wherewith the stiffe beame quaked, as affrayd,
And glauncing from his scaly necke, did glyde
Close vnder his left wing, then broad displayd.
The percing steele there wrought a wound full wyde,
That with the vncouth smart the Monster lowdly cryde.

16 He couched his steady lance, then fiercely ran at him with rigorous might. The pointed steel landed violently, but would neither pierce nor bite, bouncing straight off the impenetrable hide. Moved by such a powerful push, the wrathful beast turned quickly, and brought his tail rushing around after him, so that both horse and man were hurled to the ground.

Both horse and man rose up quickly again, and Redcross addressed the dragon with a fresh encounter. But the useless stroke recoiled yet back in vain, and found no place to penetrate the dragon's scales. Exceeding rage inflamed the furious beast, and he was determined to be avenged of so great an insult. For never did his un-pierceable breast feel such a wondrous force, from any living creature. Yet he had tested and withstood the power of many a formidable knight.

Then, with his waving wings displayed wide, he lifted himself high off the ground, forcibly dividing the yielding air with such vigorous flight, that its lack of substance was nearly too feeble to hold up his great weight. With his broad sails, he cut away and soared around. At last, swooping in low with unwieldy strength, he snatched up both horse and man to bear them away.

Long he bore them above the plain below, as far as a bow may send an arrow, till, struggling with weariness, he dropped them both before landing.

Like a wild hawk, struggling to fight with a hardy fowl beyond his strength, his weary talons exhaust themselves in vain to capture the prey too heavy for his flight which, falling to the ground, frees itself by fight.

20 Likewise, the dragon released his prey as the knight again attempted to plunge his lance into his brass-plated body. The beast felt as if three men had laid that stroke, and even the stiff shaft quaked as if afraid. Glancing from his scaly neck, Redcross glided close under his left wing, and lanced as hard as he could. The piercing steel wrought a wound full wise that, with the shock of pain, the monster cried loudly.

XXI He cryde, as raging seas are wont to rore,
When wintry storme his wrathfull wreck does threat,
The rolling billowes beat the ragged shore,
As they the earth would shoulder from her seat,
And greedie gulfe does gape, as he would eat
His neighbour element in his reuenge:
Then gin the blustring brethren boldly threat,
To moue the world from off his stedfast henge,
And boystrous battell make, each other to auenge.

XXII The steely head stucke fast still in his flesh,
Till with his cruell clawes he snatcht the wood,
And quite a sunder broke. Forth flowed fresh
A gushing riuer of blacke goarie blood,
That drowned all the land, whereon he stood;
The streame thereof would driue a water-mill.
Trebly augmented was his furious mood
With bitter sense of his deepe rooted ill,
That flames of fire he threw forth from his large nosethrill.

XXIII His hideous tayle then hurled he about,
And therewith all enwrapt the nimble thyes
Of his froth-fomy steed, whose courage stout
Striuing to loose the knot, that fast him tyes,
Himselfe in streighter bandes too rash implyes,
That to the ground he is perforce constraynd
To throw his rider: who can quickly ryse
From off the earth, with durty bloud distaynd,
For that reprochfull fall right fowly he disdaynd.

XXIV And fiercely tooke his trenchand blade in hand,
With which he stroke so furious and so fell,
That nothing seemd the puissance could withstand:
Vpon his crest the hardned yron fell,
But his more hardned crest was armd so well,
That deeper dint therein it would not make;
Yet so extremely did the buffe him quell,
That from thenceforth he shund the like to take,
But when he saw them come, he did them still forsake.

XXV The knight was wrath to see his stroke beguyld,
And smote againe with more outrageous might;
But backe againe the sparckling steele recoyld,
And left not any marke, where it did light;
As if in Adamant rocke it had bene pight.
The beast impatient of his smarting wound,
And of so fierce and forcible despight,
Thought with his wings to stye aboue the ground;
But his late wounded wing vnseruiceable found.

21 Loudly cried the monster, like the raging seas are wont to roar when a wintry storm threatens his own wrathful ruin. The rolling billows beat the ragged shore, as if to ram the earth from her seat, and drag her into the abyss of a vast and vicious whirlpool, devouring his neighboring element in revenge. And so begins earth's blustering brethren, blowing boldly, as if to budge the world off its axis, as they avenge each other in boisterous battle.

The steely lancehead stuck fast in the monster's flesh until, with his cruel claws, he snatched the shaft and broke it off. Forth flowed a fresh gushing river of black gory blood that drowned all the land whereon he stood: the stream of which would drive the water-mill. Trebly enraged, was his furious mood, that with the biting pain of his deep-rooted wound, he threw forth flames of fire from his gaping nostrils.

He then hurled his huge and hideous tail around, and enwrapped the nimble thighs of Redcross's foaming-mouthed steed, who bravely strove to kick and loosen the knot that tied him fast. But, the more the horse fought, the more the bonds entangled him, so that he was forced to throw his rider to the ground. But Redcross rose quickly from the earth, stained with blood and dirt, and reproached him for that foul fall.

Next, he fiercely took his trenchant blade in hand, and struck at the monster so furiously that nothing seemed to withstand that power. The hardened iron crashed upon the dragon's head, but his hardened crest was so well enamored, that the blade would not make a deeper dent. Yet the blow stunned him so extremely, that from thenceforth the fiend avoided the blows as he saw them coming.

25 The knight was angered to see his foiled stroke, and struck again with more outrageous might. But again, the sparkling steel recoiled, and left not a mark where it landed, as if it thrust at Adamantine rock. Impatient with his throbbing wound, and of so fierce and forcing injury, the beast thought to hover above ground, and fight from there. But, to his dismay, he found his wounded wing no longer functional.

XXVI Then full of griefe and anguish vehement,
He lowdly brayd, that like was neuer heard,
And from his wide deuouring ouen sent
A flake of fire, that flashing in his beard,
Him all amazd, and almost made affeard:
The scorching flame sore swinged all his face,
And through his armour all his bodie seard,
That he could not endure so cruell cace,
But thought his armes to leaue, and helmet to vnlace.

XXVII Not that great Champion of the antique world,
Whom famous Poetes verse so much doth vaunt,
And hath for twelue huge labours high extold,
So many furies and sharpe fits did haunt,
When him the poysoned garment did enchaunt
With *Centaures* bloud, and bloudie verses charm›d,
As did this knight twelue thousand dolours daunt,
Whom fyrie steele now burnt, that earst him arm'd,
That erst him goodly arm'd, now most of all him harm'd.

XXVIII Faint, wearie, sore, emboyled, grieued, brent
With heat, toyle, wounds, armes, smart, and inward fire
That neuer man such mischiefes did torment;
Death better were, death did he oft desire,
But death will neuer come, when needes require.
Whom so dismayd when that his foe beheld,
He cast to suffer him no more respire,
But gan his sturdie sterne about to weld,
And him so strongly stroke, that to the ground him feld.

XXIX It fortuned (as faire it then befell)
Behind his backe vnweeting, where he stood,
Of auncient time there was a springing well,
From which fast trickled forth a siluer flood,
Full of great vertues, and for med'cine good.
Whylome, before that cursed Dragon got
That happie land, and all with innocent blood
Defyld those sacred waues, it rightly hot
The well of life, ne yet his vertues had forgot.

XXX For vnto life the dead it could restore,
And guilt of sinfull crimes cleane wash away,
Those that with sicknesse were infected sore,
It could recure, and aged long decay
Renew, as one were borne that very day.
Both *Silo* this, and *Iordan* did excell,
And th'English *Bath*, and eke the german *Spau*,
Ne can *Cephise*, nor *Hebrus* match this well:
Into the same the knight backe ouerthrowen, fell.

26 Then, full of pain and vehement anguish, he brayed loudly: the like of which was never heard before. And from his wide devouring furnace-mouth, he sent a flood of fire that flashed in Redcross's beard, and startled him. The scorching flame singed his face, and his metal armor seared with such heat, that his body could barely endure such a cruel encasement, and he decided to quickly disarm and unlace his helmet.

That great champion of the Classical world, Hercules, whom famous poets' verse so much boasts, and has extolled him for his twelve huge labors, while so many furies and sharp fits haunted him, was poisoned by the garment that was enchanted with Centaur's blood and charmed bloody spells.

Similarly daunted by twelve thousand pains, Redcross now burned from the fiery steel of his armor. That which had before protected him, now harmed him. Faint, weary, sore, grieved, burnt with heat, toil, wounds, arms, pain, and inward fire: never a man endured such torment. Death were better, and death he often desired, but death will never come when he is needed.

When the dragon beheld his dismayed foe, he resolved to make him breathe his last, and began to whip his sturdy tail about, flinging Redcross to the ground.

By fortune, just behind him, unknowingly, there stood an ancient springing well. From this well, a silver flood fast trickled forth, full of great virtues and medicinal goodness. A long time ago, before that cursed dragon seized that happy land, and defiled those sacred waves with innocent blood, it was rightly called the Well of Life, and people knew of its virtues. **30** For it could restore the dead to life, and wash away the guilt of sinful crimes. It could cure those infected with sickness, and restore youth, as if one were born that very day. While the pool of Siloam and the River Jordan excelled, as did the English springs at Bath, as well as the German Spa, but neither the Cephise, nor the Hebrus, can match this well [2]

And into this same Well of Life, the knight, overthrown, fell backwards.

XXXI Now gan the golden *Phoebus* for to steepe
His fierie face in billowes of the west,
And his faint steedes watred in Ocean deepe,
Whiles from their iournall labours they did rest,
When that infernall Monster, hauing kest
His wearie foe into that liuing well,
Can high aduance his broad discoloured brest,
Aboue his wonted pitch, with countenance fell,
And clapt his yron wings, as victor he did dwell.

XXXII Which when his pensiue Ladie saw from farre,
Great woe and sorrow did her soule assay,
As weening that the sad end of the warre,
And gan to highest God entirely pray,
That feared chance from her to turne away;
With folded hands and knees full lowly bent
All night she watcht, ne once adowne would lay
Her daintie limbs in her sad dreriment,
But praying still did wake, and waking did lament.

XXXIII The morrow next gan early to appeare,
That *Titan* rose to runne his daily race:
But early ere the morrow next gan reare
Out of the sea faire *Titans* deawy face,
Vp rose the gentle virgin from her place,
And looked all about, if she might spy
Her loued knight to moue his manly pace:
For she had great doubt of his safety,
Since late she saw him fall before his enemy.

XXXIV At last she where he vpstarted braue
Out of the well, wherein he drenched lay;
As Eagle fresh out of the Ocean waue,
Where he hath left his plumes all hoary gray,
And deckt himselfe with feathers youthly gay,
Like Eyas hauke vp mounts vnto the skies,
His newly budded pineons to assay,
And marueiles at himselfe, still as he flies:
So new this new-borne knight to battell new did rise.

XXXV Whom when the damned feend so fresh did spy,
No wonder if he wondred at the sight,
And doubted, whether his late enemy
It were, or other new supplied knight.
He, now to proue his late renewed might,
High brandishing his bright deaw-burning blade,
Vpon his crested scalpe so sore did smite,
That to the scull a yawning wound it made:
The deadly dint his dulled senses all dismaid.

31 Now golden Phoebus began to soak his fiery face in the waves of the west, and his weary steeds watered in the deep ocean, where they rested from their daily labors. When that infernal monster had cast his weary foe into that Living Well, he roared pridefully from his speckled breast, louder than his usual pitch, and with dreaded countenance. Then he clapped his iron wings in victory.

From afar, the knight's pensive lady watched this sight with great woe and sorrow, believing this was the sad end of the war. She began to earnestly pray to highest God, to beg him to change her knight's luck. With folded hands and lowly bent knees, she kept vigil all night, not once lying down her dainty limbs. In her sad plight, she prayed and lamented and stayed awake.

The morrow began to appear, and Titan rose to start his daily race. But early, before sunrise, before fair Titan showed his dewy face, up rose the gentle maiden from her place. She ran to the windows and looked all about, hoping to see her beloved knight, moving his manly pace. For she had great doubt for his safety, since the last she saw of Redcross, was of him falling before his enemy.

At last she saw him rise freshly out from the well, wherein he had lain submerged all night.

Just like an eagle that has submerged into the ocean, leaving behind his plumes of gray, and taking on new and gay feathers, the newly youthful eagle mounts up to the skies, trying out his newly budded wings. There, he marvels at himself as he flies.[2]

Likewise did this new-born knight newly arise to battle.

35 When the damned fiend beheld this fresh knight, he wondered at the sight, and doubted his senses. Was it the same recent enemy, or a newly supplied knight? To test his renewed might, Redcross brandished his bright, dew-burning blade, that still shone with holy water. Then he smote the sword upon the dragon's crested scalp, so hard, that it made a yarning wound. The deadly blow dulled the dragon's dismayed senses.

XXXVI I wote not, whether the reuenging steele
Were hardned with that holy water dew,
Wherein he fell, or sharper edge did feele,
Or his baptized hands now greater grew;
Or other secret vertue did ensew;
Else neuer could the force of fleshly arme,
Ne molten mettall in his bloud embrew:
For till that stownd could neuer wight him harme,
By subtilty, nor slight, nor might, nor mighty charme.

XXXVII The cruell wound enraged him so sore,
That loud he yelded for exceeding paine;
As hundred ramping Lyons seem'd to rore,
Whom rauenous hunger did thereto constraine:
Then gan he tosse aloft his stretched traine,
And therewith scourge the buxome aire so sore,
That to his force to yeelden it was faine;
Ne ought his sturdie strokes might stand afore,
That high trees ouerthrew, and rocks in peeces tore.

XXXVIII The same aduauncing high aboue his head,
With sharpe intended sting so rude him smot,
That to the earth him droue, as stricken dead,
Ne liuing wight would haue him life behot:
The mortall sting his angry needle shot
Quite through his shield, and in his shoulder seasd,
Where fast it stucke, ne would there out be got:
The griefe thereof him wondrous sore diseasd,
Ne might his ranckling paine with patience be appeasd.

XXXIX But yet more mindfull of his honour deare,
Then of the grieuous smart, which him did wring,
From loathed soile he can him lightly reare,
And stroue to loose the farre infixed sting:
Which when in vaine he tryde with struggeling.
Inflam'd with wrath, his raging blade he heft,
And.strooke so strongly, that the knotty string
Of his huge taile he quite a sunder cleft,
Fiue ioynts thereof he hewd, and but the stump him left.

XL Hart cannot thinke, what outrage, and what cryes,
With foule enfouldred smoake and flashing fire,
The hell-bred beast threw forth vnto the skyes,
That all was couered with darknesse dire:
Then fraught with rancour, and engorged ire,
He cast at once him to auenge for all,
And gathering vp himselfe out of the mire,
With his vneuen wings did fiercely fall
Vpon his sunne-bright shield, and gript it fast withall.

36 I know not whether the avenging steel were hardened, or sharpened in that holy water in which it fell, or if his baptized hands had grown greater, or even if there were some other secret virtue. Because no mortal arm, even with molten metal in its blood, could plunge a sword like that, and until that moment, no creature had ever been capable of harming him: neither by subtlety, nor slight, nor might, nor mighty magic spell.

The cruel wound enraged the beast so sore, that he roared loudly with exceeding pain, like a hundred, raging, ravenous lions. Then he began to toss aloft his outstretched tail, whipping the yielding air so harshly, that it was obliged to yield to his force. Nothing could stand before his violent strokes: trees were uprooted and rocks torn into pieces.

Advancing with the tail soaring over his head, the monster aimed his sting at Redcross, and struck him so violently, that it flung him on the earth, as if stricken dead. No living creature would have called him living now. The angry needle shot the mortal sting right through the shield, and penetrated his shoulder, where it stuck so firmly, that he could not dislodge it, and was unable to appease the tormenting, rankling pain.

But more mindful of his honor than of the pain that wracked him, he quickly rose from the dishonorable ground, and strove to loosen the deeply embedded sting. Inflamed with wrath, he heaved his raging blade and struck the knotty tail so strongly, that he chopped off five sections, leaving just a stump.

40 The heart cannot imagine what outrage, what cries, what blaze-filled smoke and flashing fire that hell-bred beast threw forth unto the skies, until all was covered with ominous darkness. Then, fraught with malice and enflamed ire, he resolved to avenge him at once for every hurt. Gathering himself up, with his uneven wings, he fiercely fell upon the knight's shield, and gripped it firmly.

XLI Much was the man encombred with his hold,
In feare to lose his weapon in his paw,
Ne wist yet, how his talants to vnfold;
Nor harder was from *Cerberus* greedie iaw
To plucke a bone, then from his cruell claw
To reaue by strength the griped gage away:
Thrise he assayd it from his foot to draw,
And thrise in vaine to draw it did assay,
It booted nought to thinke, to robbe him of his pray.

XLII Tho when he saw no power might preuaile,
His trustie sword he cald to his last aid,
Wherewith he fiercely did his foe assaile,
And double blowes about him stoutly laid,
That glauncing fire out of the yron plaid;
As sparckles from the Anduile vse to fly,
When heauie hammers on the wedge are swaid;
Therewith at last he forst him to vnty
One of his grasping feete, him to defend thereby.

XLIII The other foot, fast fixed on his shield,
Whenas no strength, nor stroks mote him constraine
To loose, ne yet the warlike pledge to yield,
He smot thereat with all his might and maine,
That nought so wondrous puissance might sustaine;
Vpon the ioynt the lucky steele did light,
And made such way, that hewd it quite in twaine;
The paw yet missed not his minisht might,
But hong still on the shield, as it at first was pight.

XLIV For griefe thereof, and diuelish despight,
From his infernall fournace forth he threw
Huge flames, that dimmed all the heauens light,
Enrold in duskish smoke and brimstone blew;
As burning *Aetna* from his boyling stew
Doth belch out flames, and rockes in peeces broke,
And ragged ribs of mountaines molten new,
Enwrapt in coleblacke clouds and filthy smoke,
That all the land with stench, and heauen with horror choke.

XLV The heate whereof, and harmefull pestilence
So sore him noyd, that forst him to retire
A little backward for his best defence,
To saue his bodie from the scorching fire,
Which he from hellish entrailes did expire.
It chaunst (eternall God that chaunce did guide)
As he recoyled backward, in the mire
His nigh forwearied feeble feet did slide,
And downe he fell, with dread of shame sore terrifide.

41 Much was that man encumbered with his hold, fearing to lose his weapon in the monster's claw, yet not knowing how to loosen the talons. It would have been easier to pluck a bone from Cerberus' greedy jaw, than to tear the gripped token away from the dragon's cruel claw, by strength. Thrice he tried to wrench the shield free from the foot, and thrice he labored in vain. For the knight's efforts yielded nothing, and he was at a loss on how to rob him of his prey.

When he realized that no power might prevail, he finally called on his trusty sword, and fiercely assailed his foe. With double blows, he slashed so powerfully, that flickers of fire flew out of the iron claws, like sparkles from an anvil when heavy hammers are swung on a metal ingot.

At last, the knight forced the dragon to untie one of his claws to defend himself. Despite his strong sword strokes, the knight was unable to control the other foot that was fixed fast on the shield, nor could he compel the dragon to drop his prize. Then, with wondrous might, that no power might sustain, he struck his lucky sword into the joint of the free claw, hewing it in two. But his other claw continued to cling to the shield with undiminished might.

With pain and devilish despite, the dragon's infernal furnace now hurled forth huge flames that dimmed all heaven's light, enveloping it in darkened smoke and blue brimstone.

When the burning Mount Etna, erupting from its boiling cauldron down below, belched out flames and broken rocks, and ragged ribs of newly molten mountains, all the air was wrapped in coal-black clouds, filthy smoke, and choking stench.

That same ominous twilight now engulfed the atmosphere.

45 The heat and haze troubled the knight so badly that it forced him to retreat backwards for his best defense: to save his body from the scorching fire, which the dragon breathed out from his hellish entrails. It chanced that—and eternal God guided that chance—as the knight recoiled backwards in the mire, his nearly wearied feeble feet slid, and down he fell, with dread of dishonor sorely terrifying him.

XLVI There grew a goodly tree him faire beside,
Loaden with fruit and apples rosie red,
As they in pure vermilion had beene dide,
Whereof great vertues ouer all were red:
For happie life to all, which thereon fed,
And life eke euerlasting did befall:
Great God it planted in that blessed sted
With his almightie hand, and did it call
The tree of life, the crime of our first fathers fall.

XLVII In all the world like was not to be found,
Saue in that soile, where all good things did grow,
And freely sprong out of the fruitfull ground,
As incorrupted Nature did them sow,
Till that dread Dragon all did ouerthrow.
Another like faire tree eke grew thereby,
Whereof who so did eat, eftsoones did know
Both good and ill: O mornefull memory:
That tree through one mans fault hath doen vs all to dy.

XLVIII From that first tree forth flowd, as from a well,
A trickling streame of Balme, most soueraine
And daintie deare, which on the ground still fell,
And ouerflowed all the fertill plaine,
As it had deawed bene with timely raine:
Life and long health that gratious ointment gaue,
And deadly woundes could heale, and reare againe
The senselesse corse appointed for the graue.
Into that same he fell: which did from death him saue.

XLIX For nigh thereto the euer damned beast
Durst not approch, for he was deadly made,
And all that life preserued, did detest:
Yet he it oft aduentur'd to inuade.
By this the drouping day-light gan to fade
And yeeld his roome to sad succeeding night,
Who with her sable mantle gan to shade
The face of earth, and wayes of liuing wight,
And high her burning torch set vp in heauen bright.

L When gentle *Vna* saw the second fall
Of her deare knight, who wearie of long fight,
And faint through losse of bloud, mou'd not at all,
But lay as in a dreame of deepe delight,
Besmeard with pretious Balme, whose vertuous might
Did heale his wounds, and scorching heat alay,
Againe she stricken was with sore affright,
And for his safetie gan deuoutly pray;
And watch the noyous night, and wait for ioyous day.

46 But there, where the knight fell, and was fearing defeat, grew a special tree close by, laden with such rosy red apples, that they could have been dyed in pure vermilion. Great virtues were widely reported of that tree, for those who fed from it, were granted a happy life, as well as everlasting life. Great God planted it in that blessed place, and called it the Tree of Life: the crime site of our first father's fall.

No other tree in all the world could be found like that. Only in the Garden of Eden, where all good things grew, and where it freely sprung out of the fruitful ground, created by uncorrupted nature, till that dreaded dragon overthrew all. Another similar tree grew nearby where, whoever ate from it, would know good and evil. *O mournful memory of how that tree, through one man's fault, brought us death!*

From that first tree flowed forth, as from a well, the trickling stream of Balm. This sovereign and precious water still fell on fertile soil, and overflowed all the fertile plain, like water from timely rain. That gracious ointment gave life and long health, and it could heal deadly wounds, while the unconscious corpse ready for the grave, bathed in this water, was saved from death.

Seeing this, the damned beast would not draw near, for he belonged to death and detested life. Yet he often dared to invade it. By this time, the drooping daylight began to fade and yield his room to sad succeeding night who, with her sable mantle, began to shade the face of the earth and paths of living creatures. Then she set her burning torch, the moon, up high in heaven bright.

50 Gentle Una saw the second fall of her dear knight who, weary from the long fight, and faint through loss of blood, did not move. He lay as in a dream of deep delight, bathed with precious Balm, whose virtuous might healed his wound and allayed his scorching burns. Again, she was stricken with fright for his safety, and again she began her devout prayers, keeping vigil all night and waiting for joyous day.

LI The ioyous day gan early to appeare,
And faire *Aurora* from the deawy bed
Of aged *Tithone* gan her selfe to reare,
With rosie cheekes, for shame as blushing red;
Her golden lockes for haste were loosely shed
About her eares, when *Vna* her did marke
Clymbe to her charet, all with flowers spred;
From heauen high to chase the chearelesse darke,
With merry note her loud salutes the mounting larke.

LII Then freshly vp arose the doughtie knight,
All healed of his hurts and woundes wide,
And did himselfe to battell readie dight;
Whose early foe awaiting him beside
To haue deuourd, so soone as day he spyde,
When now he saw himselfe so freshly reare,
As if late fight had nought him damnifyde,
He woxe dismayd, and gan his fate to feare;
Nathlesse with wonted rage he him aduaunced neare.

LIII And in his first encounter, gaping wide,
He thought attonce him to haue swallowd quight,
And rusht vpon him with outragious pride;
Who him r'encountring fierce, as hauke in flight,
Perforce rebutted backe. The weapon bright
Taking aduantage of his open iaw,
Ran through his mouth with so importune might,
That deepe emperst his darksome hollow maw,
And back retyrd, his life bloud forth with all did draw.

LIV So downe he fell, and forth his life did breath,
That vanisht into smoke and cloudes swift;
So downe he fell, that th'earth him vnderneath
Did grone, as feeble so great load to lift;
So downe he fell, as an huge rockie clift,
Whose false foundation waues haue washt away,
With dreadfull poyse is from the mayneland rift,
And rolling downe, great *Neptune* doth dismay;
So downe he fell, and like an heaped mountaine lay.

LV The knight himselfe euen trembled at his fall,
So huge and horrible a masse it seem'd;
And his deare Ladie, that beheld it all,
Durst not approch for dread, which she misdeem'd,
But yet at last, when as the direfull feend
She saw not stirre, off-shaking vaine affright,
She nigher drew, and saw that ioyous end:
Then God she praysd, and thankt her faithfull knight,
That had atchieu'd so great a conquest by his might.

51 The joyous day began to appear early, and fair Aurora rose from the watery bed of old Tithone, her rosy cheeks blushing red in shame, and her golden locks loosely shed about her ears for haste, when Una noticed her. Climbing into her chariot, spread with flowers, Aurora was ready to chase away the cheerless dark and greet the world with the morning lark.

Then the brave knight rose, freshly healed of all his hurts and wide wounds, and dressed himself ready for battle. The dragon was already waiting to devour him, as soon as he saw that child of the day. But when he saw the knight so renewed, as if the recent fight had done him no damage, he grew dismayed, and began to fear his fate. Nevertheless, with his usual rage, the dragon advanced towards him.

In the first encounter, with widely gaping jaws, he rushed upon the knight with outrageous pride, aiming to swallow him in one gulp. But when the monster found the knight charging in return, he was pushed back like a hawk in flight. Taking advantage of his open jaw, the knight rammed his bright weapon with such brutal might, that he deeply pierced the darksome, hollow maw.

Down fell the dragon: his life breath vanished into smoke and swift clouds. Down fell the dragon: the earth underneath him groaned, as if too feeble to hold his great load. Down fell the dragon, as a huge rocky cliff, whose false foundation is washed away by waves, and with dreadful hover, is ripped from the mainland, rolling down into the sea, disturbing great Neptune. So down fell the dragon, and like a collapsed heaped mountain, lay.

55 Even the knight himself trembled at this fall: so huge and horrible a mass it seemed. His dear lady, who beheld it all, dared not approach for dread, as she was still uncertain of the outcome. But at last, when she saw that the direful fiend did not stir, she shook off her fright, drew nigh, and saw that joyous end. Then she praised God and thanked her faithful knight who had achieved so great a conquest with his might.

---

1   *pagan king: Philip II of Spain of the Spanish Armada*

2   *Cephise and Hebrus, Wells from mythology*

3   *Eagles were thought to renew themselves by plunging into an ocean*

NOTES ON CANTO XII

The wedding rituals described in this chapter date back to ancient Rome.

CANTO XII

WEDDING AND CELEBRATION

Faire Vna to the Redcrosse knight
betrouthed is with ioy:
Though false Duessa it to barre
her false sleights doe imploy.

I Behold I see the hauen nigh at hand,
To which I meane my wearie course to bend;
Vere the maine shete, and beare vp with the land,
The which afore is fairely to be kend,
And seemeth safe from stormes, that may offend;
There this faire virgin wearie of her way
Must landed be, now at her iourneyes end:
There eke my feeble barke a while may stay,
Till merry wind and weather call her thence away.

II Scarsely had *Phoebus* in the glooming East
Yet harnessed his firie-footed teeme,
Ne reard aboue the earth his flaming creast,
When the last deadly smoke aloft did steeme,
That signe of last outbreathed life did seeme,
Vnto the watchman on the castle wall;
Who thereby dead that balefull Beast did deeme,
And to his Lord and Ladie lowd gan call,
To tell, how he had seene the Dragons fatall fall.

III Vprose with hastie ioy, and feeble speed
That aged Sire, the Lord of all that land,
And looked forth, to weet, if true indeede
Those tydings were, as he did vnderstand,
Which whenas true by tryall he out fond,
He bad to open wyde his brazen gate,
Which long time had bene shut, and out of hond
Proclaymed ioy and peace through all his state;
For dead now was their foe, which them forrayed late.

IV Then gan triumphant Trompets sound on hie,
That sent to heauen the ecchoed report
Of their new ioy, and happie victorie
Gainst him, that had them long opprest with tort,
And fast imprisoned in sieged fort.
Then all the people, as in solemne feast,
To him assembled with one full consort,
Reioycing at the fall of that great beast,
From whose eternall bondage now they were releast.

V Forth came that auncient Lord and aged Queene,
Arayd in antique robes downe to the ground,
And sad habiliments right well beseene;
A noble crew about them waited round
Of sage and sober Peres, all grauely gownd;
Whom farre before did march a goodly band
Of tall young men, all hable armes to sownd,
But now they laurell braunches bore in hand;
Glad signe of victorie and peace in all their land.

Fair Una is joyfully betrothed to the Redcross knight.
Though the false Duessa tries to bar it with her false tricks.

BEHOLD I SEE THE HARBOR NEAR AT HAND, TO WHICH I INTEND TO DIRECT MY weary course. Release the mainsheet ropes and bear up, for land is coming into sight, and all seems safe from harmful storms. There, this fair maiden ship, weary of her way and at her journey's end, must land. There also my feeble boat must stay a while, till favorable wind and weather will call her thence away.

SCARCELY HAD PHOEBUS YET HARNESSED HIS FIERY-FOOTED TEAM IN THE glowing skies of the east, nor reared his flaming head above the earth, when the last deadly smoke steamed: the sign of the fiend's last out-breathed life. The watchman on the castle wall deemed that baleful beast was dead at last, and he began to call loudly to his lord and lady, declaring he had seen the dragon's fatal fall.

Up rose Una's aged father, the lord of that land, and with hasty joy and feeble speed, he looked forth to see if the tidings were true. And when the joyous news proved true indeed, he bade the brazen gate, which had long been shut, immediately opened wide, so that joy and peace could be proclaimed throughout the shire. For now their foe was dead.

Then came the sound of triumphant trumpets that sent the echoed report all the way up to heaven. Throughout the land, they sent sounds of their new joy and happy victory against the monster who had so long oppressed them, keeping them imprisoned in the fort. Then all the people gathered together to celebrate, as in a sacred festival, rejoicing at the fall of that great beast, from whose eternal bondage they had now been released.

5 Then forth came the ancient lord and the now aged queen, arrayed in somber royal robes down to the ground, while a noble crew of sage and sober peers waited around them. Next marched a fair band of handsome young men, all able to bear arms, but now bearing laurel branches in their hands: a glad sign of victory and peace in all their land.

VI Vnto that doughtie Conquerour they came,
And him before themselues prostrating low,
Their Lord and Patrone loud did him proclame,
And at his feet their laurell boughes did throw.
Soone after them all dauncing on a row
The comely virgins came, with girlands dight,
As fresh as flowres in medow greene do grow,
When morning deaw vpon their leaues doth light:
And in their hands sweet Timbrels all vpheld on hight.

VII And them before, the fry of children young
Their wanton sports and childish mirth did play,
And to the Maydens sounding tymbrels sung
In well attuned notes, a ioyous lay,
And made delightfull musicke all the way,
Vntill they came, where that faire virgin stood;
As faire *Diana* in fresh sommers day
Beholds her Nymphes, enraung'd in shadie wood,
Some wrestle, some do run, some bathe in christall flood.

VIII So she beheld those maydens meriment
With chearefull vew; who when to her they came,
Themselues to ground with gratious humblesse bent,
And her ador'd by honorable name,
Lifting to heauen her euerlasting fame:
Then on her head they set a girland greene,
And crowned her twixt earnest and twixt game;
Who in her selfe-resemblance well beseene,
Did seeme such, as she was, a goodly maiden Queene.

IX And after, all the raskall many ran,
Heaped together in rude rablement
To see the face of that victorious man:
Whom all admired, as from heauen sent,
And gazd vpon with gaping wonderment.
But when they came, where that dead Dragon lay,
Stretcht on the ground in monstrous large extent,
The sight with idle feare did them dismay,
Ne durst approch him nigh, to touch, or once assay.

X Some feard, and fled; some feard and well it faynd;
One that would wiser seeme, then all the rest,
Warnd him not touch, for yet perhaps remaynd
Some lingring life within his hollow brest,
Or in his wombe might lurke some hidden nest
Of many Dragonets, his fruitfull seed;
Another said, that in his eyes did rest
Yet sparckling fire, and bad thereof take heed;
Another said, he saw him moue his eyes indeed.

6 Unto that brave conqueror they came, and bowing low before him, they proclaimed him their lord and patron, while at his feet, they threw laurel branches. Soon after them, all dancing in a row, came the beautiful maidens bedecked with garlands, as fresh as flowers in the green meadow, when morning dew glistens on the leaves. In their hands, they played sweet tambourines, all held up high. And before them, came a group of young children, with their care-free sports and childish joy. They sang to the maidens' tambourines in well tuned notes and joyous song, making delightful music all the way.

Finally, they came to where that fair royal maiden stood, as fair as Diana on a fresh summer's day, beholding her nymphs arranged in shady woods: some wrestling, some running, and some bathing in a crystal stream. Likewise, Una beheld the maidens' merriment with cheer, and when they came to her, they graciously bowed in humble adoration at her name, lifting her everlasting fame to heaven. Then on her head they crowned her with a garland of green: half in earnest and half in fun, for she seemed such a noble maiden queen.

After that, all the common crowd, heaped together in rugged, rowdy rabblement, ran to see the face of that champion. There, they gazed upon the victorious knight, admiring him with gaping wonderment as if he had been sent from heaven.

But when they came at last to where the dead dragon lay, stretched on the ground in a monstrous heap, the sight subdued them with idle fear, and none dared approach near him, to touch or poke. **10** Some feared and fled, while others feigned fearlessness, and tried to appear braver and wiser than the rest. They teased the others and warned them not to touch, for fear that some lingering life, or hollow nest, might still lurk within a hollow breast or womb. There might be a brood of dragonets, his fruitful seed! Another warned them that sparkling fire still rested in his eyes, and another thought he saw his eyes move.

XI One mother, when as her foolehardie chyld
Did come too neare, and with his talants play,
Halfe dead through feare, her litle babe reuyld,
And to her gossips gan in counsell say;
How can I tell, but that his talants may
Yet scratch my sonne, or rend his tender hand?
So diuersly themselues in vaine they fray;
Whiles some more bold, to measure him nigh stand,
To proue how many acres he did spread of land.

XII Thus flocked all the folke him round about,
The whiles that hoarie king, with all his traine,
Being arriued, where that champion stout
After his foes defeasance did remaine,
Him goodly greetes, and faire does entertaine,
With princely gifts of yuorie and gold,
And thousand thankes him yeelds for all his paine.
Then when his daughter deare he does behold,
Her dearely doth imbrace, and kisseth manifold.

XIII And after to his Pallace he them brings,
With shaumes, and trompets,and with Clarions sweet;
And all the way the ioyous people sings,
And with their garments strowes the paued street:
Whence mounting vp, they find purueyance meet
Of all, that royall Princes court became,
And all the floore was vnderneath their feet
Bespred with costly scarlot of great name,
On which they lowly sit, and fitting purpose frame.

XIV What needs me tell their feast and goodly guize,
In which was nothing riotous nor vaine?
What needs of daintie dishes to deuize,
Of comely seruices, or courtly trayne?
My narrow leaues cannot in them containe
The large discourse of royall Princes state.
Yet was their manner then but bare and plaine:
For th'antique world excesse and pride did hate;
Such proud luxurious pompe is swollen vp but late.

XV Then when with meates and drinkes of euery kinde
Their feruent appetites they quenched had,
That auncient Lord gan fit occasion finde,
Of straunge aduentures, and of perils sad,
Which in his trauell him befallen had,
For to demaund of his renowmed guest:
Who then with vtt'rance graue, and count'nance sad
From point to point, as is before exprest,
Discourst his voyage long, according his request.

11 One mother, when her foolhardy child came too near and played with one of the talons, yelled, half dead with fear, at her little babe.

And to her gossip-friends, she counseled, "How do I know that the talon won't scratch my son, or slash his tender hand?"

So diversely, but in vain, they scared each other. Meanwhile, some of the bolder ones stood close by and tried to measure over how many acres of land the dragon was spread.

Thus, all the folk flocked around about the dragon, while the grey-bearded king, with all his attendants, arrived in front of the brave champion who defeated their foe. The king greeted him warmly and presented him with princely gifts of ivory and gold, and a thousand thanks for all the pain he had endured for them. Then when the king beheld his dear daughter, he embraced her dearly, and kissed her many times.

Next, he brought them to his palace, accompanied by flutes and trumpets and sweet clarions, and all the way, the joyous people sang, while strewing the paved street with their garments. Mounting the steps to the hall, they found a range of suitable provisions that became a royal prince's court. All the floor beneath their feet was spread with a rich, red carpet of great value, where they seated themselves and made gracious conversation.

What needs me to tell of their feast and the manner in which it was held, where there was nothing riotous or vain? What needs of dainty dishes to describe, of comely courses or courtly attendants? My narrow pages cannot contain the lengthy account of a royal prince's state, and yet their manner was then but bare and plain. For in olden days, they hated excess and pride: such proud extravagant pomp grew in later ages.

15 Then when the meats and drinks of every kind had quenched their fervent appetites, the old lord announced it was time for stories from his renowned guest. He asked the young knight to tell of the strange adventures and sad perils which had befallen him in his travels. Redcross rose and bowed, granting the king's request. Then, with grave utterances and serious countenance, from the first to the last, as is written in this story, he began to recount his long voyage.

XVI Great pleasure mixt with pittifull regard,
That godly King and Queene did passionate,
Whiles they his pittifull aduentures heard,
That oft they did lament his lucklesse state,
And often blame the too importune fate,
That heapd on him so many wrathfull wreakes:
For neuer gentle knight, as he of late,
So tossed was in fortunes cruell freakes;
And all the while salt teares bedeawd the hearers cheaks.

XVII Then said that royall Pere in sober wise;
Deare Sonne, great beene the euils, which ye bore
From first to last in your late enterprise,
That I note, whether prayse, or pitty more:
For neuer liuing man, I weene, so sore
In sea of deadly daungers was distrest;
But since now safe ye seised haue the shore,
And well arriued are, (high God be blest)
Let vs deuize of ease and euerlasting rest.

XVIII Ah dearest Lord, said then that doughty knight,
Of ease or rest I may not yet deuize;
For by the faith, which I to armes haue plight,
I bounden am streight after this emprize,
As that your daughter can ye well aduize,
Backe to returne to that great Faerie Queene,
And her to serue six yeares in warlike wize,
Gainst that proud Paynim king, that workes her teene:
Therefore I ought craue pardon, till I there haue beene.

XIX Vnhappie falles that hard necessitie,
(Quoth he) the troubler of my happie peace,
And vowed foe of my felicitie;
Ne I against the same can iustly preace:
But since that band ye cannot now release,
Nor doen vndo; (for vowes may not be vaine)
Soone as the terme of those six yeares shall cease,
Ye then shall hither backe returne againe,
The marriage to accomplish vowd betwixt you twain.

XX Which for my part I couet to performe,
In sort as through the world I did proclame,
That who so kild that monster most deforme,
And him in hardy battaile ouercame,
Should haue mine onely daughter to his Dame,
And of my kingdome heire apparaunt bee:
Therefore since now to thee perteines the same,
By dew desert of noble cheualree,
Both daughter and eke kingdome, lo I yield to thee.

16 The king and queen listened with great pleasure mixed with pitiful regard, as they were filled with compassion, hearing of his harrowing adventures. Often, they stopped his story to lament his luckless state, or to blame too grievous fate, that heaped so many wrathful wreaks on him. For never was there such a gentle knight as he, who was so tossed in fortune's cruel whims, and tears wet the hearer's cheeks.

Then the king rose to his feet, and in sober manner, he addressed him thus: "Dear son, great have been the misfortunes which you bore from first to last, in your recent enterprise, that I know not whether to praise or pity more. For there never was a living man who endured such a sea of distressful, deadly dangers. But since you have now reached the shore, and in such fine form—high God be blessed!—let us plan ease and everlasting rest.

"Oh dearest lord," then said the bold knight, "I may not yet seek after ease and rest, for I am bound by arms straight after this enterprise, to which your daughter can attest. For I must immediately return to that great Faerie Queene, and serve her for six years in warlike ways against that proud pagan king who causes her trouble. Therefore, I seek your leave, till I have completed my service.

"That hard necessity falls unhappily," replied the king, "And while the vowed foe of my good fortune troubles my contentment, I cannot justly argue against your decision. But since you cannot be released from that bond, nor can you undo it—for vows should not be made in vain—as soon as the term of those six years has ceased, you shall then return here and marry my daughter. **20** I proclaimed throughout the world that, whosoever killed that most deformed monster and overcame him in hardy battle, would have mine only daughter as his wife. And he shall be the heir-apparent of my kingdom. Therefore, since the same pertains to you, by due reward of noble chivalry, both daughter and kingdom, lo, I give to you."

XXI Then forth he called that his daughter faire,
The fairest *Vn'* his onely daughter deare,
His onely daughter, and his onely heyre;
Who forth proceeding with sad sober cheare,
As bright as doth the morning starre appeare
Out of the East, with flaming lockes bedight,
To tell that dawning day is drawing neare,
And to the world does bring long wished light;
So faire and fresh that Lady shewd her selfe in sight.

XXII So faire and fresh, as freshest flowre in May;
For she had layd her mournefull stole aside,
And widow-like sad wimple throwne away,
Wherewith her heauenly beautie she did hide,
Whiles on her wearie iourney she did ride;
And on her now a garment she did weare,
All lilly white, withoutten spot, or pride,
That seemd like silke and siluer wouen neare,
But neither silke nor siluer therein did appeare.

XXIII The blazing brightnesse of her beauties beame,
And glorious light of her sunshyny face
To tell, were as to striue against the streame.
My ragged rimes are all too rude and bace,
Her heauenly lineaments for to enchace.
Ne wonder; for her owne deare loued knight,
All were she dayly with himselfe in place,
Did wonder much at her celestiall sight:
Oft had he seene her faire, but neuer so faire dight.

XXIV So fairely dight, when she in presence came,
She to her Sire made humble reuerence,
And bowed low, that her right well became,
And added grace vnto her excellence:
Who with great wisedome, and graue eloquence
Thus gan to say. But eare he thus had said,
With flying speede, and seeming great pretence,
Came running in, much like a man dismaid,
A Messenger with letters, which his message said.

XXV All in the open hall amazed stood,
At suddeinnesse of that vnwarie sight,
And wondred at his breathlesse hastie mood.
But he for nought would stay his passage right,
Till fast before the king he did alight;
Where falling flat, great humblesse he did make,
And kist the ground, whereon his foot was pight;
Then to his hands that writ he did betake,
Which he disclosing, red thus, as the paper spake.

21 Then he called forth his fair daughter, the fairest Una, his only daughter dear: his only daughter and his only heir. She went forth with steadfast sober cheer, as bright as the morning star appears out of the east, bedecked with flaming locks, telling that dawn is drawing near, and bringing welcomed light unto the world: so fair and fresh that lady showed herself in sight.

So fair and fresh, as freshest flower in May. For she had lain her mournful black cloak aside, and thrown away the somber vestal veil, in which she hid her heavenly beauty while on her weary journey. And now she wore a garment of lily white, without blemish or pride, and which, though made of humble linen, seemed closely interwoven with threads of silk and silver. To tell of the blazing brightness of her beauty's smile, and glorious light of her sunshiny face, would be to strive against the stream. For my ragged rhymes are all too rude and base to convey her heavenly features. Even her beloved knight, who had been at her side for many days, marveled at her celestial sight. Often, he had seen her beauty, but never so fair adorned as now.

So fairly adorned, she came forward in presence and curtsied to her father, adding grace unto her excellence. Then, with great wisdom and grave eloquence, the king began to speak.

But, just before he had finished, a man came running in with seeming great purpose, looking very dismayed and carrying a letter. He was a messenger with letters, and his message confirmed this.

25 Everyone in the open hall stood amazed at the suddenness of the unexpected sight, and wondered at his breathless hasty mood. But the messenger refused to stay his passage until he was given an audience with the king himself. Falling flat, he made great gestures of excessive humility, kissing the ground where his feet were. Then, he delivered that letter into the king's hands which, after unfolding, read thus, as the paper spoke.

XXVI To thee, most mighty king of *Eden* faire,
Her greeting sends in these sad lines addrest,
The wofull daughter, and forsaken heire
Of that great Emperour of all the West;
And bids thee be aduized for the best,
Ere thou thy daughter linck in holy band
Of wedlocke to that new vnknowen guest:
For he already plighted his right hand
Vnto another loue, and to another land.

XXVII To me sad mayd, or rather widow sad,
He was affiaunced long time before,
And sacred pledges he both gaue, and had,
False erraunt knight, infamous, and forswore:
Witnesse the burning Altars, which he swore,
And guiltie heauens of his bold periury,
Which though he hath polluted oft of yore,
Yet I to them for iudgement iust do fly,
And them coniure t'auenge this shamefull iniury.

XXVIII Therefore since mine he is, or free or bond,
Or false or trew, or liuing or else dead,
Withhold, O soueraine Prince, your hasty hond
From knitting league with him, I you aread;
Ne weene my right with strength adowne to tread,
Through weakenesse of my widowhed, or woe:
For truth is strong, her rightfull cause to plead,
And shall find friends, if need requireth soe,
So bids thee well to fare, Thy neither friend, nor foe, *Fidessa*.

XXIX When he these bitter byting words had red,
The tydings straunge did him abashed make,
That still he sate long time astonished
As in great muse, ne word to creature spake.
At last his solemne silence thus he brake,
With doubtfull eyes fast fixed on his guest;
Redoubted knight, that for mine onely sake
Thy life and honour late aduenturest,
Let nought be hid from me, that ought to be exprest.

XXX What meane these bloudy vowes, and idle threats,
Throwne out from womanish impatient mind?
What heauens? what altars? what enraged heates
Here heaped vp with termes of loue vnkind,
My conscience cleare with guilty bands would bind?
High God be witnesse, that I guiltlesse ame.
But if your selfe, Sir knight, ye faultie find,
Or wrapped be in loues of former Dame,
With crime do not it couer, but disclose the same.

26 *"To you, most mighty king of Eden fair, she sends her greetings in these addressed sad lines. 'I, the woeful daughter and forsaken heir of that great emperor of all the West, bid you be advised for the best, since your daughter's engagement to that new unknown knight and guest. For that knight already pledged his right hand unto another love and another land. To me, sad maid, or rather sad maiden-widow, he was engaged a long time before, along with the sacred pledges he both gave and received. False errant knight: infamous and false promiser! Witness the burning altars on which he swore, and guilty heavens tainted by his bold perjury, which he has often polluted of yore. Yet I call them to judgment to avenge this shameful injury. Therefore, since he is mine, whether free or bound, true or false, living or dead, withhold, O sovereign king, your hasty hand from knitting league with him, I advise you. Do not use your strength to trample on my rights, through weakness of my widowhood or woe. For truth is strong: it pleads rightful causes, and shall find friends if need so requires. So bids thee farewell; your neither friend nor foe, Fidessa."*

When the king had finished reading these bitter biting words with the strange tidings that bewildered him, he sat still and astonished for a long time as in great thought, and he spoke not a word to anyone.

At last he broke his solemn silence with doubtful eyes, firmly fixed on the knight.

"Redoubted knight," he began, gravely, "you, who, for my sake alone, offered your life and honor in your recent adventures, hide nothing from me that ought to be told. **30** What do these bloody vows and idle threats mean, thrown out from an impatient female mind? What heavens? What altars? What enraged passions were heaped up here, with terms of unkind love that my clear conscience would bind with guilty bands? High God, be witness that I am guiltless. But if you, sir knight, find yourself at fault, or wrapped in loves of a former lady, do not cover the crimes of perjury, but disclose them."

XXXI To whom the *Redcrosse* knight this answere sent,
My Lord, my King, be nought hereat dismayd,
Till well ye wote by graue intendiment,
What woman, and wherefore doth me vpbrayd
With breach of loue, and loyalty betrayd.
It was in my mishaps, as hitherward
I lately traueild, that vnwares I strayd
Out of my way, through perils straunge and hard;
That day should faile me, ere I had them all declard.

XXXII There did I find, or rather I was found
Of this false woman, that *Fidessa* hight,
Fidessa hight the falsest Dame on ground,
Most false *Duessa*, royall richly dight,
That easie was t'inuegle weaker sight:
Who by her wicked arts, and wylie skill,
Too false and strong for earthly skill or might,
Vnwares me wrought vnto her wicked will,
And to my foe betrayd, when least I feared ill.

XXIII Then stepped forth the goodly royall Mayd,
And on the ground her selfe prostrating low,
With sober countenaunce thus to him sayd;
O pardon me, my soueraigne Lord, to show
The secret treasons, which of late I know
To haue bene wrought by that false sorceresse.
She onely she it is, that earst did throw
This gentle knight into so great distresse,
That death him did awaite in daily wretchednesse.

XXXIV And now it seemes, that she suborned hath
This craftie messenger with letters vaine,
To worke new woe and improuided scath,
By breaking of the band betwixt vs twaine;
Wherein she vsed hath the practicke paine
Of this false footman, clokt with simplenesse,
Whom if ye please for to discouer plaine,
Ye shall him *Archimago* find, I ghesse,
The falsest man aliue; who tries shall find no lesse.

XXXV The king was greatly moued at her speach,
And all with suddein indignation fraight,
Bad on that Messenger rude hands to reach.
Eftsoones the Gard, which on his state did wait,
Attacht that faitor false, and bound him strait:
Who seeming sorely chauffed at his band,
As chained Beare, whom cruell dogs do bait,
With idle force did faine them to withstand,
And often semblaunce made to scape out of their hand.

31 Then Redcross replied to the king, "My lord, my king, be not yet dismayed until you know well, by careful consideration, what woman, and why she wants to unbraid me with breach of love and betrayed loyalty. It was in my mishaps, as hitherward I lately travelled, that unawares I strayed out of my way, through strange and hard perils. But the day should have failed me ere I had declared every story. There did I find, or rather I was found, by this false woman so called Fidessa. Fidessa, she calls herself, but she is the falsest dame on earth: most false Duessa, so royally and richly dressed, that it was easier to beguile weaker sight. Who, by her wicked arts and wily skill—too false and strong to be opposed by earthly skill or might—wrought me unawares unto her wicked will, and betrayed me to my foe, when I least expected ill.

Then the goodly royal maiden stepped forth, and prostrated herself low on the ground.

With sober countenance, she said to her father, "O allow me, my sovereign lord, to show the secret treasons, which I know of late to have been wrought by that false sorceress. It was she who threw this gentle knight into great distress, to the point that he awaited only death in daily wretchedness. And now it seems that she has persuaded this crafty messenger, with vain letters, to work new woe and unforeseen harm, by trying to break the bond between us. She has used this false footman, humbly cloaked, whom, if you would like to discover the truth, remove his hood and you shall find he is Archimago: the falsest man alive. He who tries shall find no less than him."

35 The king was greatly moved at her speech, and filled with sudden indignation, bade that messenger be brought by force. Soon, the guard who waited upon the king, seized that false faker and bound him straight. Unhappy with his bonds, feeling like a chained bear baited by cruel dogs, Archimago fought uselessly to withstand them, and tried every trick to escape from their hands.

XXXVI But they him layd full low in dungeon deepe,
And bound him hand and foote with yron chains.
And with continuall watch did warely keepe;
Who then would thinke, that by his subtile trains
He could escape fowle death or deadly paines?
Thus when that Princes wrath was pacifide,
He gan renew the late forbidden banes,
And to the knight his daughter deare he tyde,
With sacred rites and vowes for euer to abyde.

XXXVII His owne two hands the holy knots did knit,
That none but death for euer can deuide;
His owne two hands, for such a turne most fit,
The housling fire did kindle and prouide,
And holy water thereon sprinckled wide;
At which the bushy Teade a groome did light,
And sacred lampe in secret chamber hide,
Where it should not be quenched day nor night,
For feare of euill fates, but burnen euer bright.

XXXVIII Then gan they sprinckle all the posts with wine,
And made great feast to solemnize that day;
They all perfumde with frankincense diuine,
And precious odours fetcht from far away,
That all the house did sweat with great aray:
And all the while sweete Musicke did apply
Her curious skill, the warbling notes to play,
To driue away the dull Melancholy;
The whiles one sung a song of loue and iollity.

XXXIX During the which there was an heauenly noise
Heard sound through all the Pallace pleasantly,
Like as it had bene many an Angels voice,
Singing before th'eternall maiesty,
In their trinall triplicities on hye;
Yet wist no creature, whence that heauenly sweet
Proceeded, yet each one felt secretly
Himselfe thereby reft of his sences meet,
And rauished with rare impression in his sprite.

XL Great ioy was made that day of young and old,
And solemne feast proclaimd throughout the land,
That their exceeding merth may not be told:
Suffice it heare by signes to vnderstand
The vsuall ioyes at knitting of loues band.
Thrise happy man the knight himselfe did hold,
Possessed of his Ladies hart and hand,
And euer, when his eye did her behold,
His heart did seeme to melt in pleasures manifold.

36 But they laid him low in the deep dungeon, and bound him hand and foot with iron chains, and they kept him there with continual watch. Who then would think that, by his subtle tricks, he could escape foul death or deadly pains?

Thus, when that prince's wrath had been pacified, he began to renew the recently delayed public announcement of marriage, and with sacred rites and vows to abide forever, he wedded his dear daughter to the knight.

With his own two hands, the king tied the holy knot, that none but death can forever divide. With his own two hands, for such a task most fit, he kindled and provided the sacramental fire, and holy water thereon sprinkled wide. Then, with a nuptial torch, a groomsman lit the sacred lamp that was hidden in a secret chamber, where it should not be extinguished day or night, but ever burned bright, for fear of evil fates.

Then they began to sprinkle all the posts with wine, as was the custom, and prepare a great feast to solemnize that day. They perfumed everything with divine frankincense and precious scents, fetched from far away, so that the entire house was sprinkled with fragrance. All the while, sweet music could be heard, playing with intricate skill and warbling notes, singing of love and joy, and driving away dull melancholy.

But a more heavenly melody could be heard throughout all the palace, as if it were angels' voices singing before the eternal majesty on high. While no creature knew from where that heavenly song came, each one felt secretly taken out from his ordinary senses, and ravished with rare impression in his spirit.

40 Such joy was made that day of young and old, and sacred festival proclaimed throughout the land, that their exceeding happiness could not be measured. Suffice it here, to explain with images, the usual joys at knitting a love's band. Thrice-happy man, the knight considered himself, possessed of his lady's heart and hand, and whenever his eye beheld her, his heart seemed to melt in manifold pleasures.

XLI Her ioyous presence and sweet company
In full content he there did long enioy,
Ne wicked enuie, ne vile gealosy
His deare delights were able to annoy:
Yet swimming in that sea of blisfull ioy,
He nought forgot, how he whilome had sworne,
In case he could that monstrous beast destroy,
Vnto his Farie Queene backe to returne:
The which he shortly did, and *Vna* left to mourne.

XLII Now strike your sailes ye iolly Mariners,
For we be come vnto a quiet rode,
Where we must land some of our passengers,
And light this wearie vessell of her lode.
Here she a while may make her safe abode,
Till she repaired haue her tackles spent,
And wants supplide. And then againe abroad
On the long voyage whereto she is bent:
Well may she speede and fairely finish her intent.

41 In full contentment, he long enjoyed her joyous presence and sweet company there. No wicked envy or vile jealousy could mar his dear delights. Yet, swimming in that sea of blissful joy, he did not forget that he was sworn to return unto his Faerie Queene, if he destroyed that monstrous beast. And this he shortly did, leaving Una to mourn.

NOW DROP YOUR SAILS YE JOLLY SAILORS, FOR WE HAVE NOW COME UNTO quiet anchorage, where we must land some of our passengers, and lighten this weary vessel of her load. Here, a while, she may make herself a safe abode, till her tackles and worn out rigging are repaired, and needs are resupplied. And then again, abroad, on the long voyage, whereto she is destined next.

Well may she speed and fairly finish her journey.

FINIS